"A beautifully written, lively exploration of the challenges involved in raising children — and the best we know today about how to meet those challenges. Entertaining and inspiring, this book belongs in the home of every parent — and grandparent!"

— Nathaniel Branden, PhD, author of *The Six Pillars of Self-Esteem*

"Finally, rather than a list of problems from A to Z, a refreshing, encouraging book for parents with answers from A to Z."

— Rabbi Steven Z. Leder, author of
The Extraordinary Nature of Ordinary Things and *More Money Than God*

"G is for Great! I love Dr. Jenn's *The A to Z Guide to Raising Happy, Confident Kids*. Its easy accessibility touches lightly yet profoundly on subjects we parents confront daily. Her practical advice mixed with insight on how to grow a confident, healthy individual is spot on. I will be sure to recommend this chock-full reference to my patients and friends. I know it will have a place on my shelf for years to come."

— Marilyn H. Kagan, LCSW

"*The A to Z Guide to Raising Happy, Confident Kids* is filled with wisdom and deep insight into modern parenting. From cultivating a healthy relationship with food and body to teaching your child about love and self-acceptance, this book gives parents the information they need on the issues that arise. Dr. Jenn's book is a true gift to parents!"

— Elyse Resch, nutrition therapist and coauthor of *Intuitive Eating*

"When they are all finally asleep in their beds and you have crawled into yours, *The A to Z Guide to Raising Happy, Confident Kids* is the perfect ray of hope to visit for courage, comfort, and practical solutions that will give you a restful night's sleep."

— Don Elium, bestselling author of *Raising a Son* and *Raising a Daughter*

"Reading this book is like sitting down with a trusted friend who just happens to know everything — from the intimate details of parenting to the big picture of raising a child. The chapter titles and subheads have the catchiness of pop tunes, while the content achieves breadth and depth with the grace of a superbly tuned orchestra."

— Greg Keer, syndicated parenting columnist and publisher of
www.familymanonline.com

"Parenting becomes infinitely easier if you remember that you were once a child, too. Dr. Jenn's brisk and insightful guide to child rearing provides a welcome reminder that informed parenting results in better kids. The tips and cautions alone make this book a confidence booster for handling parental pressure."

— Paul Petersen, child advocate and founder of A Minor Consideration

"A helpful, practical approach to parenting. The personal anecdotes combined with clinical research make this guide a must-have for parents. As pediatricians, we value the importance of raising a happy, healthy, and confident child. Dr. Jenn's book will help parents accomplish this goal."

— Scott Cohen, MD, FAAP, and Bess Raker, MD, FAAP,
Beverly Hills Pediatrics

The A to Z Guide to

Raising Happy, Confident Kids

The A to Z Guide to
Raising Happy, Confident Kids

Dr. Jenn Berman

Foreword by Donna Corwin

New World Library
Novato, California

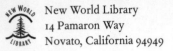

New World Library
14 Pamaron Way
Novato, California 94949

Text design and typography by Tona Pearce Myers

Library of Congress Cataloging-in-Publication Data
Berman, Jenn.
The A to Z guide to raising happy, confident kids / Jenn Berman.
    p.   cm.
Includes bibliographical references and index.
ISBN 978-1-57731-563-6 (pbk. : alk. paper)
    1. Child rearing—Handbooks, manuals, etc. 2. Parenting—Handbooks, manuals,
    etc. I. Title.
HQ769.B51885 2007
649'.1—dc22   2007002252

First printing, May 2007
ISBN-10: 1-57731-563-4
ISBN-13: 978-1-57731-563-6
Printed in Canada on acid-free, partially recycled paper

g New World Library is a proud member of the Green Press Initiative.

10 9 8 7 6 5 4 3 2 1

This book is dedicated to my incredible parents,
Barry Mann and Cynthia Weil.

Without your love, encouragement, and belief in me,
this book would not exist. You made me believe that I could
accomplish anything that I set my mind to. You taught me
that rejection and difficulty are just part of the road to success.
Thank you for always hearing me, understanding me, and loving me
with all your hearts. I aspire to be as good a parent as you both are.

CONTENTS

Foreword by Donna Corwin   xi

Introduction   xiii

A Is for Apple: Helping Your Children Form
a Healthy Relationship with Food   1

B Is for Bogeyman: Understanding and Addressing
Childhood Fears   13

C Is for Cheering: Being a Great Sports Parent   25

D Is for Double Trouble: Raising Twins   35

E Is for Eenie Meanie: Helping Children Become
Good Decision Makers   43

F Is for Free to Be Me!: Raising Kids
with Great Self-esteem   51

G Is for Gimme, Gimme: Raising Down-to-earth Children   61

H Is for Hero: Being a Great Dad   71

I Is for "I Don't Wanna Go": Helping the Child
Who Doesn't Want to Go to School   81

J Is for Jumping Jacks: Helping Your Children
Love Exercise   91

K Is for Kitty Cat: Keeping Pets in the Home   99

L Is for Lovebug: Teaching Your Child about Love   109

M Is for Mary Poppins: Finding Good Childcare   117

N Is for Noodles and Nuggets: Eating Meals Together   127

O Is for Ouch: Making Visits to the Doctor Painless   137

🄿 Is for Priorities: Spending Time with Loved Ones   143

🄠 Is for Quarters: Teaching Your Kids about Money   153

🄡 Is for Riddles and Rainbows: Promoting Creativity
      in Your Child   165

🄢 Is for SOS (Save Our Siblings): Dealing with
      Sibling Rivalry   173

🄣 Is for Teletubbies: Understanding the Effects
      of TV on Your Child   185

🄤 Is for Uno: Parenting Your Only Child   197

🄥 Is for Vegging Out: Letting Your Child Have Downtime   205

🄦 Is for Wedded Bliss: Keeping Your Marriage Strong   213

🄧 Is for X Chromosome: Raising a Girl   221

🄨 Is for Y Chromosome: Raising a Boy   231

🄩 Is for Getting ZZZs: Helping Your Child Get
      a Good Night's Sleep   241

Acknowledgments   253

Bibliography and Recommended Books   255

Index   271

About the Author   281

FOREWORD

Dr. Jenn Berman has given the alphabet new meaning. In *The A to Z Guide to Raising Happy, Confident Kids*, she offers insightful, informative advice to parents. Dr. Jenn has broken down the basics of child-rearing into twenty-six of the most important issues facing parents today. She starts with helping your children form healthy eating habits, then goes on to cover everything from childhood fears, raising twins, and sibling rivalry to family time and sleep issues. Parenting is a challenging and often frightening journey. Dr. Jenn has joined with parents in this journey and shares her vast psychological knowledge and grounded advice. She navigates the internal needs of children, and at the same time offers practical solutions to parents. Along the way, she even reminds parents to take time for themselves — a novel idea!

In the chapter "F Is for Free to Be Me!" Dr. Jenn explores parenting's most vital issue — self-esteem. She gets at the heart of what creates healthy children: their inner confidence and ego strength. Self-esteem, as she notes, forms the core of a person. As she reminds us, "Psychologically, parents are the mirrors in which kids see themselves reflected; your children look to you to figure out who they are and how they fit in the world." With sensitivity, she guides parents in making positive choices when it comes to discipline and child-rearing. Perhaps one of the most important issues is allowing children to see their weaknesses as an opportunity for growth. Dr. Jenn draws on her longtime work with children, families, and teens. She cites real-life cases to exemplify the importance of self-esteem and its core function in a child's life. She shows parents how to validate a child's feelings and to become positive role models.

Dr. Jenn is also an expert on eating disorders. In "A Is for Apple: Helping Your Children Form a Healthy Relationship with Food," she addresses a serious, pervasive problem. In the process she provides parents with strategies to help their children deemphasize diets and food obsession and to replace negative eating patterns with healthy food choices. It is worth buying the book just for Dr. Jenn's vast knowledge of the subject of eating disorders.

This essential parenting book is sure to become a classic. There is something here for every parent, on every subject. You will reread this invaluable manual over and over. I cannot recommend *The A to Z Guide to Raising Happy, Confident Kids* highly enough. It should be on every parent's bookshelf. I know it will be on mine.

— Donna Corwin, author of *The Tween Years* and
Pushed to the Edge

INTRODUCTION

Raising children is an art, not a science. The questions most parents have cannot be answered in black-and-white terms, which makes it more difficult to figure out what is right for the family and the children. There are so many different theories and approaches to consider, but most parents don't have the time to read up on everything they would like to know about. Yet they know that the more information they have, the better equipped they will be to make smart parenting decisions. This is where *The A to Z Guide to Raising Happy, Confident Kids* comes in.

I am a licensed Marriage, Family, and Child Therapist working with children, adults, and families in private practice and a parenting expert appearing on television and radio. In addition, I have written a parenting column called "Dr. Jenn" for the past five years. This column won the silver medal in parenting and child development from the Parenting Publications of America. I am also the mother of two children. Both my professional and personal experiences put me in a good position to help you master the art of parenting.

I am frequently asked for recommendations on parenting books but have never been able to find one book that covers all the questions that parents have asked me. In compiling this book, I have included some of the most important tips parents need in shepherding their children through early childhood. I have also tried to address the most frequent issues that I have tackled in my private practice, in my television and radio work and my column about parenting, and in my own parenting struggles.

My hope in writing this book is that parents will find the short, self-contained chapters easy to read and use for reference. Because each chapter is only a few pages long and can stand on its own, you can quickly read what you need, as you need it, instead of reading the book straight through. This book can serve as a helpful resource that you can turn to throughout your children's childhood as different issues arise.

One valuable idea I stress throughout this book is that sometimes raising a happy child means making your child unhappy in the short term in order to teach long-term values, such as delayed gratification, manners, and impulse control. Many parents make the mistake of thinking that raising a happy child means gratifying her every whim immediately. The challenge then is finding an appropriate balance between giving to their child and teaching important life lessons. It may seem daunting now, but rest assured, it will get easier.

Confident children tend to be those who have been given the optimal balance of freedom and boundaries, a challenge for any parent. Striking the right balance takes time, experience, and patience. But the reward will be worth it: a confident, thriving child. In *The A to Z Guide to Raising Happy, Confident Kids* I have tried to give parents all the information necessary to make the best choices for their children. There are no greater gifts you can give your kids than happiness and confidence. I hope you will find this book helpful in raising your happy, confident children.

Best wishes on your parenting journey!

Helping Your Children Form a Healthy Relationship with Food

Kaley is a slender six-year-old girl who tells me that she is "fat." She shares her food philosophies with me: Carbs are bad. Fat is bad. Sugar is bad. Fruits and vegetables are good, but only if they don't have too many carbs.

Landon is a chubby seven-year-old boy. Other kids make fun of him when he plays sports at school, so he avoids physical activity. At home he watches TV and plays a lot of video games. His family doesn't eat together, and he is pretty much on his own for meals, which he picks out of the refrigerator.

Unfortunately, I am seeing more and more children like Kaley and Landon in my psychotherapy practice. Eating disorders are striking at younger and younger ages, and obesity is now considered a national epidemic. Researchers use the body mass index (BMI), a measurement of body mass based on calculations of height and weight, to determine healthy weight, which is generally considered to be a BMI of 18.5 to 25. According to the National Center for Health

Statistics, 63 percent of Americans are overweight, with a BMI of over 25, and 31 percent are obese, with a BMI above 30. It is not surprising, therefore, that more than 27 percent of children and 21 percent of adolescents are obese. The good news is that parents have a huge influence on their children's relationship with food and their bodies, but not necessarily in the ways you might think.

Sugar, Fats, and Carbs, Oh, My!

The worst thing you can do to influence your child's relationship to food is to restrict the foods she is allowed to eat. Many well-meaning parents refuse to allow their children to eat high-sugar or high-fat foods, but what they don't realize is that food restriction creates a deprivation mentality, which just compounds the problem. Children tend to find the restricted foods more exciting and thus more preferable to the nonrestricted foods. Kids who have been kept from certain foods, therefore, have more difficulties controlling their eating when presented with those foods.

Lisa came to see me after she noticed that her ten-year-old daughter, Casey, was getting sick after spending time at her girlfriends' homes. Lisa learned from the mothers of these girls that when Casey visited she would gorge herself on potato chips, crackers, and candy. Lisa was a very slender and attractive woman who had been a chubby child and lived in fear of gaining weight. She was on a low-carbohydrate, sugar-free diet and refused to keep any foods in the house that were not on her diet. Lisa was terrified of what would happen if she was around those foods, and even more important, she wanted to keep them away from her daughter. I worked with Lisa to help her slowly bring those foods back into the house. Initially, both Lisa and Casey binged on those previously forbidden foods. Yet after some time passed, these foods began to lose their emotional charge for both mother and daughter. Lisa now stocks the home with a wide variety of groceries, and the family is able to eat a varied and healthy diet.

Most parents are terrified that if they allow their children unrestricted choices, their kids will eat nothing but gummy bears and ice cream for the rest of their lives. That is just not my experience. Children who are raised to be what Elyse Resch and Evelyn Tribole, registered dieticians and authors of *Intuitive Eating*, refer to as "intuitive eaters," or unrestricted eaters, naturally chose a variety of foods. Lisa and Casey are fairly typical. Both adults and children who are accustomed to adhering to strict food rules initially choose previously off-limits foods when they are made available but eventually tire of them when they realize that those "forbidden fruits" will not be taken away.

Don't Touch That!: The Problems with Restricted Eating

A majority of the clients in my psychotherapy practice who have food or weight problems were put on diets during their childhood. Teaching a child to follow a food plan, to ignore her hunger, or to deprive herself of foods she wants sends a powerful message to her that she cannot trust her own body. When a child learns not to listen to and obey her body's signals of hunger and satiety, she is more susceptible to eating and weight problems. This also explains why dieting in childhood is actually a predictor of later obesity.

Studies show that the risk of developing an eating disorder is eight times higher in fifteen-year-old girls who diet than it is in their peers who don't. Even though diets have been estimated to have between a 95 and 99 percent failure rate, it has been estimated that half of all American women are on a diet at any given time. So commonplace is restrictive eating in our society that one California study reported that 45 percent of all third-grade and 80 percent of fourth- and fifth-grade girls are on diets. While it was once believed that this trend predominantly affected white, teenage girls, we now know that unhealthy eating attitudes and practices affect people of nearly all ethnicities, genders, and classes, irrespective of age or geographical location.

Many theories explain why restrictive eating leads to a loss of control with food and to binge eating. Some theorists believe that it is the dieter's inability to manage powerful surges of hunger that leaves her vulnerable to erratic eating behavior. Researchers have found that the greater the degree of dietary restraint, the more severe will be the ensuing eating pathology. In addition, we now know that in addition to slowing down the body's ability to burn calories, metabolic changes have a profound impact on the brain. For the 4 percent of the population with a biological predisposition to developing an eating disorder, this spells the beginning of a serious lifetime problem.

What Is Normal?

The best thing a parent can do to fight this problem is to help her child develop the ability to read and honor her body's cues, allow her to eat a wide variety of foods, avoid labeling foods as "good" and "bad," and aid in identifying and addressing emotions so that she does not use eating as a coping strategy. The more you teach your child to trust and honor her body, the better her chances will be of avoiding an eating disorder.

Part of the reason that it is so difficult for adults to teach healthy eating to their children is that so few have mastered it themselves. Normal eating is difficult to find in this day and age. Listening to our bodies, eating when we are hungry and not eating when we are satisfied, and not eating for emotional reasons all run counter to what we have been taught by our culture, which recommends diet plans for everyone — even for young children.

In her book *How to Get Your Child to Eat ... But Not Too Much*, Ellyn Satter provides a very helpful definition of normal eating:

> Normal eating is being able to eat when you are hungry and continue eating until you are satisfied. It is being able to choose food you like and eat it and truly get enough of it — not just stop eating because you think you should. Normal eating is being able to use some moderate constraint in your food selection to get the right food, but not being so restrictive that you miss out on pleasurable foods. Normal eating is giving yourself permission to eat sometimes because you are happy, sad, or bored, or just because it feels good. Normal eating is three meals a day, most of the time, but it can also be choosing to munch along. ... Normal eating is trusting

Hunger Scale

Rate your hunger using the hunger scale, and teach your children to use it too when they are developmentally ready. The goal is to eat when you are a "3" and stop when you are a "5" or "6." If you allow yourself to get hungrier than a "3" you are likely to overeat. If you eat when you are more than a "5" or "6," you are feeding your emotions, not your body.

```
  0    1    2    3    4    5    6    7    8    9    10
◄─┼────┼────┼────┼────┼────┼────┼────┼────┼────┼────┼─►
Starving                  Neutral                Sick Full
```

0 = Starving	6 = Satisfied
1 = Empty	7 = Full
2 = Ravenous	8 = Stuffed
3 = Hungry	9 = Uncomfortably stuffed
4 = Pangs of hunger	10 = Sick to your stomach
5 = Nuetral	

your body to make up for mistakes in eating. . . . In short, normal eating is flexible. It varies in response to your emotions, your schedule, your hunger, and your proximity to food.

The good news is that children are born intuitive eaters. They come into this world eating to satisfy energy needs and being able to self-regulate calorie intake. In a study in which infants were fed formula in more diluted forms at some times and more concentrated forms at others, researchers found that the babies consumed more of the diluted formula than the concentrated one. They adjusted the volume to maintain a relatively consistent energy intake.

In *Intuitive Eating*, Resch and Tribole point out that most toddlers are intuitive eaters as well. They play until hungry and then go inside to eat a meal. They often leave food on their plates, even their favorite cookies, and then go back to play when their hunger has been satiated. If we want children with healthy attitudes about food, we need to help them maintain that intuitive ability.

Letting Go of Control

One of the biggest obstacles faced by parents who want to help their children develop a healthy relationship with food and their bodies is their own preconceived notions of what their child's body is "supposed" to look like.

Your job as a parent is to make foods available to your children, not to tell them how much to eat. You cannot control how much your child weighs or what kind of body type she has. The more you try to get your child to gain or lose weight, the more likely your plans will backfire and result in helping her develop a problem with food. You must make food available to your child when she is hungry and then let go of the outcome. I know that this is easier said than done!

When Veronica brought her six-year-old daughter, Rose, to the pediatrician she was told that her daughter was on the high end of the weight chart for her height and that it "might be a good idea to keep an eye on her." Veronica, who had been a chubby child, was terrified that her daughter would feel bad about herself and get teased by her peers, like she had. She went home that day and threw out all of the "bad" food in the house. In the beginning this approach worked; Rose lost a pound or two, and Veronica was pleased that the family was eating healthier. But soon Rose felt deprived and started asking for her favorite desserts again. Veronica told her that she couldn't have them because they didn't keep them in the house anymore. When Rose asked why, Veronica said that she was trying to help Rose lose weight. Rose began to cry. She told her mom that she must have done a terrible thing to make her mom remove all the goodies from the house. Veronica didn't know what to say. Shortly after that interaction, Veronica noticed that Rose started gaining weight again. She was still carefully controlling what she gave her daughter to eat, so she couldn't figure out how this was happening. That was until one day when she was looking for a pair of earrings she had let Rose use to play dress-up and found a drawer of hidden sweets. Veronica realized that keeping the food out of the house was not the answer, since doing so was creating the need for Rose to sneak food into the house and eat it anyway.

Shortly after this incident Veronica came to see me. We talked about how important it was for Veronica to work through her issues surrounding her own childhood weight problem so that she could be better equipped to help Rose. Then we decided that Veronica would take a more neutral stance in her approach to food at home. While she would make sure that there were nutritious foods in the house to choose from, she would not try to regulate exactly what or how much Rose ate. She would also bring the candy bars back into the house so that they would be available in the hopes that, once Rose realized they would not be withheld from her, she would stop binging on them. Veronica would encourage Rose to listen to her body's cues and to eat only when she was hungry and to stop eating when she was satisfied. She would limit television but would not try to force Rose to exercise to lose weight. In addition, she would increase the number of nights each week that the family ate dinner together, since many studies show that families who eat together have healthier eating habits.

It took a while for Rose to believe that certain foods weren't going to be taken away from her again. At first she overate, but gradually she started to eat less and to listen to her body's cues more. Because Rose learned to be an intuitive eater at a young age, as a teenager she maintained a healthy weight and never developed an eating disorder. Not every young girl is so lucky.

Risky Business

In the United States, females account for 90 percent of all people who have eating disorders. Psychology experts have found that particular personality traits — the most common being perfectionism, the desire to please, the ability to ignore pain and exhaustion, obsessiveness, and the burning desire to reach goals — make certain children more susceptible to eating disorders. Many of those same traits make children great athletes or performers. Children who participate in activities in which there is pressure to be thin such as ballet, modeling, acting, gymnastics, wrestling, horse racing, and acting are at a higher risk for developing eating disorders. Studies show that the rate of anorexia nervosa in children who participate in these activities is ten times that of the general population, owing largely to the fact that thinness is a prerequisite for success.

According to the organization Eating Disorder Awareness and Prevention (EDAP), parents should watch for three red flags that can indicate future eating-disordered behavior: body dissatisfaction, dieting behavior, and a drive for thinness. A girl who is dissatisfied with her body is very prone to dieting. If she has a high drive for thinness, she is very likely to engage in unhealthy behaviors that will lead to an eating disorder.

More Than Baby Fat

There are many reasons why children end up overweight. It is difficult to know if this is a nature or nurture issue. Sometimes there is a lack of nutritional information at home. Many parents were never taught how to feed their own bodies and therefore are not able to be good role models. Literature shows that if one parent is overweight, half the children in the family will also be overweight, and if both parents are overweight two-thirds of their children will be. One study even found that children of overweight parents had lower metabolisms than those of healthy weight parents.

Other times children are overweight because they have a sedentary lifestyle. Children tend to be as active as their parents are. Overweight children are at a disadvantage because they are often uncomfortable playing sports and therefore become less skilled, which in turn makes them less active. Another reason children end up overweight is that our culture encourages inactivity. Children often spend hours a day in front of the television, the computer, and the PlayStation. Studies show that television watching actually slows down children's metabolic rates. It is believed that the trancelike state children experience when they watch television slows down their metabolism. Normal-weight children experience a 12 percent decline in metabolic rates while watching television, while obese children experience a 16 percent decline. On top of that, eating in front of the television makes people less conscious of how much they are eating: researchers have found that people who watch TV while eating eat eight times more food.

Spoon-fed Images

Today's children are at a higher risk for developing eating disorders than those of previous generations. They are bombarded by images of unrealistic standards of beauty on television, on the Internet, in magazines, and in movies. The message being sent to children today is that beauty and thinness can change your life. Tune in to any episode of a show like *Extreme Makeover*, and you will start to believe it too.

Research shows a direct correlation between how much exposure a female has to contemporary media and the frequency of eating disorder symptoms she experiences. One study in which women viewed slides of overweight, average, and thin models found that the exposure to thin models resulted in lower self-esteem and decreased weight satisfaction. As bad as this lowered esteem is for adult women, children are even more vulnerable to it.

In the United States up to half of older elementary school girls read teen magazines at least occasionally, and one quarter read them twice a week. Often, the girls read these magazines to get ideas of how they "should" look. One study of eight- to eleven-year-old girls found that they regularly compared themselves to fashion models and other media images and felt bad about themselves as a result.

In other countries, the rate of eating disorders has risen in direct correlation to the influx of American exports, such as television programs and feature films, which bring with them new concepts of beauty and femininity as well as Western clothing, which is geared toward slimmer figures. For example, in Fiji, after being exposed to American television for only three years, Fijian teens who had never before been exposed to Western culture experienced significant changes in their behaviors and their attitudes about food and body image. Fifteen percent of Fijian high school girls started vomiting for

Tips for the Whole Family

- Eat only when hungry, and never let yourself or your children get too hungry.
- Eat dinner together as a family.
- Eat all meals at the kitchen or dining room table.
- Eat without distractions such as television, radio, cell phones, or computers at the table.
- Encourage children to listen to their bodies' cues.
- Limit television viewing.
- Expose children to a wide variety of foods, and avoid restricting your kids from eating certain foods.
- Do not use food as a reward or punishment.
- Teach your children to identify and express feelings so they don't resort to emotional eating.
- Do not criticize your own body or your child's body.
- Set a healthy example: do not diet.
- Teach self-acceptance and body appreciation.
- Encourage children to actually taste and enjoy their food.
- Do not keep any scales in your house.

weight control (a fivefold increase), 74 percent of Fijian teens said they felt "too big or too fat" at least some of the time, and 62 percent said they had dieted in the past month. In the Fijian culture, in which a comment like "you look fat today" was once considered a compliment, the standard of attractiveness has changed. As a result, the teen risk for eating disorders has doubled. In sum, the less time your children spend exposed to media images the better off they will be.

Be a Super Model

The greatest gift you can give your child is to model "normal" eating habits. A study of mothers who engaged in unhealthy dieting behaviors showed that their five-year-old daughters had more weight concerns and were twice as likely to be aware of dieting. Another study that looked at mothers who did not follow their own bodies' cues found that their daughters' eating habits mirrored their mother's. In addition, these daughters were more likely to be triggered by external cues. In other words, if they saw a cookie (even if they were not hungry and hadn't wanted a treat previously) they were more likely to eat one.

Eating practices, neuroses, and disorders are often handed down from generation to generation. If you have food issues, and most women do, you owe it to the next generation to resolve them before you pass them on.

Understanding and Addressing Childhood Fears

When four-year-old Jada awoke in the middle of the night, she knew she had to use the bathroom. Even with the nightlight on, the trail to the toilet seemed dark, scary, and fraught with danger. There could be monsters lurking around every corner waiting to grab her. Mommy and Daddy were all the way down the hall, and they might not be able to get to her fast enough if a monster actually appeared. But Jada was tough and knew that big girls handle things like this on their own. So she got out of bed, heart pounding, and started on the long journey to the bathroom. When she finally got there, she saw something move. She couldn't tell what it was in the darkness. It had to be a monster! Fearing for her life, she jumped off the toilet and ran down the hall to her parent's room, leaving a bright yellow trail on the new Berber carpet all the way from the bathroom to the bedroom.

Childhood fears are not only normal but also an important part of the developmental process. According to well-known pediatrician T. Berry Brazelton, "Fears inevitably crop up at periods of new and rapid learning. The child's new independence and abilities throw him off balance." When children first learn how to do something, even something as simple as getting out of bed in the middle of the night to use the bathroom, they don't know what the outcome will be. It takes the experience of making it to the bathroom in the dark many times before they know it is safe and that they can handle it.

Helping the Cowardly Lion

Children whose parents are able to read their distress signals and offer comfort tend to do better than those whose parents minimize their feelings. Parents are often afraid that by acknowledging their children's fears, they will only make those fears worse, but quite the opposite is true. Children whose caretakers respond to their worries, however silly they may seem to adults, grow up confident that they will receive help when they are distressed and therefore become better able to develop their own coping skills.

In addition, it can be helpful for children to understand the physiological signals that usually accompany fear. Younger children benefit from knowing that these feelings are absolutely normal and won't hurt them, while older children will often be interested in understanding why their bodies react the way they do when they are scared. Normal fear reactions usually include rapid heartbeat, butterflies in the stomach, fast breathing, shaky hands, sweaty palms, lightheadedness, and dry mouth. Of course, if your child experiences any of these symptoms regularly, you should take him to the pediatrician to rule out any other physical causes.

But what if your child is struggling with normal fears? What can you do? Here are some suggestions:

1. Normalize, don't minimize, his fears.

2. Share how you have overcome similar fears in the past.

3. Listen to your child. Reflect back what he has told you about what scares him, making sure you truly understand his concerns.

4. Help your child understand his fears.

5. Come up with ideas together that might help him. It's good for children to actively participate in this kind of problem solving: it teaches them constructive ways to cope with their anxieties.

6. Go through each strategy your child has come up with and explore possible outcomes together.

7. Encourage, but never force, your child to try to do things he is afraid of doing.

8. When your child takes brave steps to overcome his fears, reward the behavior with praise.

When Jada's parents used the eight steps listed above, they were able to help her overcome her fear. As a family, they discovered that the motion she had seen in the shadows of the bathroom was just a reflection of a tree by the window. When Jada understood that, she began to venture out of her room to use the bathroom at night again.

Keeping Monsters, Witches, and Warlocks at Bay: Fear Prevention

There are many things you can do to prevent childhood anxieties from getting out of control or to help quell fears that have already developed. Making the techniques listed below a regular part of your repertoire can be really helpful, especially if your child tends to be sensitive.

Provide Information

Knowledge is power. The proper information can often help children deal with their fears. Jack was a five-year-old boy who grew up in a house with no pets. His exposure to big dogs had been minimal, except for seeing them on television shows. When Jack went to visit his new friend, Ben, at his house and saw Snoopy, Ben's German shepherd, he got so scared that he insisted on going home right away. The dog, who was excited to meet Jack, had rushed over to smell him and lick his face, which really terrified Jack because he didn't know that dogs learn who people are by their smells. He did not know enough about dogs to be able to distinguish a friendly dog from a vicious one. Because Jack's parents knew how much Jack liked Ben, and how much he wanted to get over his fears so he could hang out at his friend's house, they decided to teach him about dogs. They bought books about dogs and read them to Jack, and they even had a friend's dog trainer come and talk to Jack to teach him about the difference between a dangerous dog and a friendly one. All this information enabled Jack to get over his fears and to spend time with Ben and Snoopy.

Give Fear Vaccinations

Preventative work on the part of parents can help inoculate their children against expected fears. Parents who prepare their children for new experiences that they know might cause their kids anxiety or make them fearful can eliminate, or at least minimize, the amount of anxiety their children experience at the event. Rachel was going to her first sleepover at her cousin's house down the street. Since her parents knew this might be a little anxiety provoking for her, they prepared Rachel in advance. Each night they told her a bedtime story that involved a character spending a night away from home. They talked to her about her fears and answered questions about how she

Recommended Books for Kids with Fears

The Goodnight Caterpillar: The Ultimate Bedtime Story, by Lori Lite (Roswell, GA: LiteBooks, 2001).

The techniques woven throughout this book help children learn to relax and help young children fall asleep.

There's a Nightmare in My Closet, by Mercer Mayer (New York: Penguin, 1968).

At bedtime a boy confronts the nightmare in his closet and finds it not so terrifying after all.

Jessica and the Wolf: A Story for Children Who Have Bad Dreams, by Ted Lobby (Milwaukee: G. Stevens, 1993).

With her parents' support, Jessica finds the strength and self-reliance to conquer a recurring bad dream.

Scary Night Visitors: A Story for Children with Bedtime Fears, by Irene Wineman Marcus and Paul Marcus (Milwaukee: G. Stevens, 1993).

When Davey realizes that his scary nighttime visitors are really his unacceptable angry feelings about his little sister projected into the world, he feels free to express his anger in a healthy way.

I'm Scared: Dealing with Feelings, by Elizabeth Crary (Seattle: Parenting Press, 1993).

This story is about a girl who is anxious to meet the new kids next door but is frightened by their big dog. Young readers and their parents can help her decide how to handle her fear by using the "choose-your-own-ending" format.

might handle things if she got scared. They gave her a photo of the whole family to take with her, and they insisted that she pack along her favorite blankie and teddy bear for comfort. It worked; all their preparations enabled Rachel to have a fun and fearless sleepover.

Teach Relaxation Exercises

Teaching your child how to relax is a gift that will last her a lifetime. At night when she is in bed, you can teach your child progressive relaxation. Progressive relaxation is a technique in which you tense your muscles and then relax them, starting at the toes and working your way up to the head. The book *The Goodnight Caterpillar* by Lori Lite talks children through progressive relaxation and can be a great tool both for teaching and practicing the skill.

Suggest Deep Breathing

Just like grown-ups, when children get nervous, their heart rate speeds up. While we can't eliminate our fears, we can slow down our heart rate when we are scared through the magic of deep breathing. In my clinical practice I have found that anxious kids love this simple exercise. Have your child sit up straight with his feet on the floor. Ask him to inhale loudly for four counts, hold his breath for four counts, and then exhale for four counts. Show him by demonstrating the technique yourself, and then count for him while he tries it. When you demonstrate you may even notice how much more relaxed you feel after doing it just once. This is a great exercise for kids of all ages. Your young child can use it after hearing a scary noise in bed, and your older child can use it before a class presentation. You may even want to use this one in your own daily life!

Put Your Child's Imagination to Work

Sports stars use imagery, or imagining a perfect performance, to help them achieve their goals. Your child can use this technique too. The concept behind imagery is that if you can imagine yourself doing it, then you can do it. Studies have even shown that with athletes, mental practice can be as effective as physical practice. In my clinical experience, children are no different.

Caroline was so nervous during the days leading up to her first day of kindergarten that her parents were afraid she wouldn't make it through the school's front door. I instructed her parents to do a guided imagery, every night for two weeks prior to her first day, in which Caroline saw herself having fun in her new classroom. By the time she went to school, Caroline wasn't nervous because she had spent so much time visualizing a positive outcome.

Teach Positive Self-talk

Positive self-talk is very powerful. According to the authors of *Monsters under the Bed and Other Childhood Fears*, "behind every childhood fear there is a series of scary thoughts and images. Children say things to themselves that either create a fear or make an existing one worse. Add a runaway imagination, and panic is a heartbeat away." For example, when a child repeatedly tells himself that monsters come out from under his bed when it gets dark, he is only adding to his fears. When he tells himself that there really are no monsters under the bed and reminds himself that he is safe and that his parents are nearby, he is more likely to overcome his fear.

When It Is More Serious Than the Bogeyman

Although every child goes through developmental stages in different ways and at different times, some children get stuck when they encounter distress. In general, children who have experienced divorce, loss, or other traumas are more vulnerable to fears than their peers, since their safety and security have been compromised. Studies have shown, for example, that children and adolescents who are exposed to life-threatening hurricanes have increased fears of water, thunder, and rainstorms. It is especially important to support children who have experienced any type of trauma in overcoming their fears without pushing too hard.

Who's Afraid of the Big Bad Wolf: Fear Milestones

There are no hard-and-fast rules about which fears your child will experience and at what particular developmental stages these fears will appear. Often a fear that disappears at one age will sprout up again years later or be replaced by an entirely new one. With that in mind, I offer you the following list of common childhood fears, the ages at which they typically arise, and some typical developmental reactions to those fears. These are very general guidelines, so don't worry if your child experiences any of these fears at different times or stages — it is not the sign of a problem.

Age	Typical Fears	Notes
Five to ten months old	Of people other than primary caretakers	Stranger anxiety often first appears around this time. Infants begin to distinguish between people they know and those they don't know or remember.
One year old	Of animals, baths, doctors, noises, separation from a parent, and strangers	Separation anxiety is common around this time. Separation anxiety may reoccur or develop at a later age when a child has experienced stress, such as the death of a relative or pet, an illness, or a major change such as moving or a family divorce.
Two years old	Of baths, bedtime, doctors, separation from a parent, toilet training	Around this age, give or take a year, children are starting to make sense of the world and are not always clear about the difference between fantasy and reality. They're apt to be afraid of monsters and other imagined threats.

Age	Typical Fears	Notes
Three years old	Of people who look different from family members (they have a beard, different skin color, etc.), bedtime, loss of a parent, monsters and ghosts, toilet training, of being hurt, and sudden loud noises (i.e., a vacuum cleaner)	Around this age, give or take a year, children are starting to make sense of the world and are not always clear about the difference between fantasy and reality. They're apt to be afraid of monsters and other imagined threats.
Four years old	Of animals, bedtime, death, divorce, loss of a parent, monsters and ghosts, noises, going to school, the dark, water, heights, getting lost, small animals, and people who look different from family members	Around this time children often start to develop more realistic fears.
Five years old	Of the dark, death, divorce, getting lost, going to daycare, injury, loss of a parent, monsters and ghosts, noises, rain and thunder, going to school, water, heights, getting stuck in an elevator, and small animals	Fears around close relationships are common at this age, along with the usual fears of both imagined and real things.
Six years old	Of real-life people (like doctors, dentists, or burglars) and things like thunder, lightning, and airplanes	There is often an increase in fears at this age because of a related increase in independence; children are more able to run off and try things they may not be ready for.
Seven years old	Of getting in trouble, of new tasks and activities.	Often at this age, children are more hesitant. They hold back until they feel they can handle things.

[Continued on next page.]

Age	Typical Fears	Notes
Eight years old	Of bodily injury, natural disaster, kidnapping, terrorism	Around this age children often have fears reflecting real circumstances that may happen to them, such as bodily injury and natural disaster. Eight-year-olds tend to enjoy mastering fears and often try to face fears themselves.
Nine years old	Of looking dumb, being unprepared, being made fun of	At this age, children are likely to fear they will not be able to handle responsibilities and are afraid of making mistakes. They are fearful about personal injury and physical destruction. Accidents, kidnapping, disease, and violence are fears that are on the minds of children at this age.
Adolescence	Of taking tests, giving oral reports, being teased or rejected by others, being embarrassed, dating, and encountering situations requiring assertiveness	The most common fears revolve around social evaluation or not being accepted by a peer group. At this age children start to have more global fears about things such as economic problems and environmental devastation.

Some children have such persistent fears that they experience genuine anxiety-related problems. Anxiety occurs on a spectrum: on one end are children who are particularly sensitive and may have a tough time adjusting to changes or new situations. The milder behavior on this end of the spectrum occurs in about 10 percent of children. One Harvard University study found this trait to be a visible part of inborn temperament in babies as young as twenty-one months old. The babies who were studied showed what therapists refer to as "behavioral inhibition," or an inhibited desire to explore their surroundings. Follow-up studies years later found that a higher proportion of this group than that of other sample groups developed anxiety disorders later in life.

On the other end of the spectrum are those who have severe anxiety that can impair their abilities on a daily basis; this accounts for about 2 percent of children. Frequently, children with more severe anxiety have a family history of anxiety and have grown up with a persistent sense of anxiety starting at an early age. It is vital to get these children professional help.

Most children grow out of their fears. With a little bit of help from parents, that process can be expedited. However, if you find that your child's fears are debilitating, last for more than six months, or prevent him from making friends, he may need assistance. If that is the case, I recommend seeking help from a mental health professional who specializes in working with children.

IS FOR CHEERING

Being a Great Sports Parent

These days parents often have trouble distinguishing between a fun game of soccer and the potential for a seven-figure Nike endorsement deal. They push golf clubs into their three-year-old's hands in the hopes of raising the next Tiger Woods and start fistfights at Little League games. While these may be the most extreme of examples, there is not a single parent who hasn't struggled with issues involving their child's athletic performance.

I have experienced the sports world from many different perspectives. I spent five years on the United States Rhythmic Gymnastics National Team, was a Junior National Champion, winning five gold medals out of five, competed in many international competitions, and performed exhibitions at the 1984 Olympic Games. During graduate school I served as a sports coach and a judge for gymnastic competitions. In addition to my psychotherapy practice, I established a sport psychology consulting business, in which I help adult and child athletes of all levels. I have been a member of the USA Gymnastics Task Force on the Female Triad (eating disorders, amenorrhea, and osteoporosis), as well as a sports psychology consultant and advisor to USA Gymnastics on the Athlete Wellness Task Force. I also perform consulting services for two groups that look out for the well-being of child performers: A Minor Consideration and the Actor's Fund.

I have witnessed firsthand the struggles that parents have helping their children become better athletes and often better people. All parents want the best for their children. And figuring out how to provide that in the sports world can be tricky. If you push too hard you may push your kid right out of sports, but if you don't help an undisciplined child learn to keep her word to the team or to herself, you may unwittingly teach her to undervalue her commitments.

Playing Young

Most parents don't want to push their children too hard, but many also feel — and this can start very early — that if they don't push at all their child will be at some sort of disadvantage. Believe it or not, this syndrome starts in utero with the "in utero classroom" and progresses to developmental toys and Mommy-and-Me classes — and keeps getting worse. Lisa Licata, vice president of community relations for the National Alliance for Youth Sports (NAYS), has noticed that kids are participating in team sports at a younger age than they used to, some as early as three years old. Many of the parents of these children assume that starting their child in sports at such a young age will give the child an advantage, when in fact the chances are greater that it will discourage him and make him resent sports activity and decline to participate in the future.

We all want healthy, active kids. The best way to help your child become active and involved in sports is to expose him to all different types of activities and let him chose what he likes best. Most kids don't know what sports they want to pursue until they have been exposed to many choices and have experience playing different sports. Many kids who specialize in one sport at a young age just end up burning out on that sport and not replacing it with another sport or activity.

Childhood is supposed to be preparation for adulthood, a time to learn life lessons such as handling disappointment, valuing hard work, and figuring out one's morals and values. It is not a performance or a competition. By definition, children are immature and cannot be expected to perform like trained monkeys. Do your best to resist the pressure from coaches, friends, relatives, and other parents to turn your kids into champion athletes and perfect children.

Self-esteem and Sports

Participating in sports can help children increase self-esteem, develop a sense of self-efficacy, learn to overcome failure, develop sportsmanship, cultivate discipline, and overcome adversity. Sports are an opportunity for children to master new physical skills, increase strength, and improve flexibility and are a great use of free time.

At their worst sports can lead to injury, feeling excessive pressure, and eating disorders and can take over a child's identity and childhood. While there can be other sources, for the most part, these bad experiences tend to come from overzealous parents or pushy coaches.

The lessons kids can learn from sports are invaluable. Athletics allow children to learn by trial and error, which is developmentally beneficial. The process of doing something over and over until success is achieved ultimately breeds self-esteem. Sports teach children that they can't always get what they want, which allows them to develop the ability to tolerate disappointment and makes them emotionally stronger.

Parents can do many things to avoid problems with their athletic children. Here are a few suggestions.

Sixteen Things Parents Should Do
for Their Child Athletes

1. Be supportive of your child, regardless of the outcome of the competition.
2. Help your child put sports in perspective.
3. Assist your child in finding a healthy balance between sports, school, and social activities.
4. Schedule activities with your child outside of sports.
5. Provide safe transportation to and from practice and events.
6. Support your child in forming an identity as an athlete and as a person.
7. Participate in team activities.
8. Help your child make sense of winning and losing by putting things in perspective.
9. Model good sportsmanship.
10. Be a good team player for your child.
11. Support the coach by giving him or her room to coach.
12. Take all problems (conflicts between players, your concern about your child's progress) directly to the coach, not to other parents or to your child.
13. Love your child unconditionally.
14. Show up for events and cheer.
15. Make sure that your child eats properly and does not try to lose too much weight; make sure she does not have an unhealthy body image as a result of her sport.
16. Never hit, curse at, or threaten a coach or another parent at your child's sporting event.

Suggest Age-appropriate Activities

While children need to be exposed to many different sports so that they can figure out their preferences, very young children should start being physical in free play. This unstructured activity is a great way to get them moving and helps them to develop coordination.

When they get to be six or seven years old, kids become capable of more organized physical activity, owing to their increased attention span and their ability to conceptualize more complex rules. Yet while children at this age are able to conceptualize at a much more advanced level, their thinking is still very black and white.

Children who are exposed to sports between the ages of six and twelve develop strength, coordination, and confidence, traits that are likely to make them more comfortable in the sports world later in life. This kind of early exposure also lays the groundwork for a healthy physical lifestyle down the road.

It is not until they are about eight to ten years old that children are developmentally ready to experiment with competitive sports. At that age they become capable of more complex thought, which gives them the ability to strategize. Most experts recommend that children stay away from high-pressure, competitive teams until the age of eleven or twelve. Children should not be pushed to be exclusive to one sport, but if they naturally gravitate to a specific sport, that decision should be supported.

Do your best to give your child as many opportunities as possible to be active and to experiment with a variety of sports and physical activities so she can find the right fit for her personality, age, and interests. Be careful not to project your own gender stereotypes about sports and physical activities onto your children. Be prepared to ask your son if he wants to try ballet and your daughter if she wants to try football. I recommend making a collaborative effort with your child to help her figure out what activity feels right and allowing the space to experiment with different activities.

Focus on the Process

Teach your child that the process and the effort put forth are far more important than the outcome. These are the only things your child can control. If your child can show some commitment to the activity, she will learn how to commit to other things as well.

According to sports psychologist Dr. Alan Goldberg, "perhaps the most common (and the most performance-disrupting) mistake is an overemphasis on winning and the outcome. Parents who get their kids too focused on the outcome of an athletic contest inadvertently participate in their child's bad performance. You can't play your best at any age if you are focused on or worried about winning or losing. In order to win, the child-athlete must concentrate on what she is doing and nothing else."

You can help your child by asking process-oriented questions like, "How did it go?" "Did you have fun?" "How did you like the game?" and "What was it like playing against that team?" instead of outcome-oriented questions like "Did you win?"

Let Your Child Set Goals

Let your child set her own goals. She just might surprise you. A few years ago a young competitive swimmer came into my office for a sports psychology consultation. During the session she told me about her goal to qualify for the national championships. We set process-oriented goals and worked on imagery to help her performance. The next day I got a call from her mother, who was very concerned. She believed that while her daughter was a very hard worker, she was not

as naturally talented as the other girls on the team. She was worried
that her daughter would be disappointed. I explained to her that it
was not her job to tell her daughter whether or not her goals were
reachable; it was her job just to support her. As it turned out, the mom
was wrong. Her daughter not only qualified for the nationals, but she
also she placed very high in the competition.

Questions Parents of Athletic Kids Should Ask Themselves

Parents with kids in sports need to examine their own motivations.
Ask yourself the following questions:

- When I talk about my child, do I find myself talking about his sports accomplishments over anything else?
- Am I looking for my child to meet my own unmet sports goals from when I was her age?
- Do I want my child to play sports so that he will be popular?
- Am I pushing my child too hard?
- Do I secretly see sports as a chance for my child to make money one day?
- Am I valuing sports over education?
- What messages am I sending my child about his performance?
- What messages is my child learning from her sports experiences?
- Is my child at a high risk for developing an eating disorder as a result of her sports experience?
- Is my child self-motivated?
- Does my child really want to be involved in sports?
- Why does my child want to play sports?
- Who wants sports for my child more? Me or my child?
- Why is my child doing sports?

Offer Unconditional Support

Sandy Connely, a former top rhythmic gymnastics coach, always told the parents of her athletes to "leave room for the coach to coach." The belief behind this statement is that kids need parents to be the support system so that the coaches can push as hard as necessary to get results. Child athletes need to be able to turn to their parents for support. Don't push — that's the coach's job — and never withhold love or display anger in response to your child's athletic results.

It is vital that you *do not add to your child's burnout*. Kids are under enough pressure as participants in youth sports, and it is not helpful for parents to add to that pressure. Most kids just want to have fun playing the game, and when parents place too much value on the outcome, their children are likely to tire of the sport. In fact, one survey of children in sports found that 95 percent of youth players were more interested in having fun than in winning. When the fun is taken out of sports, kids are ripe for burnout.

In one study focusing on the sources of stress and burnout in youth golf, some of the most frequently cited reasons for the burnout were: (1) Overtraining, (2) A lack of enjoyment, and (3) Too much pressure from self and others to do well. If you push your child to practice too much, she will enjoy that sport less and will feel pressured by you to do well. It is worthwhile to note that the greatest athletes are self-motivated. Let your child discover the love of the sport, and if she is wired to become a great athlete trust that she will pursue excellence for her own reasons.

According to a study by the Michoacán State Institute for Youth Sports of children who participate in organized sports in the United States, by the time these kids reach the age of thirteen, nearly three-quarters of them will quit. The best way to help your child to become part of the 26 percent who don't give up on their sport is to make their participation a positive experience by being supportive and not contributing to their stress.

Monitor the Coach

The coach is in a very influential position. He or she spends a lot of time with your child and is an authority figure whom your child wants to please. This gives the coach tremendous power not only to teach your child how to play but also to influence her values and beliefs. As a parent, you need to keep an eye on the coach-child relationship. Evaluate, and talk with your child about, the lessons she is learning from the coach. Don't hesitate to make unannounced visits to your child's practices and to watch the coach in action. Any coach who does not allow you to attend training sessions is hiding something, and you should be immediately suspicious.

Model Good Behavior

Your child looks to you to model appropriate behavior. If you act a certain way, your child will think it is okay to act that way too. Watch your behavior at competitions and games especially. They are a very public forum for your child. A good place to start is by demonstrating to your child what it looks like to be a good sport. Don't yell or blame specific players (including and especially your child), coaches, referees, or judges and be respectful toward whomever played well, even if he or she is on the other team. Your child will take note.

Teach your child to be a graceful winner and loser. If your child is not selected to play on a team, that is not a measure of her worth or even an indicator of her future in sports. Michael Jordan didn't even make his tenth-grade basketball team, and he still did pretty well in that sport later!

The most valuable lesson I ever learned as an athlete was not as a result of winning. In my first year at the Rhythmic Gymnastics National Championships I was one of the only people on my team who did not make the national team. To this day, I will never forget what it felt like to congratulate all my teammates who made the team, holding back my tears until I got to my hotel room. As painful as it was, I am glad I had that experience. It taught me many important lessons, such as the importance of hard work, discipline, how to lose well, and ultimately how to win well, all of which have served me well in other areas of my life

The good news is that you don't have to be a perfect parent. The most important element of being a successful sports parent is to make your child feel supported and loved by you regardless of her performance.

Raising Twins

Ten years ago it was uncommon for me to get a call at my psychotherapy office from a parent with questions about parenting twins. In the last few years, however, this type of call has become quite common. According to the National Center for Health Statistics, the number of twin deliveries has increased by 74 percent since 1980: up from 68,339 to 118,619. This increase in multiple births is due to more frequent use of fertility treatments and parents waiting to conceive until later in life, when the chances of having multiples are greater. As a result, the demand for information about parenting twins has increased dramatically as well.

Most parents recognize that the challenges of raising twins are very different from those of raising a single child but are unsure of what those challenges really are and of how to meet them. Some expectant parents believe that raising twins is the same as raising a single child, only double the effort. The truth is more complicated than that. Here are a few key issues that parents of twins should be aware of.

Independence Day: Creating Individuals

One of the greatest challenges parents of twins face is helping their children to develop independence from each other while encouraging them to maintain a close relationship. The way you relate to them and the messages you send about their relationship with each other will be one of their biggest influences early in their life.

Nancy became a client of mine when her twin girls, Mary and Carrie, were five years old. She was concerned because whenever they were separated from each other, even for a short period, they would immediately get agitated, with this agitation quickly building to fits of hysterical crying and screaming. In addition, the girls often got their names confused or referred to themselves as "Mary-Carrie." Before coming in to see me, Nancy had tried to create and nurture a close relationship between the girls, telling them that they were best friends even before they could speak. Nancy felt their twinship was truly special and liked to accentuate their togetherness by dressing them alike. Part of the reason for this was that Nancy grew up as an only child and always had trouble sharing with others. In the hopes of avoiding similar problems for her girls, she made them share everything. They shared all their toys, their clothes, and even their friends. Nancy made their entire identities be about being twins. While Nancy is an extreme example, many parents make the mistake of pushing their twins to be artificially close. Often parents project their own fantasies about what it must be like to be a twin — or what they would like the twin experience to be for their children — onto their kids instead of looking squarely at the realities of the situation and of the personalities involved.

What Nancy failed to understand is that each of her girls is a separate individual with her own likes, dislikes, and needs. In order to help Mary and Carrie, Nancy had to learn to see her daughters for who they were, not for who she wanted them to be. I encouraged

Nancy to try to avoid calling them "the twins," which had inadvertently reinforced their identity as one entity, and I encouraged her, instead, to start calling them by their names. In addition, because ownership is such an important part of identity formation, I told her to allow each daughter to have clothes and some toys that were hers alone. I instructed Nancy to stop telling her daughters they were "best friends" and to allow them to define their relationship for themselves.

While Nancy was willing to make those changes, when I told her that she needed to stop dressing them in identical outfits she was extremely resistant to making that change. When we explored her motivation it became clear that dressing them alike brought attention to them which, in turn, brought attention to Nancy, making her feel special. This celebrity status was hard for Nancy to give up. The only way for her to move forward was to find ways to make herself feel special on her own. Last, but not least, I gave Nancy a homework assignment for her and her husband to begin immediately. Both had to spend ten minutes alone a day with each child. Because the girls had spent so little time apart, the first few days were a difficult adjustment, but eventually they learned to tolerate and then appreciate time apart, first with their parents and eventually without them, which helped them become more independent individuals.

I Win, You Lose: Twins and Competition

Competition among twins is very normal, since twins grow up vying for their parents' attention. Because emotional supplies (i.e., time) tend to be in shorter supply when twins come along, often one child believes that if the other is getting the parents' attention, he or she must be the preferred twin. This belief leads to jealousy and the feeling that there is not enough of the parents' love to go around —

which is generally not the case. Parents of twins need to be sensitive to this issue.

Competition and the need to differentiate are tightly linked. Twins, like all children, always strive to figure out who they are and how they are different. When asked about the differences between her and her twin sister, Chloe, a fifteen-year-old client of mine replied, "I'm the smart one, and she's the pretty one." Because she got better grades than her sister, Chloe was labeled the "smart one" in the family which, by default, left her sister feeling like the "dumb one." This comparison also left Chloe feeling like the "ugly twin." For the sake of your twins' self-esteem, it is important for you to help them come to terms with their differences without giving them labels. Parents must walk that fine line between recognizing their children's strengths while not *defining* them by those strengths. It is

---

The Good News about Twins: Twin Advantages

Potty training. While twins tend to start toilet training a little later than their peers, they learn faster. Some believe this is because they can be role models to one another, while others believe it is the competitive nature of the twin relationship that makes them so eager to learn once they are ready.

Sharing. Because twins have grown up sharing everything from space and attention to toys, they tend to be better at sharing than other children.

Empathy. Twins generally show the ability for empathy earlier than other children.

Interaction. Because they have grown up playing with someone else, twins tend to interact with others earlier than other kids.

Love. With twins you get to give and receive twice as much love and affection.

especially important to avoid negative comparisons between siblings. Instead of saying, "You are so much better at drawing than your brother," try saying, "Wow! Your drawings are really terrific."

Competition between twins tends to heat up during periods of individuation. When children are attempting to define themselves and to prove how different and independent they are, they tend to get more competitive and to fight more often than at other times. This is especially common in the middle school years. The parents' role during this tumultuous time is not to quash their quarrelsome behavior but to make sure that their kids fight fairly.

Stuck Like Glue: Twins and Attachment

Many experts believe that twin bonding begins in utero. From the first moment of conception, twins have a completely different experience than does a single baby. Because they are born with each other as companions, their attachment to each other tends to be very strong. Often, the comfort twins find in one another's company lays the foundation for the development of other future attachments as well. A Louisville twin study that examined twin attachments found that one-year-old twins who were left with strangers adapted to the changes very calmly as long as they were with their twin.

In the early years, twins learn to strengthen their attachments to each other and to their parents at the same time, and this can complicate the bonding process. In addition, human beings are not wired to fall in love with two people at once in the same moment. It is not uncommon for mothers and fathers to start to feel a bond to one child before the other. Parents tend to feel very guilty when they feel closer to one child than the other. The reality is that even though parents love their children equally, because of similarities in temperament and personality, sometimes they may feel closer to one over the other.

In the case of twins, it is important to give both children equal attention and accolades.

Parents can run the risk of attaching to their twins as a unit. This type of unit bonding can keep parents from recognizing their children's unique attributes and feelings. To feel close to someone we must feel both seen and understood. For an infant, that means having his cries for hunger met with offers of food. For older children, it means being recognized for their strengths and having an adult who can interpret their moods.

Jane arrived at my office red eyed from a prolonged bout of crying. "I think my twin boys love my husband more than they love me," she cried. "I must have done something wrong!" In a study of the attachment patterns of twins, researchers examined the relationships of seventy-six pairs of twins and found that forty-nine pairs were classified as mother attached and twenty-seven pairs as father attached. This high number of father-focused twins is significantly higher than it is for single-birth children who have been studied. Some hypothesize that twins get tired of struggling for their mother's attention and turn to their father instead. In the case of many twins, each child bonds more closely with a different parent in order to get his or her needs met. In all these cases, both children were attached to both parents, even though they created a primary attachment to just one of them.

To help you to bond with your twin children of all ages, I recommend a few things. When speaking, make eye contact with each child and make sure to call him by name. This helps your child to connect with you and to feel as though you are focused on him alone. Try to spend some time alone with each sibling each day, even if it is just ten minutes. In addition, have a special day each month in which you spend an afternoon alone with one child at a time, while your spouse spends an equal amount of time with the other. Make sure that the next time you switch children so each child gets time alone with each parent.

Baby Talk: Twins and Language Development

For several reasons, twins tend to be slower than singletons in language acquisition. Most experts speculate that the primary reason for this is that babies learn language by hearing adults speak to them properly, and parents of twins are often overwhelmed and short on time and thus have fewer verbal interactions with their children. An Australian study measuring the length of communication times between mothers and their children found that mothers of single children averaged two minutes, while those of mothers of twins averaged only ninety seconds a child.

Many experts believe that another reason twins learn to speak more slowly has to do with the weight and development of the babies at birth. It has been estimated that 50 to 60 percent of twins are born premature, and prematurity and low birth weights are associated with early developmental delays. Not to worry, however, since the early developmental delays in twins are usually offset by a subsequent tendency among those preemie twins to grow and develop faster than other babies, helping them to catch up or surpass their peers. Studies show that any developmental or intellectual gap that may have existed tends to close by the age of six.

The most common belief, however, about why twins learn a primary language slower than other children is that twins have a tendency to learn language skills from each other. Because they spend so much time together, they tend to model language for one another, meaning that they pick up each other's mispronunciations and bad habits as well. This often accounts for what many people call the "secret twin language" but that experts refer to as "idioglossia," or autonomous language. It is estimated that 40 percent of all twins use this type of communication with each other. While outsiders may view this as a secret language, it is really just a shared type of baby talk that is a result of twins modeling incorrect language to one another. Most twins outgrow it by the age of four.

Double Duty: Parenting Twins

Parents of twins face huge challenges, but the rewards of raising twins are more than just double. The following ten tips will help you raise happy, healthy individual children who are part of a twin relationship:

1. Respond to your children's individual needs as much as possible.

2. Recognize the increase in stress on you and your spouse, and do your best to get as much support as possible.

3. Don't deny one twin what he or she needs or wants just so you can help the other. For example, if one child wants to take a class but the other does not, allow the one who wants the class to attend instead of keeping both at home.

4. When speaking to a twin, make eye contact and address the child by name.

5. Nurture your relationship with each child as well as your relationship with both of them together.

6. Insist that both children speak for themselves so that they will learn good speaking skills.

7. Teach your twins how to have alone time.

8. Prepare your twins for the fact that life is unfair and that they will each be given different opportunities.

9. Protect your twins from each other by teaching them to fight fairly.

10. Talk to your twins and read to them as much as possible to help them to develop language skills.

The greatest gifts you can give your twin children are love, support, and recognition of who they are both as twins and as unique people.

Helping Children Become Good Decision Makers

Who your child becomes, how successful he will be, where he lives, who he socializes with, how often he exercises, how strong his support system will be, who he marries, how many children he will have, and his general satisfaction in life: all are outcomes of some of the most important decisions your child will make. The choices he makes will greatly affect the quality as well as the length of his life. Considering how important it is for your child to be able to make good decisions, one would think schools would offer courses in decision-making skills. However, since the burden to teach these invaluable skills falls on parents, you need to know how to teach your kids to make responsible decisions for themselves.

Mine! Mine! Mine!: Owning Choices

When babies are born, parents make all their decisions for them. As time goes by and the children's preferences develop, parents gradually let them make an increasing number of decisions for themselves. Over time, parents transfer most of the decision making to their children.

Every choice a child makes is a testament to her autonomy and sense of self-determination. Even a choice as simple as whether to wear the red shoes or the white ones is significant for young children. Each choice they make helps to define their preferences and gives them practice making decisions.

Show your child that you have faith in her decision-making abilities by giving her the opportunity to make choices as frequently as possible. When your children are young, you should present these choices with clear limits. Allowing children to choose between two acceptable options is usually the best way to help them learn these skills without overwhelming them. For example, ask, "Do you want beans or carrots" not, "What vegetable would you like for dinner?"

Pink or Green?

To help your child develop confidence in her decision making it is crucial that you only present her with choices you can support. Terry took her six-year-old daughter, Emily, shopping before her first day of school. While in the department store Emily found a green sweater she really liked that Terry was not so fond of. Terry gave Emily a choice between the green sweater Emily liked and a pink sweater that Terry really preferred. When Emily chose the green one Terry was disappointed and asked her questions like, "Are you sure that's the one you want?" and, "Don't you think this other pretty sweater would look much better on you?" revealing that she thought Emily had made the wrong decision and that she questioned her taste. This left Emily in a bind. If she chose the sweater she wanted she knew her mother would be disappointed and think she had made the wrong choice, but if she chose the one her mother liked she would be selling herself out to please her mother.

"Oh, come on, it's only a sweater," you may be saying to yourself. But it is more than that. This type of moment is really about individuation (Emily learning to stand by her choices even when they conflict with her mom's), self-definition (Emily learning to create an image of herself), and making choices (both choices come with a consequence). By questioning her decision, Terry has sent Emily a message that (1) she cannot be trusted to make decisions, (2) there is a right and wrong opinion to have about the sweaters, (3) Emily cannot trust Terry. If you give your child a choice you must accept his or her decision, even if it is not the one you would have made.

Along those lines, it is important to choose your battles wisely. If your son wants to eat cereal instead of toast for breakfast, don't fight with him. If, however, he wants to play in the street where he could get hit by a car, that choice is not an option. Safety is one area in which parents should not budge; it is your responsibility to keep your children safe.

One of the most difficult things for children (and adults) to accept is what author Barry Schwartz refers to in *The Paradox of Choice* as the *opportunity* cost of giving up one option by choosing another. If you can teach your child to recognize and accept real-life consequences at an early age, he or she will be starting off with a great advantage. This kind of understanding leads to greater tolerance of frustration and disappointment.

Daddy Will Fix It: Facing Consequences

When you help your children understand at an early age that they are responsible for the choices they make as well as for the consequences of their actions, you promote a sense of mastery and self-confidence in them. One of the most difficult tasks for parents is allowing their kids to suffer the consequences of their choices and actions. But in order for children to grow up to become responsible adults, they need to know how to deal with these kinds of consequences. It is a crucial developmental step for them to take.

Mark, a college student, was sent to me by his parents because they were concerned about his pot smoking and poor grades. Mark, who was clearly very bright and got fantastic SAT scores, was completely unmotivated. He attended an expensive private college with a great academic reputation. When I asked him what he planned to do after college he told me he would go to law school.

"How are you going to get into law school?" I asked him. "You are barely passing your classes right now, and law school is highly competitive."

"My dad has connections. He can buy me a spot in at least three of the top schools," he told me.

Apparently Mark's dad had already bought his son's way into his current school. Up to that point, Mark had never had to face any of

---

Questions to Ask Your Child about Decision Making

During

- Would you like to hear some things other kids in your situation have tried?
- What would the consequences of your actions be?
- How would your choice affect other people?
- Is this decision in your best interests?
- If you close your eyes and imagine choosing option A, how would do you feel? If you close your eyes and imagine choosing option B, how would do you feel?

After

- How did you decide to choose that option?
- What did you learn from that experience?
- What would you do differently next time?

the consequences of his actions. If he forgot his homework his mother brought it, if he forgot his lunch the maid brought it, if he forgot to feed his goldfish and it died he was given a new fish. Now mom and dad were still getting him out of trouble, and at the age of nineteen Mark had no life skills, no discipline, and no motivation. Had Mark suffered the consequences of his actions at an earlier age, he would have learned to apply himself. Adversity leads to growth. If you allow your children to suffer the consequences of bad choices, they will learn to make better choices. Protecting kids from those kinds of consequences only retards their ability to develop into responsible adults.

If at First You Don't Succeed, Try, Try Again

Making mistakes is integral to the learning process. In a game of darts, we alter our decisions about where and how to throw the dart based on the successes and failures of our previous attempts so that we can get closer to the bull's-eye. Life is no different. You learn from past actions so that you can make different choices in the future.

When you give your child the opportunity to make a responsible decision that she doesn't take advantage of, and she suffers as a result, then she has the best possible opportunity for a learning experience. If you can respond with empathy while allowing her to suffer the consequences of her bad decision (or lack of decision), she is unlikely to make the same mistake again. When Lisa's daughter called to say she forgot her lunch, Lisa empathetically replied, "You must be hungry. I won't be able to bring you your lunch, but hopefully you will be able to find a way to get by until you get home." Lisa knew that her daughter would not starve to death by three o'clock when she picked her up. But by not rushing to the school to deliver her daughter's lunch, Lisa guaranteed that her daughter would not forget her lunch in the future.

Children also look to their parents for help in figuring out how to process a failure. How you respond to your own failures will often determine your child's tolerance for her own mistakes. If your child does not have permission to struggle and to be imperfect, she will never learn; she will be too stuck in fear to try again. If you present a mistake as an opportunity for growth and learning, your child will view it that way as well.

If children are encouraged to do only the things they are good at, they will never master new tasks. As so many of the world's greatest talents have demonstrated, to succeed people first need to learn how to fail. Ulysses S. Grant failed as a farmer, a real estate agent, a U.S. Customs official, and a store clerk before he went on to become a successful general and the eighteenth president of the United States. Michael Jordan was cut from his varsity football team in his sophomore year of high school before he went on to become one of the most revered basketball players in history. Academy Award nominee and legendary actor Rock Hudson required thirty-eight takes before he could successfully complete one line in his first movie, *Fighter Squadron*. *CBS Evening News* anchor Katie Couric was banned from reading news reports on the air by the president of CNN because he hated her high-pitched voice. If your child feels discouraged, you can let her know that even the most successful people have experienced failures.

Follow the Leader

Children look to their parents to learn how to persevere. Here are five things to keep in mind as you teach your children about good and bad decision making:

1. You can help your children by sharing your own mistakes while also teaching them how you learned from those mistakes.

2. Encourage and honor your children's repeated attempts at solving a problem.

3. Reward your children for their perseverance.

4. Pay attention to your reactions to your own mistakes. Your children will learn as much, or more, from what you do as they will from what you say.

5. Reward good decision making.

Gut Feelings: Kids and Intuition

Most people are encouraged to disregard their intuitive process in favor of a more logical one. This is a huge mistake. Great decision makers listen to their instincts. Children are born naturally intuitive because they tend to express their thoughts and feelings without a filter or without being swayed by the judgment of others.

Jamie was interviewing new babysitters for her son Ben. After she had narrowed the final choices down to two people she introduced them to Ben, who immediately took to the first candidate. The second candidate just seemed to rub him the wrong way, and, even though she seemed fine to Jamie, Ben said he just "didn't like" her and that she "gave him the creeps." That was enough for Ben's mom, who honored her son's feelings. Linda and Joe, neighbors two doors down, ended up hiring the second candidate. When they arrived home after a night out to find their new babysitter passed out on the couch with the liquor cabinet empty, they were shocked. And Jamie was glad she had listened to her son's gut feelings.

Teaching a child to trust her inner voice is a good way to help her develop good self-esteem. In his book *The Gift of Fear*, Gavin de Becker hypothesizes that our intuition is really based on our reading of hundreds of subtle logical signs around us and then drawing quick conclusions. He believes that intuition is actually a cognitive process that is superior to logical thought. De Becker recommends identifying the thirteen signs of intuition: nagging feelings, persistent thoughts, humor, wonder, anxiety, curiosity, hunches, gut feelings, doubt, hesitation, suspicion, apprehension, and fear. Teaching your child to pay attention to those signs will also help her.

Helping with the Process

Sometimes children appear to be asking for our assistance in solving problems, but in reality they only want empathy or support. We need to learn to listen quietly in order to respond appropriately to our children. Parents can be thrown off by their own anxiety and their desire to help their child avoid pain and are often too quick to offer answers.

Jim Fay, coauthor of the *Parenting with Love and Logic* series, recommends the following five steps to help children solve problems:

1. Show empathy.

2. Imply that your child is smart enough to solve the problem.

3. Ask permission to share alternatives.

4. Examine the consequences of each alternative.

5. Let the child decide whether to and how to solve the problem.

This supportive, but hands-off approach allows children the maximum learning opportunity. It is always difficult to see our kids suffer in any way, but as parents we must understand that to raise responsible children with enough self-esteem to make good decisions, we must let them learn to make mistakes.

Raising Kids with Great Self-esteem

Children with great self-esteem are secure, strong, and independent young people who, with your help, can grow up to be confident adults. All parents want to raise children who feel great about themselves and, while there are no guarantees, there are many things that you can do to give your little ones this advantage.

In his book *The Six Pillars of Self-Esteem* Nathaniel Branden, considered the father of the self-esteem movement, defines self-esteem as "confidence in our ability to think; confidence in our ability to cope with the basic challenges of life; and confidence in our right to be successful and happy, the feeling of being worthy, deserving, entitled to assert our needs and wants, achieving our values, and the fruits of our efforts." Branden believes that self-esteem is a self-fulfilling prophecy: "Self-esteem creates a set of implicit expectations about what is possible and appropriate to us. These expectations tend to generate the actions that turn them into realities. And the realities confirm and strengthen the original beliefs."

Mirror, Mirror on the Wall

Psychologically, parents are the mirrors in which kids see themselves reflected; your children look to you to figure out who they are and how they fit in the world. An infant is born without a sense of self, and parents help create his first images of who he is and what his value is in the world. As children grow older and their world becomes bigger, they discover more mirrors, people they come across one time or every day, such as friends, relatives, teachers, and childcare workers. However, for better or for worse, it is the parents, through their words and actions, who create the foundation for a child's sense of self.

Every time Sarah drew a picture, her parents smiled and commented on how smart and artistic their daughter was. They marveled at her imagination and encouraged her to explore her creativity. This positive reinforcement helped Sarah to feel good about herself and to think of herself as a creative person. Different parents might have looked at Sarah's purple trees and green clouds and told her that her drawings were inaccurate or that she was not a very good artist. Sarah now sells her abstract paintings for a small fortune at galleries around the world. Well-known pediatrician Dr. William Sears said it best when he wrote, in *The Successful Child*, "What children believe about themselves is at the heart of what they become."

There are many things that you as a parent can do to help your kids feel good about themselves. Below I suggest the most vital strategies.

Watch Your Words

Parents must be careful with their words. Name-calling, even in jest, can affect a child for life. When Jill was a little girl, whenever she got nervous, she would become very forgetful. Whenever this happened, Jill's father would jokingly call her "bubble brain." Even though he knew his daughter was smart and didn't mean any harm, for many years his insensitive nickname made Jill think she was stupid.

When your child does something that bothers you, describe the behavior, not the child. For example, say, "That was a careless thing to do" instead of, "You are so careless." This allows the child to differentiate between his behavior and his sense of self.

Be Accepting

In the late 1960s psychological researcher Stanley Coopersmith set out to identify significant parenting behaviors associated with children who had high self-esteem. One significant finding was that children with good self-esteem have parents who totally accept their thoughts, feelings, and words. These children feel loved and appreciated, despite their quirks or "imperfections." This is not to say that their parents were blind to their flaws, only that they managed to communicate to their children that they accepted them on a deep level. To let your kids know that you accept and love them for who they are, despite all their perceived flaws, is one of the most powerful things that you can do.

Grok Your Kids

In his book *Stranger in a Strange Land* Robert Heinlein uses the word *grok* to describe deeply comprehending and accepting another. I use this science fiction word simply because there is no other term that expresses the concept quite as well. It is only by developing a complete understanding of what someone is about that you can grok him or her. This means not projecting any fantasies or desires onto a person and acknowledging who he or she really is. This can be particularly difficult for a parent. Often when we see flaws in our children, especially if they are flaws we struggle with ourselves, we feel so anxious that we are not able to embrace our kids for who they really are. But if you can create a safe relationship that allows your children to really share their intimate thoughts with you, you are well on your way to helping them have great self-esteem.

Ten More Things You Can Do to Help Your Child Have Great Self-esteem

1. *Set consistent rules.* Don't announce a punishment you know you will not follow through on. Children need structure to feel safe. All rules should apply to all your children equally.

2. *Create a calm and nonviolent home atmosphere.* Children can only thrive and learn to trust when they feel safe. Make sure your home's atmosphere is conducive to your child's well-being.

3. *Ask your child for his opinions.* Show your child you value his opinions by asking questions.

4. *Spend focused time together.* Children are sensitive to an adult's distracted mind. Turn off the television, put away the Blackberry, and don't answer the phone for a few hours so you can spend some focused time together.

5. *Help your child find her passions.* Allowing your child to engage in an activity that she enjoys will bolster her self-identity and help her to develop a sense of mastery.

6. *Give honest and specific praise.* Offering this kind of praise helps your child feel seen and appreciated.

7. *Reframe your child's idiosyncrasies.* Your child looks to you to know how to perceive herself. If you let your "loud child who asks too many questions" know you see her as "passionate and curious" instead, she may see herself differently.

8. *Apologize if you say something mean or hurtful to your child.* Show your child how to make amends so that he knows how to do it himself. You don't have to be perfect, and your child will benefit from seeing how you behave when you make a mistake.

9. *Show up for your kid.* Show up when you say you will, and make sure to attend important events like school plays, sporting events, and piano recitals.

10. *Leave your child love notes.* When your child is old enough to read, leave her notes or letters encouraging her and reminding her that you love her.

Pay Attention

Providing focused attention and empathy is also vital to your child's self-esteem. Paying attention out of a desire for direct, personal involvement means being truly open to the unique qualities of your child. Showing empathy or imagining yourself in your child's shoes allows him or her to feel loved and cared for. In addition, your empathetic responses to your children teach them to have empathy for themselves.

Respect Thoughts and Feelings

It is important to show respect for your child's opinions even if you don't agree with them. Ask what she thinks, and listen attentively to her responses. Not only does this allow you to know your kid better, but it also shows her you care about her thoughts and that her opinions matter. This reinforcement helps her to believe in the value of her views and beliefs. Branden has found that the higher a person's self-esteem, the stronger her drive to express herself will be.

Teach Your Child to Fail

Children with high self-esteem can see their weaknesses and view them as opportunities for growth. Twelve-year-old Cade was a great baseball player, but when he got into the field for a game he rarely could hit the ball. Because Cade had healthy self-esteem, he was able to recognize that he was still a great baseball player but that his anxiety about performing in front of crowds was hurting his game. This allowed me as his therapist to give him some simple sports psychology techniques that helped him to relax before games, changing the outcome and allowing him to reach his potential. A child with lower self-esteem might have started doubting his worth as a result of his poor game performance. If you can tolerate your child's mistakes, you give him the opportunity to learn from them. Children who don't learn to lose don't learn to win. But more important, they get their competitive passions squashed. Competition is a great opportunity for a child to take risks, rise to a challenge, learn about himself, and perform. It is an opportunity for growth.

I have witnessed a disturbing trend in recent years: educators at elementary schools are so worried about hurting a child's self-esteem that they tell all the children that everyone is the same. This completely overlooks the truth that every child has different abilities, and it prevents children from seeing their own strengths. In addition, if a child can't see his weaknesses, how can he improve? School sports teams don't keep scores anymore, and now high schools are not likely to recognize valedictorians for fear of hurting the self-esteem of the other kids who did not win that honor. I believe this is a huge mistake.

That being said, as a parent you need to focus on process over outcome, in other words, to teach your children to learn for the sake of learning, not just to become the valedictorian. This teaches them the importance of hard work and knowledge.

Have High Standards

The Coopersmith study of parenting behaviors found that children with high self-esteem have parents with high standards and expectations of behavior and performance. These parents managed to enforce high standards without being punishing, controlling, or benevolent. Their children, to paraphrase the U.S. Army, were encouraged to "be all that they could be." Perhaps knowing that their parents cared enough to want the best for them helped them to want the same for themselves.

Parents have a hard line to walk here, because you also don't want to push *too* hard. Children tend to measure themselves against the standards their parents set for them. As Dorothy Corkille Briggs points out in her book *Your Child's Self-Esteem*, "children rarely question our expectations; instead, they question their performance adequacy." If you push too hard, your child will feel defeated before he tries.

Teach Them to Express

Teaching your children to identify and express feelings is an important way to help them build self-esteem. Children who are able to express their feelings are much less likely to act out in destructive ways. It is especially important that parents allow for the expression of negative feelings, such as anger and sadness. Many parents worry that if they listen to expression of negative emotions, they will be validating those emotions and encouraging their children to feel bad or to hurt other people. Fortunately, that is not the case. Validating your children's feelings gives them the freedom to feel but not act. This also allows your children to have ownership of their experience.

All feelings are valid, even if parents don't understand them or even accept them. The worst thing a parent can say is "You shouldn't feel that way." And here are five reasons never to say those five nasty words:

1. Your child now feels bad for having those feelings.

2. Children open up to you in a search for understanding and compassion. Telling them they shouldn't feel a certain way shuts them down and doesn't make them feel understood.

3. When your child feels free to express and explore his feelings, he doesn't need to act them out in destructive ways.

4. Telling your child to stop feeling a certain way doesn't change the fact that the feeling is still present. Now, in addition to feeling bad, your child feels guilty and frustrated for having experienced his natural emotions.

5. Energy that your child wastes trying to repress feelings is not available for more beneficial activities.

Be a Self-esteem Role Model

The best way to raise a child with healthy self-esteem is to model good self-esteem yourself. Self-esteem is one of those areas in which parents must lead by example. If you feel that you are not a positive role model, then you owe it to yourself and to your child to do everything you can do to raise your self-esteem. I encourage you to read books, attend seminars, and get therapy to work through your issues.

When we have not worked through our own problems, we are more likely to take them out on our kids. I once saw a parent in my therapy practice who kept pushing her young daughter to play tennis competitively, even though her daughter clearly hated the sport. Although her daughter regularly won ribbons, she really wanted to play soccer instead. After exploring the issue with the mother I asked her if she had ever wanted to be a tennis player. The mother told me that she had always regretted not playing tennis as a child and wanted to give her daughter the chance to have what she had never had. When I asked her why she didn't start tennis lessons now, as an adult, she burst into tears and told me she was too "fat and dumb" and that she had missed her chance, clearly all messages she had received from her own family of origin.

This mother had lost track of where she ended and where her daughter began. She was not giving her daughter the fantasy tennis experience she herself had desired and missed. Instead, she was ignoring her daughter's wishes and creating a negative experience that made her daughter feel like she had to continue to play tennis to be loved by her mother. After examining her own self-esteem issues, the mother ultimately allowed her daughter to switch over to soccer and started playing tennis again herself. She even won a ribbon in the adult division at her club.

[F]

To help your child develop strong, positive self-esteem you don't have to be the perfect parent. You do, however need to be a conscious parent who is accountable for her own emotional imperfections and who consistently shows her child that he is loved. If your child knows that he can count on you to be there for him and to validate his thoughts and dreams, then you are on the right track.

 IS FOR GIMME, GIMME

Raising Down-to-earth Children

Eighty percent of people polled think that kids today are more spoiled than kids ten or fifteen years ago. Two-thirds of parents think their own children are spoiled.

— Results of a 2001 *Time*/CNN poll

We live in an era that has glamorized the "spoiled princess." Your child can turn on the television to see role models like Paris Hilton and Nicole Richie in *The Simple Life* or Ally Hilfiger and Jamie Gleicher in *Rich Girls*. These scions and heiresses have made their careers out of being spoiled rich girls and even take pride in that designation.

Because I practice psychotherapy out of my office in the affluent city of Beverly Hills, you might think that I see many spoiled children. While that is partially true, I have discovered that wealth does not guarantee that a child will be spoiled. I have seen families with extraordinary amounts of money with unspoiled children and families with money problems whose children are difficult and entitled, as well as the reverse, which is more what you might expect.

One thing that unifies all these parents, however, is that none of them set out to create a monster who believes that his or her every desire should be met right now. Most of these well-meaning parents just want their children to have the advantages they never had and to save them from pain. While that is a noble cause, the disappointment, frustration, and pain that come from delayed gratification help build your child's character, and they bolster moral and ethical values, along with patience, determination, and adaptability. Children who are spared the ordinary difficulties of daily life end up at an emotional and developmental disadvantage.

In fact, spoiling your children is more dangerous to their well-being than you might imagine. According to a nationwide study of over one thousand families, girls who describe themselves as "very spoiled" are three times as likely to have driven drunk and twice as likely to have smoked marijuana. They are also at high risk for getting poor grades, having bulimia, smoking cigarettes, cheating on tests, and skipping school. According to that same study, boys who considered themselves "spoiled" were found to be at a higher risk of behavioral problems like lying, cheating, being anxious and/or depressed, skipping school, underachieving academically, using steroids, and driving while drunk.

We all want to raise children whose self-worth is not based on the brand of jeans they wear. So let us turn to some of the important issues involved with raising a down-to-earth kid.

Presence, Not Presents

In order for children to form healthy attachments, they need to be able to self-regulate, which, in turn, makes them more resilient and more capable of dealing with adversity. And to form good attachments, children need to have caregivers who are consistently available both physically and emotionally.

You cannot spoil a child with too much love. Giving your child attention, love, and affection does not make her entitled, but giving her every material object she desires does. Children look to you to teach them how to delay gratification. This ability to delay gratification, once they are adults, translates into lower rates of drug and alcohol abuse, a stronger work ethic, and generally having more patience. To develop good self-esteem children need to know that they are loved by their parents. Giving a child a toy or game does not replace spending time with her. She needs to know a parent loves her enough to spend time with her and cares enough to ask about her thoughts and feelings.

In addition, spending time together allows you the opportunity to be a role model. Your child absorbs everything you do and say. If you buy impulsively, even at the supermarket, your child is likely to learn that behavior. Children are very aware of their parents' values and behaviors.

Setting Clear Boundaries

Giving your children rules to follow shows them you care about their well-being and safety. Setting boundaries makes your children feel safe. Imagine driving your car in a world with no rules or regulations to aid drivers; it would be chaotic and scary. A home without consistent rules for a child would be the same as a lawless road. Without rules to live by and the ability to follow the "laws" of the family, children grow up anxious and disrespectful. They believe it is permissible to behave however they choose because no one has taught them otherwise.

Many parents care more about being their children's friends than being their parents. Often this dynamic gets in the way of their being able to set rules and be firm with their word. The truth is, your child has plenty of friends; what he needs most is a parent. It is part of your job to be the final word. Children sense when you are ambivalent about what you're saying and will almost always try to take advantage of this. They don't try to take advantage to be "bad" or malicious, but because they need to test you. When you are firm with your word despite tantrums, tears, or threats from your child, you send a message not only that you care about him but also that you are not going to be bullied.

The truth is that even though, in that moment, your child wants his way, he never wants to feel more powerful than you. If you have allowed him to scream his way out of a decision you have made, he will feel too powerful for his own good and is likely to develop "little emperor syndrome." In many families in which both parents lavish excessive attention and resources on their child, the child becomes increasingly spoiled and gains a sense of self-importance and entitlement. The last thing you want to do as a parent is to create this type of attitude in your child.

Parents also need to be consistent with punishments and follow-through. When children know what the consequences of their actions will be, they make better decisions about their behavior. This challenge is the Achilles heel for many parents. As noted above, many parents want to be their child's friend and, as a result, have a hard time following through on punishments. Other parents are just too busy to follow through.

Parents need to be consistent with punishment. If they can't be, children have no reason to respect them, much less to be law-abiding citizens when they are older. Phil and Becky had many rules in their house. Their six-year-old son, Kevin, broke most of them. His parents would tell him what his punishment would be but would never follow through on it.

At the first parent-teacher conference, it shouldn't have been a surprise when Kevin's teacher told them that he was a disruptive child who had trouble with being penalized for his actions. Because Kevin never expected his punishments to be carried out, he felt free to do whatever he wanted. This made it difficult for him to make friends and to get along with authority figures.

Teaching Cause and Effect

I'll say it again: Children must learn the important psychological lesson that their actions come with consequences. Jill made lunch for

What a Character!

Our culture largely chooses flash over substance. Kids today are encouraged to wear the "right" shoes, carry the coolest lunch box, and wear designer clothes before they are even old enough to walk. Character development is being overlooked, and as a result we are raising a generation of apathetic children. Here are ten of the most important characteristics for your child to develop:

1. Values and morals

2. The ability to delay gratification

3. Understanding and expectation of the consequences of his actions

4. Empathy toward others

5. A strong work ethic

6. A willingness to face consequences

7. The ability to learn from failures

8. An ability to take responsibility for mistakes

9. A tolerance for negative feedback

10. The ability to tolerate frustration

her six-year-old son, Dillian, every day and left it by the front door. She made it clear that it was his responsibility to remember to take it to school with him. Every few days Dillian would call home to say he had forgotten his lunch, and Jill would race over to his school and drop it off. When I asked her why she did that, she said that Dillian needed his nutrition and that he might not be able to concentrate if he didn't have his lunch. I asked if Dillian had any medical problems like diabetes or hypoglycemia, which he didn't.

Even putting aside the fact that Dillian wasn't studying rocket science in first grade, one day without his lunch wouldn't hurt him. He was likely to scrounge around and get leftovers from other kids. What Jill didn't realize was that she was sending Dillian a subtle message that he did not have to face the consequences of his actions, that she would always fix things for him. This choice prevented Dillian from learning about cause and effect. While bringing him his forgotten lunch may not seem like a big deal, the cleanup left for a parent who does not teach her son this valuable lesson only becomes larger as time goes on. One of the greatest lessons parents can teach their children is to be accountable for their actions.

Contributing to the Family

It is ideal for children to learn at an early age that they can contribute to the family. Allowing a child to be helpful, to feel needed and valued in the family, helps create a sense of importance that benefits the child's sense of self-efficacy and the well-being of the whole family.

Contributing teaches the child the dynamics of give-and-take. In his book *Choking on the Silver Spoon*, Gary Buffone describes this psychological dynamic well: "Narcissistic entitlement occurs when children remain forever on the receiving end without being expected to give in return. When parents teach their children to earn things they receive, and to appreciate what they have, they help them avoid developing a sense of entitlement."

Another way for your children to contribute is through volunteer work. Studies show that people who do volunteer work develop increased self-esteem and a sense of self-efficacy. By helping others, your children learn that they can make a difference in the world as well as the important truth that not everyone lives like they do or has all their advantages.

Give Your Child Something to Work Toward

Even if you can afford to give your child everything she wants, you should not. Give your child something to work toward. The children I have seen who are given everything they want never learn the value of a dollar, grow up to have a poor work ethic, and are often depressed. These children feel there is no reason to have goals or to work at anything because they can always ask Mom or Dad to give them what they want.

Give your child the opportunity to save up for a toy or game she really wants. If you do, she is most likely to value it more. Caroline loved Barbie dolls and everything associated with them. She had the Barbie house, car, and a large wardrobe for all her dolls. When she asked her parents for the Barbie camper, they told her that if she wanted it she would need to save up for it and buy it herself. They showed her how many weeks it would take given her current allowance and offered her additional ways to earn money around the house and then stood back to see what she would do. It took her one month to save up for the camper. Not too surprisingly, Caroline treated it better than any of her other toys because she had worked so hard to acquire it.

Give your child a financial education. Children should start learning simple money management skills as soon as they are old enough to do basic addition and subtraction; allowing a child to save up for a toy he wants is a great way to start teaching these skills. You don't want a child to think of money as being an endlessly supplied resource. Children who think that way grow into adults who spend beyond their needs, rack up credit card debt, and don't understand the value of a dollar.

The Importance of Failure and Frustration

Children today have a lower tolerance for frustration than those of previous generations. Because society today is so geared toward instant gratification — with cell phones, instant messages, iPods, and cars with DVD players — children are less likely to develop the ability to tolerate delayed gratification. The ability to tolerate frustration is crucial to development, and the only way to master that skill is through practice. It is through experiencing failure and frustration that children develop resilience. Even though it is painful for parents to watch their child suffer from frustration that they could easily rescue him from, it is crucial for the child's development to let him experience the frustration. Children who do not learn to handle frustration become adults who cannot handle stress and are ill-equipped to face the real world.

Six-year-old Ming-Ling was involved with the Brownie Girl Scouts. Her troop was selling cookies to raise money for a field trip. Each girl was expected to sell at least twenty boxes. Many of the parents of this well-to-do troop bought dozens of boxes from their children, or they sold boxes at their offices instead of letting their daughters do the hard work themselves. Ming-Ling had only sold six boxes, while her best friend had sold fifty. She was really frustrated and wanted to give up or get her parents to buy her remaining boxes.

They recognized that doing so would not teach her anything about working through frustration and told her that they would do anything to support her in selling the cookies but that they would not buy them.

Ultimately Ming-Ling worked through her frustration and came up with some great ideas about where to sell her cookies, and her folks helped her by taking her where she needed to go. Ming-Ling was really proud of the seventy-two boxes she sold, and she learned a valuable lesson about hard work.

In order for children to develop ambition, they must experience some level of deprivation. While they do not have to experience hunger or poverty, they do need to experience being left wanting for goods not necessary for survival. Desire breeds motivation, and we all want to have motivated, proactive kids.

Pain Inoculation

Don't always rescue your child. This is the hardest parenting skill to learn. We all want to spare our children pain and give them the best that life has to offer; but pain teaches kids about life. While undue suffering is not the goal, emotional pain teaches empathy. Trying to protect children from all pain usually backfires, and the children become avoidant and poorly equipped to handle life's challenges.

Jane is a seventeen-year-old girl who was too busy shopping with her friends to focus on her schoolwork and as a result began getting terrible grades. When I asked her what she was planning to do about college, she told me that her father has a connection at an Ivy League school and would "make a call" to get her in. By making that call for her, Jane's father will be teaching her that she does not have to work hard like everybody else, that there are no consequences to her negative behavior, and that his expectations for her are low. Unchallenged, those are the beliefs Jane will continue to live by.

In sum, how well your children function as adults is largely dependent on the tools they are given when they are young. It is in childhood that we acquire important qualities such as tolerance for frustration, ability to delay gratification, development of ambition, capacity to work past failure, and empathy toward others. Parents must be willing and able to provide their children with the framework in which to learn these lessons.

IS FOR HERO

Being a Great Dad

Today's fathers are very different from the fathers of previous generations. A recent study found that men spend twice as much time caregiving their children today than they did just twenty years ago. In addition, a whopping 80 percent of fathers today want to take a more active role in parenting than their own fathers did. In addition to being more involved, modern dads consider their families more of a priority than ever before. Studies show that three out of four fathers consider family to be the most important aspect of their lives, and more than 70 percent of married men, ages twenty-one to thirty-nine, report that they would be willing to give up a portion of their pay to be able to spend more time with their wives and children. According to a 2004 poll commissioned by the men's cable network Spike TV, 56 percent of men would consider being stay-at-home dads. The number of men who are actually giving up their jobs to be at home with their kids is growing at a surprisingly fast rate. According to recent census data, nearly 2 million fathers in this country are primary caregivers in their households, a much larger number than has ever been reported in the United States.

Dad Power

Fathers have a huge influence on their children's well-being. Study after study shows the importance of paternal presence in children's lives. Here are some of the findings:

- Infants who spend time alone with their dads show more varied social and exploratory behavior than other children, are more curious, and are better at dealing with stressful situations.

- One-year-olds whose fathers are more involved protest separations from their parents less than those with more absent dads.

- Babies whose fathers play with them regularly become better problem solvers as toddlers.

- Children with involved fathers show greater cognitive aptitude and on average score six points higher on IQ tests.

- Daughters with involved fathers score higher on math competency tests.

- Sons with fathers who take responsibility with limit setting and discipline and who help them with personal problems and schoolwork display a greater capacity for empathy.

- Children whose fathers perform 40 percent or more of the childcare engage in less gender-role stereotyping.

- Teenagers who live in two-parent families and have good relationships with their dads are at a 40 percent lower risk of smoking, drinking, and using drugs than teens from single-parent households.

- Children who feel close to their fathers are twice as likely as those who do not to enter college or to find stable employment after high school, 75 percent less likely to become pregnant as teenagers, 80 percent less likely to spend time in jail, and half as likely to experience depression.

Lasting Influence

A child's relationship with her father is the template for her relationships with men in the future. For the heterosexual woman, this is one of the biggest determinants of the type of man she will be attracted to and the kinds of relationships she will have; the effects of her relationship with her dad will linger in her psyche forever. Whatever deficits she felt in her relationship with her father she will be likely to feel in her romantic relationships with men until that wound is healed. Having a healthy loving relationship with her father can set the stage for more positive future relationships. A boy's relationship to his dad is most likely to shape his relationships with and expectations of other men.

In addition, the dynamics between father and mother influence both boys and girls in terms of their future romantic relationships. A father and mother's interactions become what he or she expects in romantic relationships. If children witness consistent loving interactions between parents, they are most likely to create that dynamic in their own future relationships.

What Keeps Men from Fathering

Often men find more impediments to being involved fathers than they had expected. Below we'll explore some of the challenges faced by these men.

Moms

In the beginning new moms are often ambivalent about handing over their newborns to anyone else, even their own husbands. Many moms feel such a strong bond with their babies that they have a hard time sharing that crucial bonding time — even with the baby's father. As their children grow, many moms have such specific ways of taking care of their children (i.e., how they bathe them, put them to bed, get them dressed) that they can be critical of their partners when they don't do it exactly the same way.

But fathers have their own ways of approaching childcare tasks that may be different from that of the moms. While it is important for parents to share information and techniques with one another, it is also wise for moms to give dads the room to do things their own way, as long as they are not posing any danger to their children.

Dan always looked forward to bath time with his daughter, Amy, and repeatedly asked his wife, Barbara, to let him take on that task. On the rare occasions when Barbara let him, she criticized his technique. She told him he wasn't using enough shampoo or was using too much, told him that he had brought the "wrong" bath toys to the tub, or that he was letting Amy splash too long. This constant criticism turned the bath-time ritual into an unpleasant task. He became more and more hesitant to be in charge of Amy's baths and eventually stopped altogether. While Dan missed this intimate connection that he so enjoyed with his daughter, who really lost out in this situation? Amy. She was missing out on important bonding time with her dad. It wasn't until Barbara was willing to let go and let Dan share this ritual with his daughter in his own way that Dan and Amy were able to enjoy that wonderful time together again. The only way to learn how to be a good parent is through experience. Moms need to give dads the latitude to do things their own way.

Misconceptions

There is a common misconception that fathers are somehow less able than moms to care for kids or that their instincts are somehow inferior to that of mothers. Margaret Mead, the well-known anthropologist who focused her studies on child-rearing and personality, was quoted as saying, "Fathers are biological necessities but social accidents." Unfortunately many people still adhere to this belief. But the truth is that men are very capable parents, just as capable as women.

Take, for example, the ability to read a child's behavioral cues — one of the most important aspects of taking care of a child. Psychologist Ross Parke conducted a study in which he found that fathers and mothers are equally able to interpret their child's cues indicating hunger, gastric distress, and fatigue. In addition, they are equally able to respond appropriately. Another study showed that fathers and mothers experience an identical elevation in blood pressure in response to a crying infant. In sum, men are capable caregivers and should be treated as such.

Lack of Role Models

Unfortunately, few men have good role models to show them what an involved, active dad looks like. There aren't "Daddy and Me" classes or other social circles for men to learn from one another, so without a model or a good guiding structure, many men don't share their parenting struggles and joys with each other and are often left in the dark. Mass media don't help much either. In 1998 the National Fatherhood Initiative studied prime-time programming of the five major networks and found that fathers are central recurring characters on only fifteen out of 102 comedies and dramas. Even more discouraging was the finding that men were portrayed as competent and caring on only 4 percent of these shows.

Many men had uninvolved fathers themselves and therefore don't have a good frame of reference for how to be an involved and nurturing father. Studies reveal that men without involved fathers are at a disadvantage when it comes to creating close relationships with their own children. In fact, a study conducted by Michael Cox found that the quality of a man's relationship with his father is the greatest predictor of his sensitivity to his own child and the appropriateness of his responses to his child's actions and behaviors.

Websites for Dads

American Coalition for Fathers and Children (www.acfc.org)

Brand New Dad (www.brandnewdad.com)

Dads and Daughters (www.dadsanddaughters.org)

Dads at a Distance (www.daads.com)

Dads Divorce (www.dadsdivorce.com)

Dads Today (http:dadstoday.com)

Daily Dads (www.daddydaily.com)

Family Man (www.familymanonline.com)

Father Magazine (www.fathermag.com)

Fathers.com (www.fathers.com)

Fathers Direct: The National Information Centre on Fatherhood (www.fathersdirect.com)

Fathers Network (www.fathersnetwork.org)

Father's World (www.fathersworld.com)

Fatherhood (www.fatherhood.org)

Fatherhood Coalition (www.fatherhoodcoalition.org)

Fatherville (www.fatherville.com)

Funky Stork (www.thefunkystork.com)

Executive Dads (www.executivedads.com)

Grateful Dads (www.gratefuldads.com)

Great Dad (www.greatdad.com)

Interactive DAD Magazine (www.interactivedadmagazine.com)

Military One: Dads (www.militaryonesource.com)

Mr. Dad (www.mrdad.com)

National Center on Fathers and Families (NCOFF) (www.ncoff.gse.upenn.edu)

Postpartum Dads
    (home.comcast.net/~ddklinker/mysite2/Welcome_page.htm)
Rebel Dads (www.rebeldad.com)
Slowlane Dads (www.slowlane.com)
TV Single Dads (www.tvdads.com)

Work

Job demands are probably the most common obstacles to good parenting. For example, whether by choice or by necessity, in the United States only 1 to 3 percent of men take advantage of paternity leave when it is available. And even though men are increasingly requesting this leave, it is still uncommon enough that it is frequently unpaid, employers discourage their employees from taking it, and men who consider it are often fearful of being put on the "daddy-track." Fathers who want to leave work early to attend a child's school play, soccer game, or graduation are often given a hard time by their supervisors and fellow employees. No one wants to be perceived as not being a "team player" at work, and few can afford to be perceived as lacking commitment to their job or, worse yet, to be fired.

Despite all these challenges, most men today realize that there is no more significant job in a man's life than being a father. Most men want to overcome the obstacles that prevent them from being better parents, but they need help and support from those around them.

What Men Can Do

All is not lost for men who want to be great dads. The following suggestions can help men have a big impact on their kids.

Get Involved

Do everything you can to be involved in your child's life. Doing simple things like showing up at important events carries a lasting impression and shows your child that you care enough to be there. Create nightly rituals, like reading a bedtime story together, to ensure that you have one-on-one time with your child every night. In addition to being a good way to bond, reading together can make a big difference in your child's verbal skills. In one of the first studies of children who spend time with their fathers, it was found that children whose fathers read to them had better verbal abilities than those with fathers who did not. (Interestingly, the study also found that when mothers read to their children, it does not result in improved verbal skills in their kids.) The more face-to-face time you can spend with your child, the better off he or she will be.

Set the Standard

As a father, the greatest gift you can give to your child is a healthy, loving relationship. This relationship, as mentioned above, is the template for his or her relationships with men for a long time to come. According to a report by the National Fatherhood Initiative, father love (measured by children's perceptions of paternal acceptance/rejection and affection/indifference) is as important as mother love in predicting the social, emotional, and cognitive development and functioning of children and young adults. In other words, having a loving and nurturing father is as important to a child's happiness, well-being, and social and academic success as having a loving and nurturing mother. It has also been shown that children with involved, loving fathers are significantly more likely to perform well in school, to have healthy self-esteem, to exhibit empathy and prosocial tendencies, and to avoid high-risk behaviors such as drug use, truancy, and criminal activity than children with uninvolved fathers.

Be a Relationship Role Model

Modeling a loving relationship with your spouse is another great way to be a super dad. The absence of familial hostility is the most consistent predictor of a child's healthy adjustment, whereas marital conflict is the most consistently reliable predictor of his or her maladjustment. This is not to say that every fight with your spouse is going to harm your child's well-being — quite the contrary. Constructive marital disagreements may be a positive way to teach children valuable lessons about conflict expression and negotiation. The problem occurs when there is consistent anger, hostility, and discord in the home. If you are experiencing this in your home, I implore you to explore marital therapy. If you cannot do it for yourself or your spouse, do it for the sake of your child.

A better relationship between parents can foster a better relationship between the parents and the child and between the child and others. Research shows that fathers in close, confiding marriages have more positive attitudes toward their three-month-old infants and toward their roles as parents than do fathers in less successful marriages. The same studies showed that mothers in close, confiding marriages were warmer and more sensitive.

Really Listen to Your Child

It is all too easy to make assumptions, to project your own feelings onto your kids, to zone out after a long day, or just to stop listening to your children altogether. But listening is one of the most important parenting skills. Feeling seen, heard, and understood by primary caregivers is vital to a child's self-esteem. In addition, your sensitivity and ability to evaluate a child's signals and respond appropriately is a crucial way to be involved and to build closeness. Many studies dealing with paternal influences show that the closeness of the father-child relationship, itself a consequence of extensive and sensitive interactions, has a crucial influence on the child's development and adjustment.

Helping the Child Who Doesn't Want to Go to School

Gwen had been looking forward to her first day in kindergarten for months, but when the morning of her first day arrived, she said her stomach hurt and that she couldn't go to school. Her parents suspected that something else was going on.

Benjamin is a six-year-old boy who cries every day before school and asks to stay home. Every night at dinnertime he starts begging to skip school the next day.

Carmen is a third-grader who cries for her mother every day halfway through the school day. She rarely makes it all the way through a day without trying to go home at least a few times.

Every fall, millions of children go with their parents to buy a back-to-school wardrobe and to collect supplies for the upcoming school year. Some kids eagerly look forward to seeing their friends and playing on the playground, and many are filled with a combination of excitement, anticipation, and some nerves as they approach

81

the new academic year. But there is another group of kids for whom school is a more frightening proposition. And many of these children are quite resistant to going to school.

What Is School Refusal?

The term *school refusal* is often used to describe a child's resistance to attending school or his or her difficulties remaining in class an entire day. This pattern includes a wide spectrum of behaviors: being completely absent from school; attending school for only part of the day; attending school following misbehavior at home in the morning (throwing tantrums, clinging, dawdling, complaining of stomachaches, being aggressive); and attending school under great duress and with lengthy pleas each day to not have to go in the future.

It is commonly believed that 28 percent of children and adolescents display some kind of school refusal. For the families of these children, every school day is met with dread. School refusal violates a parent's basic expectation of his or her child, and this behavior can create tremendous stress in a family.

Reading the Writing on the Chalkboard

School refusal doesn't just come out of nowhere; there are usually signs and symptoms long before this behavior becomes a problem. To nip the problem in the bud, parents should be aware of some of the behaviors that may be precursors to school-attendance problems:

- expressing excessive worries or fears
- talking on Sunday nights about dreading school
- frequent complaining about friends or lack of friends
- talking about a bully who has made threats

School Anxiety Scale

It can be helpful to everyone involved for parents to have their children rate their anxiety on a scale from 0 to 10. This way the children can view their fears on a continuum, and parents can gain a greater understanding of their anxiety. Have your child create his own descriptions for each number in the scale so that the scale will be accurate and so that you can get a better idea of what your child's anxiety looks like as it escalates. Here is one child's example:

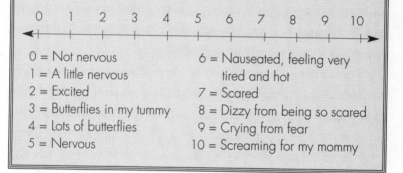

0 = Not nervous
1 = A little nervous
2 = Excited
3 = Butterflies in my tummy
4 = Lots of butterflies
5 = Nervous

6 = Nauseated, feeling very
     tired and hot
7 = Scared
8 = Dizzy from being so scared
9 = Crying from fear
10 = Screaming for my mommy

- refusing to get out of bed in the morning

- resisting getting ready in the morning

- being very rigid about breakfast foods

- throwing tantrums

- having nightmares

- refusing to take the school bus

- having difficulty getting out of the car in the morning

- clinging to you when it is time to leave the house

- having difficulty going to a friend's house

- crying before school

- having difficulty entering the school building

- having difficulty separating from parents in social situations

Why Does It Happen?

There are many causes of school refusal. While the reasons for it vary in severity, and not all are agreed on by professionals, as a parent you need to rule out the most serious possible causes before looking at the more typical ones. I have worked with children who avoided school out of fears of tangible dangers such as school violence, extreme cases of bullying, and physical, mental, or sexual abuse. At other times their avoidance can be a sign of a more serious emotional problem, like an anxiety disorder, post-traumatic stress disorder, depression, obsessive-compulsive disorder, or agoraphobia. These more serious issues will require professional help.

Certain personality traits make some children more vulnerable to school refusal. Children who are worriers, for example, tend to be more vulnerable in general. These kids find themselves ruminating about worst-case scenarios and have a difficult time calming themselves down when agitated. Children who are passive or shy are also likely candidates for some form of school anxiety. These children do not ask for help when they need it and, as a result, by the time they express their anxiety it has often snowballed. Highly sensitive children, who are easily overstimulated by classrooms, noise, and social situations, are often susceptible to school refusal as well.

Another factor, especially in young children, is a lack of understanding of the passage of time. For these children, anxiety comes on suddenly. Since they do not realize that the next school day is so close at hand, they may not worry about going back to school until the morning when they are faced with the prospect of getting ready.

While there are probably as many reasons to skip school as there are children who do it, there are some common, less serious, reasons why kids are motivated to ditch. Some try to avoid school simply because they find it unpleasant. They may not like a classroom, a teacher, certain students, or a subject they are studying. The children who miss school for these types of reasons tend to be younger and to have a difficult time explaining what is bothering them. Often older children find themselves avoiding school to escape social situations or circumstances in which they will be evaluated (such as tests, presentations, and homework evaluation). These children will go to extremes throwing tantrums, clinging to their parents, locking themselves in their rooms, running away, or complaining of bogus physical ailments.

Secondary Gains

Another reason kids refuse to go to school is to reap rewards, such as sympathy from their parents, attention from doctors or family members, and getting to watch television during the day or to play video games. In psychology we call these "secondary gains." Lola started first grade problem free. A few months into the year she caught a bad case of the flu and had to stay home. Her parents kept her out for a few extra days to prevent her from relapsing. Lola found she really enjoyed being home with her mother, Mona. None of her siblings were there, so she didn't have to share her mom with anyone, and she got to watch cartoons, while Mona, who worked part-time out of the house, caught up on her work. The first day that Lola was supposed to go back to school, she started complaining that she had a sore throat. She had no temperature, and her pediatrician recommended sending her to school. That was when the trouble began. Lola began throwing tantrums every morning and refusing to budge. It wasn't until Lola's parents realized what was going on that they were able to put an end to the behavior.

When Lola went back to school and attended regularly, they started giving her positive reinforcement by creating opportunities for special one-on-one times with each parent individually. They also let her know that in the future when she stayed home she would have to stay in bed the whole time and would not be allowed to watch any television. Miraculously, her sore throats and tantrums went away.

Mommy, Don't Go: Separation Anxiety

There is a strong connection between school refusal and separation anxiety. Separation anxiety is defined as an unrealistic and excessive anxiety caused by a separation from a child's major attachment figures. The child's worry is usually focused on harm coming to him, his parents, or his loved ones. Children who suffer from separation anxiety often try to avoid situations in which they will have to be apart from their caregivers, such as play dates without at least one of their parents, having sleepovers with friends, going to bed alone and, of course, going to school. It has been estimated that 75 percent of children with separation anxiety exhibit some form of school refusal behavior as well.

What You Can Do

There are many different ways to treat the problem of school refusal. Cognitive behavioral interventions tend to be the most useful in changing these habits. Of these interventions, I have found the most effective to be the behavioral reward chart, which parents can use to reward positive behavior changes. Depending on his previous behavior, the child gets a star for every time he does something such as make it to school without complaints, stay in school the entire day, take a test without leaving, or complete a presentation in class. Parents plot the chart in advance so the child will know how many stars he needs to earn before he gets a specific treat. The child needs to know exactly how to earn a reward, and the rewards should be things the child actually cares about. Children who experience a lot of fear or anxiety at school can also benefit from learning some basic relaxation or deep breathing exercises.

Different techniques work with different children, since they all have different needs. Here are some things that may help:

1. Take your child to school a few days before the school year begins so that the facility will start to feel more familiar to her. Go inside and walk the halls if the school is open.

2. Introduce your child to her teachers before the first day of school.

3. Give your child a transitional object (like a special bracelet, a photograph of the family, or a small toy) to take to school.

4. Have older children who are capable of abstract thoughts rate their anxiety on a scale from 0 to 10 so you can get an accurate idea of how fearful they are and help them calm themselves down.

5. Teach your child relaxation techniques.

6. Help your child identify specific stressors, including things like bullies, strict teachers, and difficult classes.

7. Help your child make a list of the ten scariest things about school. Then put them in order of the least scary to the scariest, taking time to talk about each item on the list to help desensitize him.

8. Find extra support for your child at school.

9. Help your child identify anxiety-provoking self-talk.

10. Make morning time more structured so that your child feels contained. Finding time for personal or group relaxation, prayer, or meditation can help calm nerves for everybody before school.

11. Help your child identify and express emotions.

12. Give your child longer transition times between morning activities like waking up and leaving for school and between evening activities like reading a bedtime story and turning all lights out. Try not to rush.

Relaxation Exercises

1. *Rhythmic Breathing.* Instruct your child to inhale for four counts, hold the breath for four counts, and exhale for four counts. This will slow down your child's breathing and, in turn, her heart rate, which can alleviate many of the physical symptoms of nervousness. This is a particularly effective exercise, and it is simple enough that a young child can do it on her own at school if she has the need.

2. *Guided Relaxation.* This exercise takes about twenty minutes and is best done at home in a quiet room with privacy. Have your child get into a relaxed position on the floor or in bed, while you read the following out loud in a calm, clear voice:

   - Breathe in through your nose and out through your mouth.

   - Allow your eyes to close whenever you're ready.

   - I am going to count slowly from one to ten. You are going to inhale each time I read a number and then exhale slowly.

     One: Inhale all the way through your chest.

     Two: Focus on your breathing.

     Three: Allow your body to relax.

     Four: Notice your limbs getting heavier with each breath.

     Five: Allow yourself to get more and more relaxed.

     Six: Notice your lungs expanding with each breath.

     Seven: Notice how each breath you take helps you become more relaxed.

     Eight: Notice how much more relaxed you are now.

     Nine: Allow your body to melt into the bed or the floor.

     Ten: Notice how calm you feel.

   When you are ready, picture yourself someplace safe, someplace that is really relaxing and comfortable. This place can be real or imaginary. It can be indoors or outdoors. When you have chosen your safe place, allow yourself to take in your surroundings. Notice any sounds or smells. Notice how warm or cool it is in your safe place. Notice what you are wearing and how you are feeling. Know that you can always return to this safe place any time you need to be relaxed.

Now I am going to bring you back into the room. When I do, you will feel well rested and clearheaded. I am going to start counting from ten to one. Listen to your breath with each count.

Ten: Allow yourself to become aware of the movement of your chest while you inhale and exhale.

Nine: Become aware of the feeling of your body in the room.

Eight: Listen to the sound of your breath.

Seven: Notice yourself becoming more alert.

Six: You feel more awake.

Five: You feel more energetic.

Four: You start to notice sounds in the room.

Three: You start to feel aware of other people in the room.

Two: Notice how awake you feel.

One: Allow yourself to open your eyes whenever you are ready.

13. Get involved at your child's school.

14. Do your best to get your child assigned to a teacher whose temperament is compatible with your child's.

15. Try role-playing at home.

16. Talk your child through a visualization of a "good day at school."

17. Listen to your child's fears without minimizing them.

18. Don't compare your child to other children, especially siblings, who are having an easier time getting to school. Also, don't compare your child's school accomplishments to those of other kids.

19. Minimize secondary gains.

20. Stay at school after dropping your child off if necessary.

Sometimes children who struggle with school refusal need professional help. To begin with, you should always rule out physical causes with a knowledgeable pediatrician. A therapist can help by using talk therapy or more complex techniques like systematic desensitization or cognitive restructuring. Alternatively, a good therapist can teach parents better ways to handle the kind of acting out that comes with this kind of problem.

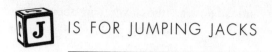 IS FOR JUMPING JACKS

Helping Your Children Love Exercise

Your job is to support your child's natural inclinations to move so he can get the body that is right for him. Your job is *not* to get your child to be active as a way of preventing or curing overweight. Children are born loving their bodies, curious about them, inclined to move and driven to be as physically competent as they can possibly be. The goal of good parenting with respect to physical activity is to preserve your child's positive attitudes about his body and his joy in moving it. Joyful activity is sustainable.

— Ellyn Satter, from *Your Child's Weight*

When Opportunity Knocks

As your child grows older it is your job, as a parent, to give him the opportunity to try many different types of activities. This will help him find the activities he enjoys most, ones he is most likely to be enthusiastic about. Children who find activities they love are far more likely to be active now and later as adults. Children need a safe space to run, throw a ball, and roll around on the grass. They need to be able to use their bodies and fall down without worrying about hurting themselves.

Once they get older they should have the chance to try short-term classes and lessons in different sports. These should be opportunities for your child to experiment with movement, not a chance for you, as a parent, to push a sport onto your child. This is a crucial point. As Satter points out in *Your Child's Weight*, parents of older children are responsible for providing a safe experience for their children to exercise and enjoy movement, but it is up to the children to decide whether to move and how much movement they will do. The more you push your child to be active when he does not want to be, the less likely he is to associate exercise with pleasure.

Emphasize Fun

The only way to get a child to exercise is by making it fun. As Rae Pica points out in her book *Your Active Child*, "children should never be encouraged to exercise because it will make them look good, even if obesity is an issue. Emphasizing exercise for the sake of appearance places the wrong value on physical activity — and appearance!" Children are not born with a critical awareness of how their bodies look. That kind of criticism is a learned behavior. Parents who emphasize the functionality of their children's bodies are more likely to raise active children who feel good about their bodies than parents who focus on the way their kids' bodies look. Children who feel good about themselves feel freer to move about uninhibited. Overweight children need that acceptance and encouragement from their parents even more. A focus on process over outcome is an important philosophy for parents to adopt in general. A child cannot control whether she wins a race, but she *can* control how hard she trains for it.

It is important to keep exercise age appropriate. Children who are given activities that are too difficult become frustrated and give up, while those who are given activities that are too easy become bored; we will discuss this in more detail just below. Set your child up to succeed, so she can feel good about herself and about physical movement.

According to the authors of *Fit Kids*, researchers have come up with several key reasons why children find physical activity fun. Exercise provides kids with:

1. positive interactions

2. praise from their peers and coaches

3. support

4. mastery

5. recognition

6. enjoyment of physical sensations

The Importance of Play

Children's physical activity should start with free play. When they get to be six or seven years old, kids become capable of more organized physical activity, owing to their increased attention spans and ability to conceptualize more complex rules. It is not until they are between eight and ten that they become developmentally ready to experiment with competitive sports. It is at that age that they become capable of conceptualizing and implementing strategy. Even though most kids have developed some of the basic skills necessary to compete, most experts recommend that children should stay away from high-pressure, competitive teams until they are eleven or twelve.

Children should not be pushed to participate in one sport exclusively, unless they naturally gravitate to one; in that case, you should support their decision. Every child has a "right fit" sport for both her mind and body. Allow your child to find that fit for herself. Maddie was an eleven-year-old girl who played soccer and ice-skated. Her father loved soccer, and her mother was a former figure skater. Maddie really wanted to play basketball but she was afraid of disappointing her parents. She continued to skate and play soccer long after she stopped enjoying both sports because she wanted to please her parents, who never got to fulfill their own athletic dreams. It wasn't until she told them how she felt and started playing basketball that she rediscovered the pure

Tips to Having an Active Family

1. Encourage the enjoyment of physical activities.

2. Plan parties, outings, and vacations around physical activities.

3. Create physically active family rituals like going for a walk after dinner.

4. Get your children gifts, such as Rollerblades, that promote physical activity instead of ones that encourage a sedentary lifestyle, such as video games.

5. Limit television, video game, and computer time.

6. Be a role model; have an active life style yourself.

7. Have an activity-friendly home. Keep jump ropes, balls, and other equipment handy at all times.

8. Keep the television out of the bedroom.

9. If your child asks to participate in sports classes or lessons, find a way to make it happen.

10. Compliment your child's physical strengths and encourage body acceptance.

11. Provide opportunities for your child to be active.

12. Allow your child to find sports he enjoys without pushing him to excel at the sports you want him to like.

joy of movement. Parents must be careful not to pressure their children to participate in a particular sport. In a healthy atmosphere, children will organically gravitate to sports that interest them.

Telechubbies

Studies show that the more television children watch, the heavier they tend to get. There are three primary reasons for this. The first, and most obvious, is that children are sedentary when they watch television. Every hour that they sit in front of the television is an hour in which they are not moving around and playing. The second reason is that television actually slows down children's metabolic rates. When children watch TV, they go into a trancelike state. Studies show that normal-weight children experience a 12 percent decline in metabolic rates, while obese children experience a 16 percent decline. The third reason is that when children watch television, they tend to eat unconsciously, which leads to overeating. An article in the *Journal of the American Dietetic Association* reports that the average person eats eight times more food during prime-time television hours than at any other time of the day.

The American Academy of Pediatrics suggests that no child under the age of two be allowed to watch any television, since TV habits picked up early in life tend to persist. Two-year-olds who are heavy TV watchers are two and a half times more likely to become excessive television viewers by the age of six. Children over the age of two should be limited to one or two hours of TV watching a day. Computer and video game time should be counted toward that total as well. In fact, a 1999 study of children's habits found that children spend an average of over six and a half hours a day engrossed in various types of media, time when they could be involved in some sort of physical activity.

If you want to whittle down your child's usage to the recommended two hours a day or less, here are a few tips that can help you achieve your goal:

- Take the TV, computer, and PlayStation out of your kids' bedrooms. Enforce the rule that they are only to be used in common rooms, and only during certain hours.

- Establish a nightly limit.

- Eliminate daytime usage.

- Help your children create a TV-viewing schedule so that they can plan in advance what they will watch during their permitted times.

- Monitor their viewing.

- Turn on the TV when the scheduled show starts, and turn it off as soon as it ends.

- Provide creative and intellectual alternatives (i.e., arts and crafts, storytelling, hobbies, and reading).

- Keep your home exercise friendly. Stay well stocked with jump ropes, balls, hula hoops, bicycles, racquets, and other child-accessible equipment that will encourage movement.

Mind, Body, and Soul

Children develop basic skills during critical growth periods. For basic motor skills, that time is from the prenatal stage until about age five. It is believed that the period between ages two and eleven is the window of opportunity for the brain's motor neurons to be developed; allowing your child appropriate movement during that time gives her the best opportunity for healthy motor skill development. Research shows that children who do not develop the ability to perform basic motor skills are three times more sedentary than their more skilled peers.

Because our brains become activated during exercise, exercise can make your child smarter. A Canadian study found that children who engaged in five hours of vigorous activity a week had stronger academic performances in math, English, natural sciences, and French than children who partook of only two hours of activity.

We are all born with a natural ability to internally regulate our food intake. In other words, we are born understanding our body's cues to eat (hunger) as well as its signals to stop eating (satiety). In *Intuitive Eating*, authors Elyse Resch and Evelyn Tribole cite the average toddler as the quintessential intuitive eater. According to Resch and Tribole, left to their own devices most kids play until they are hungry and then come inside to eat. Physical activity actually aids your child's ability to sense these cues. It helps those internal regulators to be more accessible, making it easier to detect cues of hunger and satiety, therefore making it easier to feed the body what it needs without overeating.

In addition, physical skill and acuity are positively associated with peer acceptance, and even leadership, in children from elementary school age through adolescence. Studies of five- and six-year-olds found that those with the highest levels of motor skills were more popular than those with the lowest levels. This was especially apparent among boys.

In child development, the physical, social, intellectual, and emotional elements are intertwined. Each area influences the others and can create either a negative or a positive cycle, depending on the skills developed. Children lacking in any one of these areas could find that they are developmentally left behind their peers as a result.

Do as I Say; Do as I Do

Self-critical children tend to be inactive children. They don't move because they fear that they will do something wrong or look foolish trying. Children most often learn this type of self-criticism from their parents, and it is usually learned in one of three ways:

1. Seeing a parent be critical of herself (e.g., hearing a parent say, "I am so fat that nothing looks good on me!")

2. Witnessing a parent being critical of others (e.g., hearing a parent say, "Did you see how terrible Aunt Janice looked at Thanksgiving?")

3. Being criticized by a parent directly (e.g., hearing a parent say, "You are stupid.")

On the flip side, parents who model self-acceptance teach their children to be more accepting of themselves. They teach their offspring the valuable lesson that they don't have to be perfect to be loved and accepted. Children who grow up with this understanding feel good about themselves and are willing to take risks, such as trying new sports, since they know that their self-worth is not at stake if they do not perform well.

As affected as children are by what you say to them, studies show that they are more affected by what you do. Telling your kids to be active when you sit in front of the television renders your words totally ineffective. A child who has an active parent is six times more likely to be physically active himself. In fact, the *Australian Journal of Nutrition and Dietetics* reported that children with active mothers are twice as likely to be active than children with inactive ones. Kids with active fathers are three and a half times more likely to be active than those with inactive dads. And children with two active parents are six times more likely to be active.

Children tend to enjoy the activities their parents enjoy. It is especially nice when kids can share exercise with their parents. Taking a walk after dinner or throwing a ball around in the backyard are great ways to enjoy being physical as a family. Not only do these activities help your child become healthier, but they help your family become closer.

 IS FOR KITTY CAT

Keeping Pets in the Home

Sooner or later, every parent is faced with the question of whether to bring a pet into the home. Most often it is a child who makes the request and promises to take care of the animal for life. Before you answer with an automatic no, fearing that you will end up taking care of the animal yourself, there are some issues you might want to consider first. Pets can add tremendous joy to your household; they provide physical, emotional, and intellectual benefits to every family member. But in order to receive all the possible gains, parents must be willing to handle the responsibility of pet ownership, to pick the right pet, and to prepare the family correctly.

Talk to the Animals

According to Dr. Marty Becker, veterinarian and author of *The Healing Power of Pets*, approximately 99 percent of kids from the ages of three to thirteen report wanting a pet. Pets offer children unconditional love and constant companionship. Many children even prefer their pets to people. A German study found that 80 percent of children surveyed considered their dog to be a close friend and confidant. A 1985 Michigan study of ten- to fourteen-year-olds found that 75 percent of them turned to their pets when they felt upset. These kids gave their animals high scores for their abilities to listen, reassure, show appreciation, and provide companionship.

Sometimes children are able to open up to an animal and get things off their chests when they are struggling to share their feelings with people. Joshua came to see me because he was being teased at school and his parents were worried about his level of anxiety. He wasn't very talkative during our sessions. Even play therapy didn't seem to help much. One day Joshua noticed a picture of my German shepherd, Stella, who has been trained to aid in psychotherapy, on my desk. He seemed really interested in her and asked lots of questions. I asked Joshua if he would like to meet her at our next session. He seemed very excited at the prospect.

At first when I introduced him to Stella Joshua was very intimidated. After all, she weighed more than he did! But soon enough he was petting her. Although he had been very guarded with his parents and me about his feelings, he told Stella all about the teasing at school and how bad it made him feel. Stella became a tool that helped me communicate with Joshua and ultimately to reduce his anxiety.

I Promise I'll Take Care of Him Forever

When pleading with you to get a pet, most children at some point promise a lot of things, such as "I'll be good," "I'll do my homework," "I'll do my chores without your asking," or my personal favorite, "I'll take care of him." Many parents, in the hopes of teaching their child responsibility, fall for the last one. Months later, when little Benjamin is too busy with baseball practice to feed the dog, his parents are faced with the choice of whether to take over the responsibility themselves or to teach poor Ben a lesson and get rid of the pooch.

No parent should ever get an animal with the expectation that a child will take care of it. After all, you wouldn't give your child a baby and expect him to take care of it, would you? Even if he promises with the utmost of sincerity, do not expect your child to take care of an animal until he has demonstrated that he is mature enough to take care of himself. In other words, don't give him that responsibility when he is still a child. If you chose to add a pet to your home, it must be with the understanding that it will be your responsibility. Children should be encouraged to participate in the care and feeding of your pet, as well as in age-appropriate activities with the animal, but parents must be realistic about their child's ability to make and keep this type of long-term commitment. Many parents are eager to get a pet to teach their child responsibility, but they have it backward; children need to learn responsibility so that they can have a pet. It is the parent's job to teach that responsibility, and a pet can be helpful as a catalyst to that lesson.

The Circle of Life

Children can learn about life cycles through their pets. Through their animals, kids are exposed to birth, cognitive and physical development, illness, and death. Some adults take this a bit too far, however, wanting their children to learn about the birds and bees by watching pets mate, become pregnant, and give birth. As you might imagine, this is a terrible idea. Responsible pet owners have their dogs and cats neutered before the animals reach sexual maturity. There are so many homeless animals in the world, and children learn a far more valuable lesson about compassion and altruism by going to a shelter and adopting an animal before it is euthanized.

Unfortunately, almost all the animals we choose as pets have shorter life spans than human beings, so every family is faced with the death of a pet. However, this can be a positive learning experience, giving your child the opportunity to learn about grief and sadness. Telling your child that Spot went to live at a farm, when in fact he died after being hit by a car, is to deny your child the chance to learn about loss. In addition, one lie leads to another because any child who cares about her pet is going to ask a lot of questions, such as, Where was he taken? Who took him there? Can I visit him? and, Why was he taken there? One lie will lead to ten more, and eventually when your child discovers the truth she will wonder what else you have lied about. Children need to learn how to grieve and to tolerate uncomfortable feelings. Shielding them from loss only puts them at an emotional disadvantage.

The Power of the Pooch: Emotional Benefits

Children of all ages reap emotional benefits from pet ownership. Kids who know enough about their pets to describe their routine and behavior generally rank themselves higher in competence than those who cannot. The ability to care for an animal and receive affection helps enhance children's well-being. A Swiss study of 540 children ages four, six, and eight found that the children who cared for cats scored higher on measures of self-reliance; in addition, a 2000 study of ten- to twelve-year-old children that explored the relationship between pets and children found that dog owners showed much higher levels of empathy and self-esteem. It appears that the positive effects can last far beyond childhood, as demonstrated by a recent study of university students. According to the researchers, those who had owned dogs or cats in childhood turned out to be more self-confident than those who did not.

Pets can also improve children's overall behavior. The parents

Age-appropriate Pet Responsibilities

Age	Responsibilities
Three	Can help fill food and water bowls at mealtime
Five	Can perform basic grooming tasks and help keep the pet's area clean
Ten	Can walk a dog that is less than one-fifth of the weight of the child in a safe or supervised area
Tweens	Can go to veterinary visits and help give medicines when the animal is sick
Teens	Can participate in obedience training
Any age	Can research their pet on the Internet (with a parent's supervision) and can read about their pet

of kindergarten-age children who were very attached to their pets reported that their kids displayed fewer behavior problems and that their kids' teachers had an easier time with them in class. In another study, children who said they received substantial emotional support from their pets were rated by their parents as less anxious and withdrawn than other kids.

Relationships with pets can also help children deal with trauma. A five-year-long study of six hundred children aged three to eighteen revealed that children who are slow learners or whose parents have divorced and who also own pets cope better with life than do children in similar circumstances who do not have a pet. Animal ownership can even help children who have suffered from severe trauma: pet-owning children who survived violence in Croatia reportedly had the lowest levels of post-traumatic stress disorder after the war, when compared to non-pet-owning children.

Benefits of the Beagle: Increased Communication

Children with pets appear to have better communication skills as well as deeper empathy for others. Perhaps it is because they have had to learn to interpret nonverbal cues from their dog or cat. It may also be due to their early practice of relating to another living creature and being sensitive to its needs and feelings. Developing these skills increases self-esteem and a sense of self-efficacy as well. A heightened ability to pick up on the subtler cues, such as the kind we receive from animals, was demonstrated in a study of 455 school children between the ages of eleven and sixteen, which revealed that children with pets had a greater ability to understand nonverbal communications both from other children and from adults. Studies of children who scored high on the animal-bonding scale (a scale that assesses the quality of the relationship between a child and her pet) found that those kids also scored the highest on their ability to reassure others and they scored the lowest on being uncooperative. And a New Mexico study that looked at the effect of dog ownership on ten- to twelve-year-old boys and girls found that preadolescents who owned dogs scored higher in both empathy and self-esteem.

Clever as a Fox: The Academic Advantages of Pets

Children with pets actually have an academic advantage; they even have higher school-attendance rates. Studies show this is apparent in all grades but is particularly pronounced in students from kindergarten through third grade, who received up to eighteen extra half-days of schooling per year than their non-pet-owning counterparts. If that doesn't convince you of the benefits of owning pets, maybe this will. Robert Poresky, a professor of human development and family studies at Kansas State University, surveyed eighty-eight children and found that those with higher scores on his companion animal-bonding scale also scored, on average, five points higher in IQ tests. In another study he conducted, Poresky found that children from families who owned pets scored higher in tests determining cognitive, social, and motor skills development. Some parents are already able to see the academic benefits to their children of their family pet. In a German study, 90 percent of parents thought that their dogs played an educational role with their young children and improved the children's quality of life.

Strong as an Ox: The Physiological Benefits of Animals

The physical benefits of having a pet in your home start early in life. Doctors used to think that children who grew up with pets were more likely to experience allergies, but that has now been disproven. Studies have shown that children who live with two or more dogs or cats in their homes during their first year of life, when the immune system is still developing, have a 50 to 77 percent reduction in both pet allergies and in common allergies such as to pollens and mold. Studies of IgA (a class of immunoglobulins, including antibodies found in bodily secretions like saliva, tears, and sweat) levels found that the levels among young pet owners were more stable, indicating that these kids are better able to fend off illness.

Kids who own pets, especially dogs, have more motivation to run and play outside. This physical activity is good for both your children and your pets. In addition, young children with pets have an opportunity to improve their motor skills by performing simple tasks, such as scooping food into the pet's dish, pouring water into the pet's bowl, or brushing the pet.

Preparing Fido for Your New Child

1. Start training your pet long before you bring home a new baby.

2. Keep your dog on the same schedule as much as possible.

3. Keep any dog-on-dog play for outdoors only (no playing inside).

4. Keep all toys that you could slip and fall on outside.

5. Make sure your dog understands the rules, and don't change them suddenly when the baby arrives. In other words, if Fido has had access to the furniture, don't suddenly tell him he can't jump on the couch anymore. Change any rules that need to be changed prior to the new arrival.

6. Practice walking the dog with a stroller before baby comes home.

7. Get your dog accustomed to how things will be by practicing with a baby doll. Carry the doll around the house, push it in a stroller, and talk to it. Don't allow your dog to paw the doll or walk on it.

8. Make sure your dog understands commands such as "stop," "no," or "get back" before you bring your child home so that you will be able to prevent serious problems.

9. Get your dog used to the sound of a crying baby by playing a recording of one.

10. Encourage your friends with babies and children to visit to help your dog become adjusted.

11. After the baby is born, bring home a blanket or a piece of clothing with the child's scent, and let your dog smell it so that the smell becomes familiar to him.

12. When you first come home with a baby, make sure to greet your dog without the baby in your hands.

13. Include the dog in safe activities with your baby.

14. If you have any doubts about your dog's behavior, or if he has ever shown aggressive behavior toward children, consult a professional immediately. Don't wait until you bring the baby home.

For Your Health, Pets Are the Cat's Meow

Pets don't just help kids, they also benefit adults. Researchers at the State University of New York at Buffalo found that married couples who owned pets had lower heart rates and blood pressure, regardless of whether they were at rest or undergoing stress tests than those who did not have pets. In fact, pet-owning adults have cholesterol levels that are on average 2 percent lower than those of non-pet owners, reducing the risk of heart attack by 4 percent. Pet owners who have heart attacks also stand a better chance of surviving them, as indicated by a U.S. Department of Health study, which revealed that 28 percent of heart patients with pets survived serious heart attacks, compared to only 6 percent of heart patients without pets.

One Big Happy Family

Before welcoming an animal into your home, be sure to make your home pet friendly. Here are a few steps you can take:

1. Always supervise interactions between pets and children.

2. Be aware that young children can be aggressive toward animals without realizing it; be watchful for aggressiveness from a pet as well.

3. Teach your children how to play appropriately with an animal.

4. Teach children not to disturb an animal that is sleeping, eating, or chewing on a toy.

5. Make sure children understand where it is okay to touch an animal.

6. Choose the right pet for your family based on its temperament and needs.

7. Make sure to wash your hands after playing with your pet, and teach your children to do the same.

8. Make walking the dog a family activity.

9. Teach children the safest way to approach animals.

10. Take your pet to the vet regularly for immunizations and checkups to ensure good health.

Even with all the fantastic benefits of pet ownership, you should never impulsively decide to get a pet. Adding an animal to the family should be a well-thought-out decision. Animals, especially dogs, take a lot of time and attention. The cute puppy you cuddle with at the kennel can turn into an unruly problem without the proper care and obedience training. On the flip side, finding the right animal for your family can bring great joy and improved health to everyone.

IS FOR LOVEBUG

Teaching Your Child about Love

Children learn how to love and be loved from the messages and examples set forth by their "primary love objects," traditionally the mother and father. Sometimes these examples are subtle, such as an expression of affection between family members. Other times they are more overt, such as a frank, sit-down discussion between a parent and a child about relationships or sex. While most parents recognize that learning to love and be loved is valuable for their children to learn, they also need to understand that the real impact of these early, unconscious lessons will last their kids a lifetime.

Love in the Bank

Children look to their parents to know if they are lovable. Psychologically speaking, parents are the mirrors that reflect back their children's self-concept. They create the foundation for a child's sense of self, especially through words and actions. If a child feels loved by his parents he is more likely to feel lovable in general and, when he is an adult, he is more likely to seek out people who behave lovingly toward him.

To have the strength, self-esteem, and resilience a child needs to thrive he must experience unconditional love from his parents. Unconditional love, which affirms the child for who he is, not for what he does, is the currency that fills the "love bank." Sometimes a parent is unable to convey all that she feels toward her child because she is not paying attention to how the child responds to her gestures of love. To succeed in conveying your feelings to your child, you need to pay attention to how your child responds to you. Reflect on what seems to be the most effective way of communicating your emotions.

Gloria's mother baked cookies for her every day when she got home from school. When Gloria became a parent she couldn't wait to do the same for her daughter, Carmen. But Carmen didn't care for cookies; she liked ice cream better. Because Gloria so desperately wanted to re-create the feeling she'd had when her mother made her cookies, she wasn't able to see that this was not the most effective way to reach her daughter. In the end, Carmen responded much better to hugs and kisses when she got home from school than she did to the baked goodies.

According to Gary Chapman and Ross Campbell, authors of *The Five Love Languages of Children*, children (and adults) speak and understand emotional love through five things:

1. physical touch

2. words of affirmation

3. quality time

4. gifts

5. acts of service

Different people, even within the same family, respond to different expressions of love. You should never assume that your partner or child will respond the same way you do to a certain love gesture. It is, however, safe to assume that once you figure out the best way to reach out to a family member, whether through spending time with him or her or giving small gifts, that person will feel loved and understood by your gesture — more love in the bank!

Teach Your Children Well

From infancy through adulthood, your children need to learn many important things about relationships. Children are like sponges, constantly absorbing what you say, do, and show them. Here are a few suggestions about areas that are especially vital.

Mirror a Loving Relationship

The relationship between you and your spouse is the blueprint for all your children's future intimate relationships. Set a good example for your children. This does not mean you have to have a "perfect" relationship to show your children how to do it. It is far more valuable to show them how couples deal with disappointment, hurt feelings, anger, misunderstandings, and conflict in a loving way in a normal, healthy relationship.

Model Conflict Resolution

Children count on adults to model conflict resolution. While some arguments and disagreements should take place behind closed doors, children do need to see couples work through differences so that they can learn how to do that with their peers and later with their intimate partners. Your children need to learn how to assert themselves without diminishing others. They need to learn how to express their needs and to tolerate hearing opposing views.

There is a misconception that partners should never fight or disagree. Yet it is abnormal in any type of relationship never to disagree. In my clinical experience, couples who never experience conflict are avoiding sharing their honest feelings and opinions with one another either because they don't know how to work through conflict or they are afraid of what the other will think. This dynamic invariably leads to resentment and larger problems down the road if the issues are never addressed and worked through. So engage in healthy conflict, and teach your kids to do the same.

Share Feelings

Demonstrate the open sharing of feelings regularly. When you show respect for other family members' feelings, there is more likely to be open communication and therefore healthier interactions within the family. When you honor each other's feelings, you teach your children that emotions are important, which in turn raises their self-esteem. In addition, when family members feel heard and cared about, it makes them feel good and reduces the chances that they will act out. An important adage to remember is that there are only unacceptable actions, not unacceptable feelings.

Listen

Truly listen to those in your family. This is more challenging than it sounds. To really know your child you need to listen to him without any preconceived notions, judgments, and projections getting in the way. This allows him to truly tell you what is going on in his mind and heart. Your children are always watching to see how you interact with your partner in anticipation of how you will act and react with them. You would be amazed at how sensitive kids are to your behavior, tone, and body language.

When eight-year-old Irina told me about some girls teasing her

Love Myths and Realities

Myth	Reality
Love means never having to say you are sorry.	Love means being willing to put your ego aside enough to admit when you are wrong or to apologize when you have hurt someone you care about. Love is about learning new ways to say you're sorry every day.
Never go to bed angry.	Staying up to resolve a conflict isn't an effective way to resolve a problem. Getting a good night's sleep can do wonders for conflict resolution. We tend to think more clearly after a good night's sleep, and a new day can bring a perspective on and greater distance from a heated outburst.
We should all live happily ever after.	There is no such thing as "happily ever after." Good relationships take work. If you are honest and open with your partner you are likely to have conflicts, but working through them creates greater understanding.
Couples in good relationships don't fight.	All couples fight. Research shows that the most important predictor of the success or failure of a marriage is not whether a couple fights but the ratio of positive to negative interactions. The magic ratio appears to be 5 to 1, with five positive interactions for every negative one.

at school, I was curious about how her mom had responded when she told her about the teasing. I was very surprised when she replied that she hadn't related the incident to her mom. When I asked her why, she very matter-of-factly answered, "Because the other night I heard my dad telling her about some problems he was having with some people at the office, and she just told him to 'buck up' and not let them get to him." When I asked Irina what that meant to her she said, "I could tell that she was disappointed with him for being weak, and I think that if I tell my mom about this problem I am having with people at school she will probably think the same of me and will tell me the same thing." It was hard to argue with Irina's logic.

Trust Instincts

Trust your instincts, and teach your children to trust theirs as well. This invaluable lesson will benefit your kids in all areas of their lives. Most people are born with good instincts but are taught to ignore them to be polite or to fit in. Children need to be taught that trusting their instincts is more important than pleasing others. Instincts are some of the clearest guides that people have when it comes to picking a partner or steering clear of a dangerous situation.

Tell the Truth

We all, children included, count on those closest to us to tell us the truth. Children want to know when they are doing a good job. They need to be able to trust your opinions and to count on you for your honesty. I have always admired the level of honesty and openness between my parents, which is even more important for them because they also work together. In their collaborations they are extremely honest, yet respectful, of one another's work. While their honest opinions have not always been easy to hear from one another, they both know when they receive a compliment, it is genuine. As a result of growing up in this environment, I have always valued that kind of trust and openness, and I have always known that if I ask either of them for their opinion about something, I will get an honest answer. This has only made me trust them more.

Help Your Child Speak Up

Many years ago I did some work for the Los Angeles Commission on Assaults against Women as a rape and battering hotline counselor. During one of our training sessions, this group of intelligent and outspoken women participated in an exercise to help them understand the dynamics of date rape. After a long discussion, it became apparent, in several of the scenarios that were brought up, that although they made all the women uncomfortable, many would not have said anything out of fear of hurting their date's feelings or of making their date not like them. The problem with this kind of thinking is that it only leads to more behavior that is uncomfortable and can quickly spiral out of control. The truth is that a really great guy would want to know when he is making a woman feel uncomfortable.

Teach your children to speak up for themselves. While date rape is an extreme example, often when you repress your desires or needs, those around you never have the opportunity to meet your needs or to truly get to know you. Kids are no different. When they don't express themselves, they are unlikely to have satisfying relationships with peers or adults.

Be There

For children to feel safe they need to know their parents will be there for them and that their family is an important priority to all its members. The primary way they know this is from experience. When you are there for them and for your partner, they will feel secure and cared for. Constantly having their needs met and feeling loved helps children develop healthy self-esteem. This also makes it more likely that they will seek out others who are supportive as well.

Teach Your Kids to Expect Respect

Marlene was a seventeen-year-old client who had some truly inconsiderate friends. When I asked her why she put up with them, she told me that her mother always told her to be nice to everyone and that it was really important to be liked. This put Marlene in a position to be mistreated and resentful. It also eroded her self-esteem. When people consistently treat you poorly and you believe that you have to put up with their behavior, your self-esteem takes a hit. Marlene was no different. It wasn't until she started to adopt a new philosophy in which she created standards for herself that she was able to find better friends and insist on being treated better.

In addition to reflecting on how you allow people to treat you, you should also examine how you treat others. Try to be open and communicative. Whenever you make promises, do your best to maintain your integrity by following through. Keep in mind that your children are watching. Teach them to be conscious not only of what people say, but also of what they do. It is easy to say nice things and make promises, but actions speak louder than words.

One of the greatest gifts you can give your children is to teach them healthy lessons about love and relationships. Although maintaining open and honest communication can pose a great challenge to parents, the benefits are immense.

Finding Good Childcare

For many parents the decision to hire a childcare professional is difficult, but finding a person with whom you feel safe leaving your children can be even more challenging. Whether you are a working parent who needs childcare so that you can provide for your family or you are a stay-at-home parent who recognizes your limitations and needs additional help, the challenges are the same. Regardless of your situation, you need to first come to terms with your need for help so that you can find the right person for the job. If you do not make peace with your need for childcare, you are likely to let your ambivalence affect your ability to pick the right person for the job.

Fear Factor

All you have to do is turn on the local news or pick up a newspaper to learn about some childcare horror stories. You probably even know parents who have had bad experiences. A friend of mine, Jill, spent weeks looking for a nanny for her two young sons, ages four and six. She was visibly relieved when a neighbor who was moving recommended her

117

nanny, Sara, whom her family no longer needed. Jill met with her and immediately loved her. Sara had come so highly recommended that Jill saw no need to ask for references, and it never dawned on her to do a background check. She figured that if Sara was good enough for her neighbor's kids, she was good enough for hers.

Jill's boys had no complaints about Sara, and she seemed to handle the boys quite well. One day Jill came home from work early to find both of her normally rambunctious boys sleeping on the living room couch in the middle of the day. This unusual behavior worried her, but she didn't want to jump to conclusions. She wanted to find Sara and figure out why her sons were so tired. When she couldn't find the nanny, she walked around the house calling her name, eventually following the strains of music to the closed bedroom door. When she opened the door she found the music blaring and her naked nanny having sex with her boyfriend. It turned out that Sara was giving the boys cough syrup to make them sleep so she could have uninterrupted time with her beau.

I share this story not to scare you off of finding childcare but to impress on you the importance of doing your homework. To find high-quality childcare, you must be willing to devote all your time and resources to finding the right person and later to maintaining a positive relationship with that person.

Where's Waldo's Nanny?

There are many different places to find a nanny. Your approach will most likely depend on a combination of the practices in your area, your financial resources, and your relationships with people who have access to the type of help you are looking for. Whatever method you choose, the most important things you can do are to check references and to perform a background check. Some of the most popular ways to find a nanny are:

The Internet. The Internet has many nanny specific sites as well as general sites where people can post Job Wanted or Help Wanted ads.

Nanny agencies. Nanny agencies can screen for the specific training and qualification of their nannies for you, and many also offer background checks as part of their services. While you should always perform your own background checks, a nanny who comes through an agency recommendation is usually someone who is comfortable giving out the information you will need for that kind of investigation. The one negative aspect of going through an agency is that it can be expensive. Most agencies will charge you a fee, which is commonly 12 percent of what you will pay the nanny for one year of work.

Au pair services. Hiring an au pair can be a good way to get live-in childcare at a greatly reduced rate. An au pair is generally an eighteen- to twenty-five-year-old person from a foreign country who exchanges childcare services for a chance to live and study in the United States. The service is run through a government agency called the U.S. Information Agency (USIA), which also sets many rules, such as au pairs can only work up to forty-five hours a week, they can only stay in the country for a maximum of twelve months, and they must be taken to two cultural events a month and be allowed to attend some kind of classes. The disadvantages of hiring an au pair is that you are hiring someone young, the au pair will have to be replaced after twelve months, you cannot interview your candidate in person, and you have little or no say about who you are assigned.

Word of mouth. Word of mouth can be an effective tool for finding a good nanny. Sending out a mass email to friends, co-workers, family members, and other moms can be a great way to learn about a prospective candidate. The more resources you come up with, the more likely you are to have a large pool from which to choose.

Childcare experts. Ask the experts if they can make any recommendations. Pediatricians, lactation consultants, teachers, clergy members, or obstetricians often hear of great candidates.

Nanny schools. Schools where people are trained to become nannies can be a great supply source for new nannies.

College bulletin boards. College bulletin boards can be a terrific place to put a posting for a nanny or to find someone looking for a job, if you are comfortable with a college-age student taking care of your child.

Newspapers. Looking in the paper, especially local and college papers that have Help Wanted or Job Wanted sections, can be a good place to start your search.

The nanny grapevine. This is a particularly great resource. Nannies often develop relationships with one another at parks, playgrounds, and other local child hotspots. As a result they often know when another nanny is planning to leave a job and look for a new one even before it happens.

The Other PP: Parenting Philosophy

I recommend to all parents that they start the process by first getting clear on their own parenting philosophy. Although it may seem obvious, figuring out your parenting approach and what values and methods of upbringing are important to you can help you more easily identify a nanny candidate with similar values and approaches to children. It is not enough to hire someone just because she comes highly recommended and knows infant CPR. To have a lasting relationship with your nanny, you need to be on the same page philosophically. This philosophy should include your ideas about what helps a child develop healthy self-esteem, your beliefs about physical punishment, and how you believe disagreements between adults and children should be handled. I recommend spending some time discussing these issues with your partner and committing your ideas to paper. Be honest with yourselves about your philosophy and approach, because the next step will be sharing it with viable nanny candidates during the interview process. If you are not honest with yourself or you are too embarrassed to share your views with the potential nanny, you are likely to be disappointed.

Securing Your Mary Poppins

To find the perfect person for the job, you must have clarity about what you are looking for in a childcare provider and what you are going to expect of her. It is a good idea to create a detailed job description as well as a list of job requirements before speaking with your first candidate. You may want to divide these lists into categories such as *want*, *would like to have*, and *must have* qualities. That way you can narrow down the field quickly and avoid wasting your time and the candidate's. Before you start interviewing nannies, you should have a salary range in mind as well. A discussion of salary can be an effective gauge of the person's experience. For example, a nanny who offers her services at far below what you are willing to pay should be approached with caution, since her low rate is either a sign of inexperience or of something else being off.

When thinking about the qualities you want in a caregiver you should include personality, temperament, skills, and philosophical beliefs. The ideal nanny is someone who will be a role model to your child as well as someone your child will love. I recommend giving all candidates an application form. This forces them to write down their answers and to stand by the information they supply. Having this piece of paper in front of you also ensures that you won't forget to ask a question.

You need to do everything in your power to ensure the safety and well-being of your kids by asking the difficult questions and performing proper background checks. Experts recommend that you let all candidates know before their interview that you will be doing extensive background checks including, but not limited to, criminal records, driving records, and financial records. This can help weed out people from the start who are hiding something. Even if you pay a service to run a background check on a candidate, no matter how highly recommended someone comes, you *must* check his or her references yourself. Security expect Gavin De Becker recommends getting what he calls a "developed source," or someone who knows the applicant but was not briefed to expect your call. You can go about getting this kind of reference by asking primary references if they know anyone else who knows the candidate with whom you could speak.

Security experts recommend making intentional mistakes about facts on an application when speaking to references in order to ensure that they are real references, not friends who have been coached. In addition to verifying the facts of employment, you want to get a sense of the candidate's strengths and weaknesses and how she handles emergencies. Always ask why the candidate stopped working for the family and if they would hire her again. If not, find out why.

More Than Chitchat: The Interview

During the interview it is crucial for you to trust your instincts. After all, the primary reason we have instincts is to alert us to danger. In his book *Protecting the Gift* De Becker says that "intuition about your children is always right in at least two ways: It is always based on something, and it always has your child's best interest at heart." Make note of your initial impression, and listen to any gut feelings you have on meeting your candidate.

Interviews should always be in person so that you can notice body language and facial cues. During the interview you should take notes so that you'll be able to keep all your candidates straight.

During the interview you will be asking a range of questions. You will need to ask the typical questions about job expectations, salary, and experience. In addition, you will need to ask the more difficult and sensitive questions (see sidebar) that tend to be more revealing but that can be difficult to ask. While it can be uncomfortable to ask these types of questions, any candidate who truly cares about children will recognize that you are only doing your best to protect your kids.

Some Interview Questions to Help Get You Started
Standard Questions

- Why are you interested in applying for this job?
- Are you currently working? What do you like/dislike about your current job? Why is your employment ending?
- What have your previous nanny experiences been like?
- What other types of jobs have you held?
- What degrees or special training have you received to help you do your job?
- Can you tell me about your education? Did you attend college or graduate school?
- What are your feelings about children?
- Why did you choose to become a nanny?
- What do you think are the three most important things to know to care for a child?
- What age children do you prefer to work with?

(Continued on next page.)

- What are you looking for in a job?
- Are you infant CPR certified and first aid certified?

Touchy Questions

- What in your life has prepared you for this kind of job?
- Aside from childcare, what have you accomplished that you are proud of?
- Can you please tell me about your relationship with your parents?
- What is your worst memory?
- How do you believe children should be disciplined?
- Have you ever had a problem with drugs, alcohol, or eating disorders? If so, how did it get resolved?
- Have any of your friends or family been convicted of a crime?
- As a child did you suffer from abuse of any kind?
- Have you ever been convicted of a crime?
- Will you provide us with a list of recent references?
- Do you smoke?
- Do you foresee any personal or family situations that may impair your ability to do this job?
- How do you think children should be disciplined?
- How would you handle it if you found my child touching his genitals?
- Have you ever suspected a child in your care was being abused? How did you handle that?
- Do you answer your cell phone while on duty with a child?

Specific Questions

- What activities would you organize for a four-year-old on a rainy day?
- What are three nutritious meals you could prepare for a six-year-old?
- What kinds of projects do you like to do with eight-year-olds?

- Tell me about a typical afternoon with children.
- How do you promote certain behaviors (e.g., sharing, kindness)?
- Describe how you would spend a typical day with my child.
- What might you do with my children on a rainy or snowy day?
- What kind of activities do you like to do with children my child's age?

Nanny Contract

Once you have your Mary Poppins, I recommend that you create a "nanny contract" to be signed by you and her. While this document is not intended to be legally binding, it does help to establish a professional relationship and will prevent confusion and misunderstanding between employee and employer.

The contract should spell out all the following:

- childcare and household responsibilities
- vacations, holidays, and sick-day policies
- salary and benefits, including when payday is
- employment terms
- daily schedule
- living arrangements (if employer is providing living accommodations)
- household values (curse words, religious values)
- food (Are you providing breakfast, lunch, or dinner for your nanny, or do you expect her to bring her own food?)
- termination policy
- discipline (e.g., no physical punishment)
- kid rules (food allergies and preference, TV rules)

Although there are many great Poppins-like childcare providers, when you launch your own search it can feel as though you are looking for a needle in a haystack. But by putting in the time, energy, and due diligence you are likely to find the perfect person for your family.

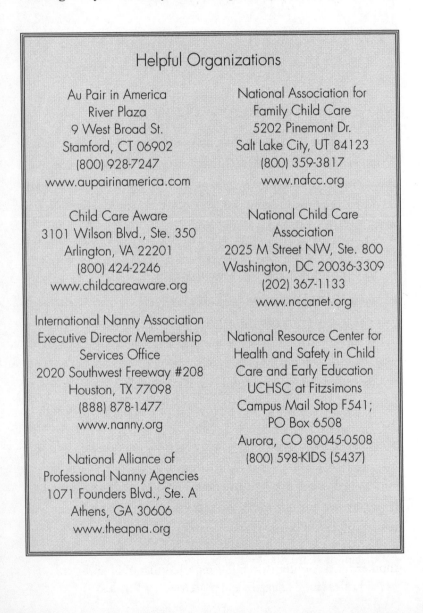

Helpful Organizations

Au Pair in America
River Plaza
9 West Broad St.
Stamford, CT 06902
(800) 928-7247
www.aupairinamerica.com

Child Care Aware
3101 Wilson Blvd., Ste. 350
Arlington, VA 22201
(800) 424-2246
www.childcareaware.org

International Nanny Association
Executive Director Membership
Services Office
2020 Southwest Freeway #208
Houston, TX 77098
(888) 878-1477
www.nanny.org

National Alliance of
Professional Nanny Agencies
1071 Founders Blvd., Ste. A
Athens, GA 30606
www.theapna.org

National Association for
Family Child Care
5202 Pinemont Dr.
Salt Lake City, UT 84123
(800) 359-3817
www.nafcc.org

National Child Care
Association
2025 M Street NW, Ste. 800
Washington, DC 20036-3309
(202) 367-1133
www.nccanet.org

National Resource Center for
Health and Safety in Child
Care and Early Education
UCHSC at Fitzsimons
Campus Mail Stop F541;
PO Box 6508
Aurora, CO 80045-0508
(800) 598-KIDS (5437)

Eating Meals Together

P arents often ask me what they can do to help give their children as many advantages as possible. They want to know how to keep their kids away from drugs, prevent eating disorders, help them get good grades, help them be healthy both physically and emotionally, and reduce the chance that they will develop depression. And they are especially interested in inexpensive, quick solutions.

What would you think if I told you that I have one: the family meal. No, I am not talking about some nostalgic throwback to the days of *Leave It to Beaver*. But study after study does show that eating dinner together can actually deliver on all the above. With children's increased participation in after-school activities and the parents' expanding workdays, modern families are finding it more and more difficult to make time for a family dinner. A 2005 *New York Times* article, titled "Benefits of the Dinner Table Ritual," reported that even though 87 percent of parents say that it is "very important" or "extremely important" to eat dinner together as a family, 30 to 40 percent of families do not eat dinner together five to seven nights a week. Another far less optimistic study reported that only approximately half of nine-year-old children ate dinner with their family every day, compared with only one third of fourteen-year-olds. Yet despite the challenges involved, families really need to make an effort to dine together. I believe that the renowned dietician and psychotherapist Ellyn Satter said it best when she wrote "meals are as essential for nurturing as they are for nutrition."

Sex, Drugs, and Cigarettes

In 1996 the National Center on Addiction and Substance Abuse (CASA) at Columbia University did a study to see what factors differentiated children who engaged in destructive behaviors like taking drugs, drinking, and smoking from those who did not. They talked to 1,200 adolescents, ages twelve through seventeen, as well as to 1,200 sets of parents. The results surprised even the most experienced researchers. They found that even more than religious ceremony attendance or grades, the most significant predictor of positive behavior in kids was eating dinner with their parents. CASA found that kids in that age group who had dinner with their families five or more nights a week were

- 32 percent likelier never to have tried cigarettes.

- 45 percent likelier never to have tried alcohol.

- 24 percent likelier never to have tried marijuana.

CASA has continued to perform their surveys each year, refining the questions as they learn. They have consistently found dinner to be the top predictor of good behavior in kids. The researchers have found that the number of teens who participate in family dinners drops by 50 percent as their substance abuse risk increases by 700 percent. The CASA reports show that kids who have some dinners with their families still do better than those who have none.

A University of Minneapolis study of five thousand teens found similar trends in their study of "family connectedness." They too found that the frequency of shared family meals was inversely associated with tobacco, alcohol, and marijuana use.

Fuzzy Wuzzy Wasn't Chubby, Was He?

Sandra came to see me because she was concerned about Jeni, her six-year-old daughter who was "chubby." Jeni grew up on educational television and videos; her parents were adamant that she watch only "good TV." The family was very busy chauffeuring Jeni's older siblings to soccer games and gymnastics practices, and the ritual of family dinner had all but disappeared in their home. Jeni was usually plunked down in front of the television set to watch "smart" TV while she ate. Even though Jeni was a moderately active kid, her weight kept increasing above her pediatrician's recommended levels.

Children who watch television while they eat don't pay attention to their body's signals of hunger and satiety. Knowing how to read these signals is one of the most important foundations on which healthy eating is built. If you do not learn to read your body's cues, you cannot respond to them. This applies to both adults and children. In the groundbreaking book *Breaking Free from Emotional Eating*, author and eating expert Geneen Roth recommends eating without distraction — that is, with no television, newspaper, books, music, or emotional conversations — so that we can learn to read our body's cues. What Sandra didn't realize was that by putting Jeni in front of the television while she ate, she was essentially teaching her to take her focus from her body and onto the entertainment. It is hard to taste and enjoy your food when your focus is elsewhere.

A study done by the Children's Nutrition Research Center (CNRC) correlating television watching with childhood obesity found that children who were overweight ate 50 percent of their dinners in front of the television, whereas normal-weight kids only ate 35 percent in front of the tube. Clearly a meal or two in front of the television does not condemn a child to obesity, but a lifetime of this behavior just might.

Studies show that kids who eat with their families tend to have a

Family Dinner "Don'ts"

- Don't be an eating-disordered parent. Do not discuss dieting or body dissatisfaction at the table. If you have an eating disorder, get help immediately so that you don't pass it on to your child.

- Don't make your child "clean her plate." Children should be encouraged to listen to their bodies' cues. Food should never be used as a reward or punishment.

- Don't use dinnertime as a time to argue, create conflict, or work through problems. Mealtime should be as tension free as possible so that family members can listen to their bodies' cues and digest easily.

- Don't drink heavily. You are a role model for your child when it comes to alcohol consumption. Families with heavy drinkers or alcoholics tend to have more tension-filled family meals.

- Don't push "healthy" menus on your family. Choose a variety of foods you know everyone likes, and start adding new dishes. If a family who normally eats hotdogs and potato chips is suddenly presented with a spinach-and-tofu casserole someone is going to start sneaking food after dinner.

- Don't be Martha Stewart. Each meal does not have to be a four-course affair with linen napkins and crystal. Make it easy.

- Don't allow distractions at the table. Turn off the television, cell phone, and the ringer on the phone. Don't allow MP3 Players, Game Boys, computers, or any other disruption at the table.

lower body mass index (BMI). A 1996 Harvard Medical School study found a strong correlation between a lack of family dinners and obesity. The researchers found that the more dinners children ate with their families the lower those kids' BMIs were. Another study, published in the May 2005 issue of *Obesity Research*, found that children who reported eating dinner with their families on "most days" or "every day" were 15 percent less likely to be overweight than those who said they ate dinner with their families "some days" or "never."

Avoiding ED (Eating Disorders)

Eating meals regularly with parents provides children with the security they need to create a sense of nutritional abundance, which allows them to make choices based on their body's cues and not on a fear of scarcity or deprivation. In her book *Your Child's Weight*, Satter says, "If they don't know they will be fed and allowed to eat as much as they want at frequent and predictable times, they will eat as much as they can whenever they can. Their fear of going hungry will override their cues of hunger, appetite, and satisfaction and make them eat until they can hold no more." Food insecurity creates food preoccupation, overeating, and eating disorders. Eating meals together as a family is an excellent preventative measure.

In a study called Project EAT (Eating Among Teens), printed in the *Journal of Adolescent Health*, researchers reported that adolescents who claimed to eat more frequent family meals, who gave family meals high priority, who experienced a positive atmosphere at family meals, and who had a more structured family meal environment were less likely to suffer from eating disorders. Nearly 18 percent of the girls in the study who ate only one or two family meals each week showed signs of developing an eating disorder. This number fell to 9 percent as the girls reported having family meals three to four times a week. Girls who ate five or more family meals weekly had an even lower risk of developing an eating disorder.

Family meals allow children to learn from their parents' attitudes and behaviors about food and nutrition. Parents with healthy attitudes toward food and their own bodies tend to raise children with the same attitudes. Providing a positive role model to your kids, especially to girls, is vital in preventing eating disorders.

Smart Food

A variety of independent studies show that children who eat regular meals with their families enjoy more academic success and have higher grade-point averages then their more solitary peers. They tend to have better vocabularies, which can lead to increased reading skills. Researchers found this to be particularly apparent in young children; they believed these youngsters enjoyed an academic head start as a result. Because dinner is a time of family sharing and discussion, kids have the opportunity both to practice and to learn new words. Boston researchers examined the correlation between reading acquisition and vocabulary among three-year-old children from low-income families by using tape recorders and interviews of children and their parents. In the first two years of the study researchers found two thousand "rare" words. More than one thousand of those words came from the dinner table, whereas only 143 came from stories that were read to them. In the book *The Surprising Power of Family Meals*, one of the researchers from the study, Catherine Snow, was quoted as saying "The frequency at which they [the children] were exposed to rare words at three and four [years of age] predicted their kindergarten vocabulary. We found vocabulary at kindergarten was a very good predictor of reading comprehension throughout the rest of their lives."

Family Dinner "Do's"

- Eat while sitting down at the dinner table without any distractions.

- Start having family dinners when your kids are young. The younger your children are, the easier this transition will be. You can start eating together when your child is as young as six months old.

- Serve foods your family likes, and add healthier additions once the family ritual has been established.

- Make things that are easy to prepare. There is nothing wrong with using prepared food now and then.

- Make attendance mandatory. All family members should be present. Try to plan around everyone's schedules, even if this means a late dinner (make sure your kids have snacks earlier if that is the case).

- Use the meal as an opportunity to get to know your family members better and to connect with them.

- Allow older children the opportunity to be responsible for meal preparation sometimes, and make sure to help them so they can succeed. Allow kids to make what they are able to. It is fine if your family eats peanut butter and jelly sandwiches for dinner once in a while!

- Eat "family style" and offer everyone the same food. Give family members four or five dishes (e.g., a plate of chicken, one of baked potatoes, one of string beans, one of baked beans, and a salad) so people can pick what they like and so that dinner doesn't turn into a big power struggle. This way family members can choose from what is already on the table.

- Allow children to determine how much they are going to eat and what they are going to eat.

Mind, Body, and Tummy

The access to parents that the family meal gives children has been shown to reduce stress and to improve the emotional and therefore the physical well-being of children. Even teens, who you would not expect to want a regular family gathering, thrive when they share family meals. Recently Dina, a thirteen-year-old, complained to me about how her family never has meals together. Her parents are well-intentioned but are far too busy with their own careers and other aspects of parenting to find the time to sit everyone down together at a meal. They spend their evenings driving Dina and her brother to various activities. When I approached her parents about setting up a regular time to eat a meal together as a family, I was met with resistance.

Both parents were overwhelmed and exhausted and felt that they were already meeting their obligations by feeding their kids on the run and making sure they had what they needed. Eventually we reached a compromise: the family started out eating dinner together one night a week. They had to eat a little bit later than they would have liked to allow everyone to return home from their activities. Eventually they started adding additional nights and then reached a plateau at four nights a week. It made Dina feel really good to be heard by her parents, and ultimately all family members got to know each other better, and they felt better as a result. Mom even put the kids to work, making each one responsible for meal preparation one night a week!

Dina is not alone. In a study of five thousand teens performed by the University of Minnesota School of Public Health, three-quarters of those surveyed said that they enjoyed eating meals with their family, and 62 percent agreed with the statement "In my family dinnertime is about more than just getting food." Since we know that food-related conversation (e.g., "This chicken is really good") only accounts for one-third of family dinner conversation, dinner is a time for family members to get to know each other better and to connect.

In a study of families who eat dinner together called "Of Ketchup and Kin: Dinnertime Conversation as a Major Source of Family Knowledge, Family Adjustment, and Family Resilience," researchers found that when they measured the children's self-esteem, those with the highest self-esteem also turned out to know the most about their families. In addition, kids who knew more about their families also thought their families functioned well. In other words, kids with high self-esteem knew more about their family members and as a result viewed them as higher functioning and more able to tackle problems.

The Minnesota study mentioned above found that the more a family eats together and the more connected a family feels, the more self-esteem in kids went up as negative factors like depression, suicidal ideation, and suicide attempts went down. The benefits even translate to the physical. In a study of eighty-six families, half of whom included asthmatic children, researchers found that families who used family routines, specifically mealtimes together, had lower levels of anxiety, which correlated with fewer school absences, fewer hospitalizations, and fewer medicinal interventions.

Apples and Oranges: Nutrition

Aside from all the emotional and psychological benefits that derive from eating together, dinnertime is an opportunity for children to learn about portion size, food combinations, and nutrition from their parents. Children learn more from what we do than from what we say, and this is as true at the dinner table as it is everywhere else. When parents supervise or cook the family dinner, their children are more likely to be getting more complete nutrients. Study after study show that children who eat with their parents get more folate, fiber, calcium, iron, and vitamins A, B6, B12, C, and E. They also consume fewer soft drinks, less fat, and fewer fried foods.

Raised by Wolves: Manners

Family dinners are also an opportunity for children to learn appropriate behavior and to develop conversation skills. Children rely on their parents to teach them proper behavior so they can go out into the world and be accepted. They must learn age-appropriate manners so that they can go to dinner at their friends' homes, attend parties, and so on. Children take pride in learning new behaviors and in pleasing their parents.

As you can see, the benefits of eating dinner with your family far outweigh any potential negatives. The family meal can help your child physically, emotionally, and academically. The icing on the family cake is the shared memories and time together. What parent wouldn't want that?

Making Visits
to the Doctor Painless

G oing to the doctor can be an anxiety-provoking experience for children of all ages. Often they are intimidated by doctors, afraid of shots, and scared of invasive or painful procedures and of undressing in front of a stranger, or they simply don't know what to expect. No parent likes to see her child distraught, and often parents themselves become anxious, only exacerbating the child's anxiety. But there is a lot you can do to make a visit to your child's doctor a more pleasant experience for everyone.

The Doctor Is Your Friend

Let your child know that the doctor is her ally. If you portray the pediatrician as a helpful, friendly person who solves problems, your child will go into the appointment with that positive expectation. Explain that the doctor is there to keep her healthy and make her well when she is sick. Since doctors know all about the body you can encourage her to ask the doctor questions. You can even help your child come up with a list of questions to ask (making a list is a good idea for parents, too, helping you avoid forgetting to ask specific things). Anything you can do to help your child develop a rapport with the doctor is a good idea.

Explain to your child what she can expect during her doctor visits. The more she knows, the less anxious she is likely to be. Children who attend their regular wellness visits tend to be less fearful during sick visits.

Set a good example with your own doctor visits. Let your child know when you are going to your appointments so she can see that you are not frightened. You can even ask her if she would like to join you, if it is appropriate, so you can show her that you take good care of yourself, too.

Relax

Margaret was a young mom whose daughter, Rose, would start screaming in the car the moment she realized she was going to the doctor. As soon as Rose arrived at the doctor's office she would throw a huge tantrum, go into hysterics, and seem utterly inconsolable. This ordeal was so upsetting and embarrassing to Margaret that she would rush right home, close the door to her room, and collapse, crying, on her bed. As a result of all this, Margaret became so anxious whenever she had to take Rose to the doctor that she would begin hyperventilating.

To help them break this cycle I asked Margaret to change her attitude about taking her daughter to the doctor. Margaret actually liked her daughter's doctor quite a bit and found the visits reassuring except, of course, for all the drama involved. I advised Margaret to start telling Rose how much she liked the doctor and how much she looked forward to seeing her. On the day of the next appointment, Margaret made a big deal about how she hoped they would get to spend a lot of time with the doctor that day. She also encouraged Rose to talk about her anxieties and feelings about going to see the doctor. Once Margaret realized that Rose was acting out because she was scared, she was able to address Rose's fears, which immediately helped to reduce her anxiety. After the appointment Rose made sure to take extra time to talk to her daughter about the experience. It only took about three appointments using this protocol for the tantrums to disappear completely.

I believe the combination of Margaret's lowering her anxiety, showing compassion for her daughter, changing her approach to the appointment, and reframing the doctor as a friendly person was largely responsible for the change in Rose's behavior.

Tell the Truth

It is commonly said that "the truth will set you free." This is particularly appropriate when it comes to kids and doctor appointments. One of the most common lies I hear parents tell their kids is that "the shot won't hurt a bit." Children need to know they can count on you to tell the truth. Letting them know what to expect allows them to prepare emotionally for the experience. I recommend a more honest approach like, "The shot will probably hurt. It will feel like a pinch, and then the pain goes away. I promise I will be there to hold your hand the whole time."

You don't want to let very young children know about a doctor visit too far in advance, because their anxiety will only mount the longer they think about it. But you should let them know the truth if they ask, and make sure you let them know they are going to see the doctor on the day of the appointment. If you lie about where you are going, and then you suddenly arrive at the pediatrician's office, your kids won't trust you in the future. This will also reinforce their notion that the doctor's office is a bad place where strange and painful things happen. If you lie to your children or don't tell them that they are going to see the doctor, not only do they have to deal with the anxiety of a doctor's appointment but they also have to deal with the disappointment of having been lied to by a parent.

Recommended Books for Children Preparing for a Doctor Visit

For babies through preschool-age children:

- *Froggy Goes to the Doctor*, by Jonathan London and Frank Remkiewicz (New York: Puffin [Penguin], 2004)

- *It's OK: Tom and Ally Visit the Doctor*, by Beth Robbins and Jon Stuart (New York: Dorling Kindersley, 2001)

- *Pooh Plays Doctor*, by Kathleen Zoehfeld, A. A. Milne, and Robbin Cuddy (New York: Disney Press, 1997)

- *My Friend the Doctor*, by Joanne Cole and Maxie Chambliss (New York: HarperCollins, 2005)

- *Going to the Doctor*, (Usborne First Experiences) by Anne Civardi (Tulsa, OK: EDC Publishing, 1992)

- *Going to the Doctor*, by T. Berry Brazelton, Alfred Womack, and Sam Ogden (Reading, MA: Addison-Wesley, 1996)

For children ages four through eight:

- *The Berenstain Bears Go to the Doctor*, by Stan and Jan Berenstain (New York: Random House Books for Young Readers, 1981)

- *Doctors Help People*, by Amy Moses (Plymouth, MN: Child's World, 1997)

- *I'm Going to the Doctor: A Pop-Up Book*, by Maxie Chambliss and Kathryn Siegler (New York: HarperCollins, 2005)

- *The Big Blue House Call* (Bear in the Big Blue House), by Kiki Thorpe and Tom Brannon (New York: Simon Spotlight, 2000)

- *Captain Kangaroo: Just Say "Ahhh!"*, by Ronnie Krauss (New York: HarperPerennial, 1998)

- *DK Readers: Jobs People Do — A Day in a Life of a Doctor*, by Linda Hayward (New York: DK Children, 2001)

Tears for Fears

It is completely natural for a child to be scared of going to the doctor's office. Here are some very common fears that children experience:

1. *Fear of pain.* Most kids are afraid the doctor will have to give them painful shots or that the exam itself will hurt.

2. *Fear of being separated from their parent.* Many children are afraid that they will be left alone in an exam room or will have to get a shot alone. This fear is especially common among children under the age of seven.

3. *Fear of the unknown.* Many kids don't know what to expect when they go to the doctor, which increases their anxiety. Children who are sick worry that they are sicker than they are being told or that they might die.

4. *Fear of the doctor.* Not every doctor has a great bedside manner. If your pediatrician is not good with kids, find someone who is. Putting your child at ease is part of the job.

5. *Fear of the doctor doing something that will make them sicker or make them die.* For example, young children who are told the doctor will be "taking blood" may worry that the doctor will take all their blood and need to be informed that the body has a lot of blood and that only a small amount will be used for testing.

Playing Doctor

A great way to help your child feel more comfortable going to the doctor is to re-create a normal visit to the doctor at home. A play doctor kit should provide you with all the tools you need. Take turns being the doctor and then the patient, and let your child's dolls or action figures be the patients as well. Play is a healthy way for children to work through their anxieties. This is also a great way to teach young children to identify body parts.

Reading children's books about going to the doctor or being a doctor is a great way to teach children about the experience. Often children who read books about the doctor's office come into appointments proud that they are able to identify tools or that they know why the doctor is doing certain things, like listening to their hearts. This sense of mastery can make the whole experience more pleasant.

Tips for Visits

You can do many things to prepare your child for a visit to the pediatrician:

• Bring a transitional object like a blanket or a doll.

• Have the doctor examine a doll first to show your child what she is going to do.

• For older kids, bring coloring books, a portable video game, or even an MP3 Player.

• Give tasks to your child that will force him to focus, such as counting, saying the alphabet, or even sitting still for discrete periods of time.

• Go without siblings so your child can have your complete attention.

• Allow your child to sit on your lap, if possible.

• Set up a pattern you can continue. Make sure that if you make a new ritual of a postdoctor trip to the toy store that you will be able to do that in the future.

• Prepare for long periods of time in the waiting room by bringing things to distract your child.

Going to the doctor doesn't have to be a nightmare. By using the tools listed here you can have your child eager for her next appointment!

IS FOR PRIORITIES

Spending Time with Loved Ones

When asked about priorities, most parents will tell you that family is number one on the list. But our actions don't always reflect our hearts' desires. In this day and age it isn't easy to find a balance between work and family. Even the most family-oriented parents find it difficult to stay connected.

More of us work today than we did in previous decades, and, to top it off, we are working much longer hours. In the United States today, more than 50 percent of all households have two working parents. According to one research company, 32 percent of the labor force works more than thirty-two hours a week, and one out of every five employees works close to fifty hours a week or more, not including commute time, which can easily be one hour in each direction every day. These statistics beg the question, "How do we find time for the most important people in our lives, our family members?"

Since it can be difficult to know where to begin, below I offer some helpful suggestions.

Create Family Rituals

Because our society has become less formal and more hurried, most of us have increasingly less time for rituals and traditions. As a result we have less significance and connection in our day-to-day lives, which is not only damaging to our family dynamics, but it is also a developmental hindrance to our children. A fifty-year study in the *Journal of Family Psychology* found that consistent family rituals encourage the social development of children and increase feelings of family cohesiveness by more than 17 percent.

What are family rituals, and how are they helpful? A family ritual is any repeated, shared activity that has meaning and is rewarding to family members. That fifty-year study showed that family rituals are associated with marital satisfaction, adolescents' sense of personal identity, children's health, academic achievement, and stronger family relationships. They provide families with the framework for maintaining and strengthening their relationships. In addition, family rituals

- promote family health and well-being.
- create a sense of predictability, comfort, and safety.
- aid social growth.
- store and convey family identity from generation to generation.
- facilitate the transmission of core values and beliefs.
- provide support and containment for strong emotions.
- help navigate change.
- provide members with warm memories.
- create connections between individuals, families, and communities.

One Columbia University study even found that rituals provide neurobiological benefits. The researchers founds that rituals produce positive limbic discharges, which create feelings of warmth and close-ness among participants. Because rituals stimulate both the left and the right sides of the brain, participants can experience reactions on both an emotional and a logical level at the same time.

Rituals don't have to be daily, and they need not be religious, like going to church on Sunday or having a Friday-night Shabbat dinner. My favorite childhood ritual was a once-a-year "date" that I had with my father. For this date we would get dressed up and go out for a re-ally nice dinner, just the two of us. It made me feel really special, and I loved having my dad's undivided attention. Your rituals can be any-thing your family creates that is meaningful to you. One family I know has a special dinner ritual. At the end of the week they start the meal by going around the table, with every family member sharing the best and the worst thing that happened to them during the week.

Anyone can incorporate rituals into her family life. Creating a ritual generally involves three steps. The first is preparation, which may involve sharing information, making mental notes, cooking, or whatever else is necessary to set up the ritual. The next stage is the ac-tual event or action. The final stage is connectedness or celebration. This stage can be subtle (e.g., feeling connected with the family at the end of a family movie night) or dramatic, like dancing the hora at the end of a Jewish wedding. If the event is enjoyable and mean-ingful for the participants, you can plan to do it again at whatever in-terval makes sense, whether it is daily, weekly, or yearly.

Schedule One-on-one Time

Make sure that there is a time of day, every day, when your children know they have your undivided attention. This gives children struc-ture and assures them they will be heard by you. Cynthia, a success-ful makeup artist, spends fifteen to thirty minutes every day, as soon as she gets home from work, talking and playing with her three-year-old son: "We talk about his day, what he liked about it and what he didn't like. Now he asks me, 'How was your day, Mom?'"

Sara, mother of twin daughters, created a one-on-one washup time with each of her girls. She sits in the bathroom and talks to each of her six-year-old daughters alone while they wash up, allowing each time to connect with her and be heard. Parents should use this kind of time to promote open dialogue between themselves and their children. One study found a direct correlation between optimism and open communication between a parent and child. It is also believed that a feeling of safety and a sense of being heard promote a more positive attitude in children.

Avoid Overscheduling

It is hard to spend time together as a family when, in addition to school, your child has soccer lessons, gymnastics practice, piano lessons, foreign language class, and art classes to go to when she is only six years old. That was the weekly schedule of activities for Olivia, one young girl I know. Even though she enjoyed many of the activities, she found herself overwhelmed and exhausted by the end of first grade. Yes, she had asked to do each of the activities she participated in, but her parents never made her pick one or two to focus on for a few months before trying something else. Because of our competitive culture and the difficulty today's parents have setting boundaries, more and more children are becoming overscheduled and burned-out.

According to a national survey performed by the University of Michigan, since the 1970s children have

- lost twelve hours a week of free time.

- decreased free-form play time by 25 percent.

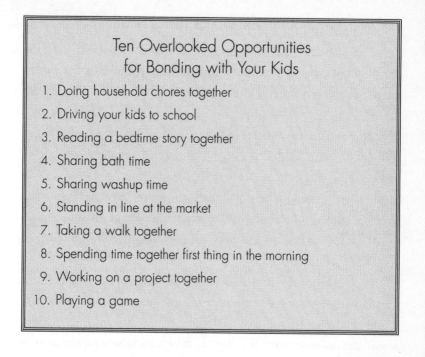

Ten Overlooked Opportunities
for Bonding with Your Kids

1. Doing household chores together
2. Driving your kids to school
3. Reading a bedtime story together
4. Sharing bath time
5. Sharing washup time
6. Standing in line at the market
7. Taking a walk together
8. Spending time together first thing in the morning
9. Working on a project together
10. Playing a game

- experienced a 50 percent decrease in unstructured outdoor activity.

- increased their structured sports time by 100 percent.

- increased spectator time (i.e., watching others play) from thirty minutes to more than three hours.

In other words, kids have never been busier with structured activities. As a result they have very little time for family dinners, outings, and vacations.

The National Association of Elementary School Principals recommends that young children only participate in one activity at a time and that they limit that activity to no more than twice a week, with clearly delineated "on" and "off" seasons. If your child wants to try more than one activity, the study recommends that she try a different one each season.

Turn Off the Technology

One easy way to regain some meaningful time together is to limit the use of things that gobble up your time and your child's. Restrict the use of the computer and the television, not just for the kids but for the adults as well. You are probably groaning right now, but each hour spent online or in front of the tube is one less hour spent interacting with your child. It is easy to get online or to turn on the television when you get home from work because you "just need to look something up," or you need to "check the score," or you need to see who got booted off a reality show, but before you know it, it is time to put the kids to bed. In addition, your viewing behavior influences your child's future habits.

Turn off the television and initiate a game, an activity, reading time, an arts-and-crafts project, or talking among family members. Often children who are used to parking themselves in front of electronic entertainment are at a loss for things to do when parents pull the plug. If this is the case with your kids, they will need help coming up with new things to do. Don't just restrict their access and leave them to their own devices; help them to find other activities, and participate if you can.

Enforce strict rules about the amount of time your kids are allowed to spend watching television or on the computer. I also recommend forbidding the use of handheld electronic games and MP3 Players in the car. Spending time in the car together can be a great time to connect with your kids. You won't be having any conversations if they have earphones in their ears.

Enforce Bedtime

To create focused family time at bedtime, you need to be consistent. Children should know when their bedtime is, and younger kids, who may not be able to tell time yet, should be given periodic warnings to help them wind down. If children do not have a clearly established bedtime, the evening hours will be consumed with negotiations and power struggles between parent and child, which will rob you of time to connect. In addition, two-parent homes should have an established system so that the child knows who will be tucking him in. This way when the mother tucks him in, the night will not be ruined by the plaintive wails of a child crying, "But I want Daddy to tuck me in," and vice versa.

Connecting with your children before bedtime can be a truly precious time. After a long day, most kids are open to connecting and cuddling, if they are not too cranky or overtired. Some great bedtime rituals to share are reading a story, taking turns making up a story, praying together, or giving your child a back or foot rub. Saying goodnight together to all friends and family members out loud is a great way for you to know who is on your child's mind. Many parents and children look forward to the nighttime reading ritual. One father told me, "We have given up a lot of evening activities we enjoy in order to put our children to bed. We love our evening ritual. My wife reads a story to our son, and I read one to our daughter every night." Simple time together is often the most valuable.

Eat Together

It has been estimated that only between 37 and 50 percent of American families eat together each night. For most families, mealtime is often hectic and difficult to coordinate among all family members. Many families find it helpful to set a consistent dinnertime and to expect everyone to attend. It is also helpful to commit to stopping all work-related activities (phone calls, emails, and so forth) during a specific and predetermined window of time every day. One busy mom says, "We eat dinner at 6 p.m. year-round. This was very important when the kids were young as well as through their teenage years. [It promoted] continuity and conversation. After dinner I would go back to work."

As I have stressed already, dinner is a really significant time to connect with family members. A University of Minnesota School of Public Health study found that teens value and enjoy dinner with their families. Sixty-two percent of the teens surveyed recognized that dinnertime is about more than just food. The study also found that the more family meals that were eaten together and the more connected a family felt, the higher individual self-esteem went up, while negative factors such as depression, suicidal ideation, and suicide attempts went down. In addition, researchers have found that children whose families ate together had more positive feelings about themselves and their families and tended to be more connected and to know more about the other members of their families.

Give Family History Lessons

A great way to help children feel connected to their families is through telling them some family history. Studies have shown that sharing family history produces higher levels of interest and concern for their family members among children and increases the likelihood of the children's happiness. Creating a family tree to put up in the house, sharing stories about family members, paging through scrapbooks, and even creating a book of family photos and stories are all great ways to help a child connect with her roots.

Take Vacations

Vacations are very healthy for families. Aside from the chance to have fun and to create shared memories, vacations also provide opportunities to spend time together in a relaxed and unhurried atmosphere. Despite all the positive data about family vacations, according to a study conducted by the University of Michigan's Survey Research Center, since 1985 there has been a 28 percent decline in family vacations. Many families cite lack of time, money, and energy as the reason they do not go on more vacations.

But planning a trip together gives your family something to look forward to. If money is an issue, save up air miles and visit someone with whom you can stay. Traveling together is exciting for children and gives family members time to unwind together.

Volunteer

Volunteering is a great way to bring family members closer together and to give back to the community. There are age-appropriate opportunities for volunteer work, even for the youngest of children. Whether your family makes visits to a geriatric home, feeds the homeless at a shelter, or helps raise money for orphans, there are always ways to give back. Volunteering as a family can lead to a new appreciation of one another, spark meaningful conversation, increase communication, and prompt discussions about values and feelings, all of which increases closeness within the family. Doing volunteer work also allows kids to learn about different people, acquire new skills, develop new perspectives, and increase their appreciation of the things they own. Volunteering often leads both children and parents to good feelings about self and family. Children who learn early in life that they can make a difference develop a sense of self-efficacy that, in turn, leads to increased self-esteem.

 IS FOR QUARTERS

Teaching Your Kids about Money

Most mothers-to-be take folic acid to help ensure that they will have healthy babies. Many fathers-to-be start thinking about the best way to teach their kids to throw a ball long before conception. But very few parents think about how to raise financially healthy children. While three-quarters of U.S. parents agree that providing financial guidance to their children is very important, only slightly more than one-third believe that they know how to impart the necessary skills.

This may be due to the fact that, judging by the average American family's credit card debt, oversized mortgages, and other out-of-control spending issues, a large percentage of parents do not have a firm grip on their own finances. To complicate matters further, money matters are such a taboo subject, probably even more so than sex, that most parents shy away from having fiscal discussions with their children. Many hold to the misguided belief that everything will fall into place naturally. But the truth is that children, now more than ever, need parental guidance through that murky maze of personal finances. In addition to the basics we all have to learn as children, modern kids have readier access to cash and a dizzying number of items to spend it on, which makes learning about managing money increasingly valuable at an earlier age.

In her book *Silver Spoon Kids*, Eileen Gallo compares teaching children how to handle money with teaching them to drive. If you gave a sixteen-year-old a BMW for his birthday but didn't bother teaching him how to drive it, is it reasonable for you to be surprised when he gets into an accident? Well, the only way to avoid financial car wrecks is to start educating your child early about handling money.

The Power of Money

The more control parents exert over their children's finances, the less their children will learn about handling money responsibly. For a person to learn about money he must have the freedom to make mistakes, and it is ideal for him to make those errors during childhood when the stakes are low. The best way to ensure that your children learn from their blunders is to give them the opportunity to suffer the consequences of their financial mismanagement.

Eight-year-old Lexi really wanted an American Girl doll named Jess, so her parents bought it for her. She was thrilled. For a few days she took Jess with her everywhere she went, but, unfortunately, somewhere along the way she misplaced the doll. Lexi was distraught. Her parents, who couldn't bear to see their daughter in pain and who could afford to buy her a new doll, were very tempted to replace it for her. However, they realized that if they did, Lexi would not learn a lesson about being more careful with her possessions. They empathized with Lexi, but they held strong and did not buy her a new Jess doll. As a result Lexi saved up her allowance and bought it for herself. That was the last time Lexi ever misplaced a toy. Had her parents rushed in to help her, Lexi would not have learned these valuable lessons about taking care of her possessions and saving up so that she could buy something she dearly wanted.

Having some financial freedom allows children to weigh and prioritize their desires and to make difficult choices. It also encourages them to value money. This process will help your kids make good decisions as adults.

Financial Education

It is a parent's job to introduce his children to money. Most parents take for granted that children understand how things work. If your child doesn't see you deposit your paycheck but does see you withdraw money from the ATM, do not assume that she will understand where that money came from. Young children tend to think that the bank just gives you the money when you ask for it, like the proverbial money tree. The same goes for paying for purchases with a credit card. If your children never see you pay the bills, they will not understand that you have to pay for what you charge. Explain how these things work. Similarly, don't assume that older children know how to balance a checkbook or pay bills. Let them sit with you and help you pay the bills so that they will understand how it works and can grasp the value of money.

Communicate with your children about your family's financial values. In addition to having conversations, you need to be a good role model. According to Dan Fienberg, a Beverly Hills wealth management advisor and certified financial planner who frequently lectures about family and finance, "Lead by example. If parents mismanage money, their kids are more likely to follow — especially when it comes to credit cards and debt."

Many parents struggle with their own finances and worry about their children's financial futures. Statistics show that 55 percent of parents carry over credit card debt each month, that only 45 percent stick to a budget, and that one in eight parents report they have nothing saved in work-related retirement plans. Parents need to get their own financial matters in hand so that they can teach their children and be a positive example. But you don't have to be perfect to teach your kids about money.

Knowledge Is Power

Most kids are ignorant about money because they have never been taught about it. A survey of 5,775 high school seniors in thirty-seven states done by Jump$tart Coalition for Personal Financial Literacy found that the average score on a questionnaire about basic finances was 52.4 percent. In other words, the average student who graduates from high school lacks basic skills in managing personal finances, is unable to balance a checkbook, and has no insight into the basic survival principles involved with earning, spending, saving, and investing.

We need to teach our kids in two ways. The first, as Fienberg points out, is by example. Children are constantly watching their parents' actions and learning from them. The second is through what we actively teach them. Children need to be taught the basics and then to build on the information they have acquired. In this way they can grow up to be financially savvy adults. The most important financial lessons you can teach your young children are

- how to identify coins and paper money and each of their respective values.

- how coins and bills add up.

- how to manage a cash allowance.

- how to save for a short-term goal.

- how to analyze a commercial or ad.

- how to compare prices.

- how to calculate correct change.

- how to spend wisely.

- how to make an ongoing budget.

- how to tip.

- how to double-check a restaurant bill.

- how coupons and sales work.

- how to save for a long-term goal.

The most important financial lessons you can teach your older children are

- how to manage a checking account.

- how an ATM works.

- what interest is.

- how to make money grow.

- how to get out of debt.

- how a credit card works.

- how taxes, such as sales tax, work.

- how to invest.

Money Doesn't Grow on Trees: Earning an Allowance

There is no better way to help children learn the value of a dollar than by giving them an allowance, yet in the United States only 46 percent of children ages nine to fourteen receive one. An allowance is the best financial teaching tool you can give your child. Fienberg, who is also a parent, is a big believer in giving an allowance: "It allows freedom, expression, and responsibility for a child." Depending on your child's level of maturity, you can start giving an allowance when she is as young as three years old; you should begin when she is no older than seven. It is recommended that parents begin giving children an allowance as soon as their kids

- are aware of the relationship between money and purchasing.

- can differentiate between coins.

- are able to count, add, and subtract.

- have an opportunity for spending.

- begin to ask you to buy them things when you are shopping together.

- ask for an allowance or money.

The two biggest hot-button issues pertaining to allowance are whether it should be tied to chores and how much to give. When deciding whether your kids should work for money or whether they should receive a regular weekly allowance not tied to any duties, keep in mind that there are pros and cons to both options.

Tying chores to payment has the advantage of teaching children the link between work and financial reward, which can help create a strong work ethic. This philosophy prevents children from feeling too entitled and allows them to gain a sense of responsibility, since they are contributing to the household. It can even help children appreciate how hard you work for your money. On the flip side, linking allowance with chores has the potential of creating mercenary children who are less willing to help around the house without financial compensation. This dynamic can get complicated. What if, for example, little Joey does five out of six of his chores? Do you pay him for five chores, or do you pay him nothing, since he did not complete all his chores? It can also be difficult to keep track of all the chores that are expected of your kids, especially in multiple-child homes. In addition, what do you do if Joey doesn't need the money that week and decides to forgo his duties until next week when he does need the money?

Giving a regular allowance that is not tied to chores has the advantage that it is easy to keep track of. This system keeps children helping out with family chores because they are contributing members of the family and not because they are trying to earn more cash. With this system children know exactly how much money they will receive each week, and they can start to learn how to make a budget for themselves, with a parent's help, of course.

Many parents are unclear about how much money they should give their children. The amount should be large enough that your children can learn money management but small enough that any splurges will not be disastrous. In figuring out how much to give your child you should also take into account how much your family can afford to give, what other children in your neighborhood are getting, what financial responsibilities your child will be taking on, what other financial resources your child has, and whether his payment will be linked to chores.

Most financial experts recommend giving children anywhere from the equivalent of half their age per week (in other words, an eight-year-old would get four dollars a week) to their full age per week (that eight-year-old gets eight dollars a week). Whatever you choose to do, give them the money in easily dividable denominations so they can more easily save some and spend some. Help your children find a safe place to keep their money so that it will not get lost or stolen and so they can watch it grow. Most important, you need to determine in advance exactly what you expect your children to use their allowance for. That is a key part of helping your children learn money management.

Tia and Sasha live only a block from each other. They are both

Fun Games That Teach Children about Money

Game	Company	Skills Taught	Age Range
Presto Change-o	Educational Insights	• Making change	Four and up
Little Spender	Creative Teaching Associates	• Making change	Five to eight
Monopoly Junior	Hasbro	• Math skills	Five to eight
Pit	Parker Brothers	• Investing • Understanding the stock market	Seven and up
Cashflo for Kids	Cashflow Technologies (Rich Dad Poor Dad)	• Investing • General financial education	Seven and up
The Allowance Game	Lakeshore Learning Materials	• Earning money • Saving • Smart spending	Eight to eleven
Payday	Parker Brothers	• Household finances • Paying bills	Eight and up
Monopoly	Hasbro	• Math skills • Real estate	Eight and up
The Game of Life	Hasbro	• Decision making • Finances	Nine and up
Let's Go Shopping!	Super Duper Publications	• Smart consumerism • Math skills	Nine and up
Hot Company	Independent Means, Inc.	• Business finance • Understanding profits and losses	Twelve and up

Check out sites such as www.EducationalLearningGames.com to learn more about games that teach children about money.

seven years old. Tia receives four dollars a week from her family, and Sasha gets ten. At first glance you might think that Sasha's family is being extravagant and that Tia will be better equipped to handle money, but in this case neither assumption is true. Tia's family never outlined for Tia what her allowance should be used for. As a result Tia constantly asks for more money, which she always gets, and she doesn't have any real responsibilities. Sasha, on the other hand, pays for all her own toys (except for those she receives as gifts), buys her own supermarket treats, buys gifts for her friends, and donates 10 percent of her income to charity each month. Who do you think is learning more about financial management?

The Three Little Piggy Banks

Many parents have their children divide their allowance into three categories: money for saving, money for spending, and money for charitable giving. This allows parents to impart their own financial values to their children and to teach their children useful money-management skills. There are even special piggy banks with three compartments, such as those created by Moonjar (www.moonjar.com), which come in plastic or cardboard and have passbooks for children to keep track of their deposits. Other companies take this system a step further and have four categories: spending, saving, charity, and investing. Money Saving Generation (www.msgen.com) makes two four-compartment banks for kids: the Money Savvy Pig and the Moolah Cow Bank. Prosperity 4 Kids (www.prosperity4kids.com) makes a bank called Money Mama and the Three Little Pigs that has four connected pigs, each with coin slots.

The problem with forcing kids to save their allowance or to give to charity is just that — you are forcing them to do it. When you make them divide their money the way you see fit, your kids never develop a sense that the money is theirs, and they never make the mistakes that all kids need to make in order to learn how to handle money. If you force your child to save, any potential for imparting values is lost because then your lesson is just about following house rules and not about their doing what they believe is best. The concepts of delayed gratification and working toward long-term goals are foreign to children (and to many adults!), and therefore early childhood is the right time for children to practice these valuable skills. Children need to know what it feels like not to have money available, just as much as they need to know what it feels like to have the financial security that money in the bank can give you.

Many parents match their children's savings to help inspire healthy saving behavior or to teach them about how interest works. But what if your kids want to make a withdrawal? Most experts agree that it is good for kids to be allowed to take money out of their own accounts. The pros conclude that if your children are going to make financial mistakes (and they will), it is far better for them to make small mistakes now rather than bigger ones later. However, if you are matching funds to your child's account, I recommend not adding any money until the balance is back up to the amount they had before the withdrawal. You will never be able to teach your child the value of money and of savings if you replenish the account every time your child depletes it. You need to strike a balance, so to speak, and you need to be responsible to your child.

When it comes to charitable contributions, it is far more meaningful for a child to choose to give money away than it is for her to be forced to do it. If a child is told she has to give away 10 percent of her allowance to charity, then it is the parent who is really giving, not the child. Parents are better off showing children how they give and talking about how it makes them feel to help others. If your child decides she wants to make a donation, help her find an organization that will be meaningful to her.

Go Out and Buy That Toy Right Now: Advertising

In 2006 children between the ages of four and twelve spent more than $50 billion dollars and influenced an estimated $200 billion that their parents spent. These numbers are not lost on advertisers. According to Fienberg, "Kids are more vulnerable to creating debt then ever before because they are being marketed to very directly. The advertising business is really catering to children. Everything is geared towards kids because they have so much purchasing power, both direct and indirect."

If you are going to raise smart consumers, you must educate them about how commercials and ads work. You can make this fun by, for example, asking them to create a commercial to convince you to buy a product they know you don't want, to analyze TV commercials, and to do blind taste tests at home to see if the name-brand products really are any better.

It is crucial that you teach your children to become savvy about how advertising works. We have all seen, or been the parent of, a child in a store having a fit because she wants something she saw on TV that she is being denied. Don't buy things for your child just to appease her. Children don't know the difference between wants, needs, and wishes; they need your help in learning how to evaluate spending choices and how to react to all the commercials geared toward them.

With the help of aware parents, children will become savvy about their finances, will make good choices, and will know how to make their money grow.

Promoting Creativity in Your Child

Stephanie Taylor was eleven years old when she read about a New Jersey police dog that was killed in the line of duty. Stephanie decided to start an organization called VEST-A-DOG to raise money to provide bulletproof vests to police dogs. She started by making donation boxes and flyers, which she distributed in veterinarian's offices and pet stores. She then contacted her local newspaper to inform them of her program. Within three weeks she had raised enough money to provide vests for six police dogs. She has now provided thousands of dogs in the United States and Canada with bulletproof vests.

Akiane Kramarik, from a small town in Idaho, is considered by many to be one of the most successful young painters in the world. Akiane began drawing at age four and painting by age six. She is self-taught in both painting and poetry and is currently compiling a book of more than three hundred of her poems, with corresponding paintings. She is considered a genius in both mediums. Akiane made her first appearance on *Oprah* at the age of nine.

Jason Brown was twelve years old when he wrote his first play, *Tender Places*, about a boy caught in the middle of his parent's divorce. His script was made into a TV movie, which won an award from the Foundation for Dramatists Guild. A *New York Times* drama critic called his movie "astonishing."

All parents want their children to be creative. While the examples above are extreme — they are of child prodigies — they each demonstrate a different type of creative thought. Creativity is not just about producing a product; it is a way of thinking. Creative children are great problem solvers because of their unique way of looking at things. They use their imagination to create beauty and to come up with innovative solutions to problems. In her book *Growing Up Creative*, Teresa Amabile defines a creative activity as something that is "substantially different from anything the child has done before and anything the child has seen or heard before."

How to Promote Creativity

Although it may sound obvious, homes that value creativity tend to spawn creative children. Children look to parents to be creative leaders, and parents can do a lot to foster their children's creativity. Below I provide some suggestions for some basic things you can do.

Believe in Them

Conveying to your child that you believe in his abilities is an important starting point. A study focusing on the preconceptions associated with labeling children tested a group of kids' IQs using a standard test and put them in groups according to the results. Teachers were told which kids scored the highest, but in reality the children were randomly assigned. By the end of the year the children whom the teachers thought had done well on the test were performing well, and the ones they did not think were as bright were not performing as well. This study shows how assumptions can become self-fulfilling prophecies. If you treat your children as if they are creative beings, they are far more likely to be creative. If little Nicky draws purple trees and you respond to that as a creative choice by asking her questions or commending her on her creativity, she is likely to continue thinking outside the box.

Value Process Over Results

Focus on process over outcome. If you teach your child to paint for the sheer enjoyment of painting, he is more likely to feel motivated to create and to love the process of painting. Jason Brown was inspired to write his script when his mother came to him and asked if he would like to enter a contest for young playwrights. Even though it was a contest, his focus was on the process of writing; the fact that it was a contest was unimportant to him and to his mother. He was excited about developing his first play and having it read by other people. Jason wrote for the love of writing and because he wanted to have a new experience. The more pressure a parent puts on a child to produce something, the harder it can be for that child to get in touch with his creativity.

Give Support

Support your child's desire to be creative, and help her accomplish what she sets out to do. When Stephanie Taylor needed to get to the veterinary offices and pet stores to drop off her donation boxes and to pick them up, her parents had to help her. Had they been unwilling or too busy to help, or if they had discouraged her, she never would have had her vision come to fruition and would not have learned what a difference she can make in the world.

Specific Things Parents Can Do to Inspire Creativity in the Home

1. *Keep art supplies well stocked and available.* Your home should have drawing paper, colored pens and pencils, paint, child-safe scissors, rubber cement, glue, crayons, clay, Play-Doh, yarn, thread, cardboard, dress-up clothes and shoes, makeup that kids can play with, dolls, toys, blocks, Legos, and musical instruments (plastic flutes, drums, and so on).

2. *Tell stories, and encourage your child to make up stories too.* A bedtime story doesn't have to be read from a book. You can make stories up for each other or take turns completing a story.

3. *Make music part of your family life.* Listen to CDs together, try writing a song, or put together a band using materials from around the house, like tin cans for drums.

4. *Play dress up.* Keep a trunk full of clothes, makeup, and accessories that your children can use to play dress up.

5. *Give your children a wide range of experiences.* Bring your kids to museums, zoos, and photography exhibits. Expose them to different cultures and cultural experiences.

6. *Encourage your children to put on a show.* Let them make a play, puppet show, or a movie.

7. *Allow your child to be bored.* Children need unstructured time so they can daydream and learn to create their own fulfillment. Send your kids outside to play, or give them some free time by themselves.

8. *Provide a workspace for your kids.* Designate an area of the house where your kids can get dirty and where you don't have to worry about paint on the carpet, furniture, or walls.

9. *Encourage creative writing.* Let your kids write stories, scripts, poetry, songs, and plays.

10. *Play games.* Make doing puzzles and playing board games a regular part of the family repertoire. These activities encourage children to think in new ways.

Support your child's uniqueness and creative thinking. My parents, who make their livings as creative people, always valued original thinking. When I was four years old I put on a Barbie play in the living room with my cousins Valerie and Jill. In the beginning of the play each of our characters appeared from behind the couch and introduced herself. Jill's doll appeared and said, "Hi, my name is Cindy." Valerie's introduced herself and said "Hi, my name is Carol." Then my doll said, "Hi. My name is Tucksculpa." Other parents might have corrected my doll's strange name and tried to convince me to use a more "normal" name, but my family loved Tucksculpa. This incident, among other things, encouraged me to think outside the box.

Respect the Creative Instinct

Raise your children to listen to their instincts. In his bestselling book *The Six Pillars of Self-Esteem*, Nathaniel Branden wrote, "Creative people listen to and trust their inner signals more than the average. Their minds are less subservient to the belief systems of others, at least in their creativity." Akiane Kramarik is a perfect example of that. Many of her paintings contain religious symbols, even though her parents were atheists. They support her creative work, regardless of its form, and encourage her to listen to her instincts. Her website mentions that when it comes to criticism, Akiane pays little attention.

A child needs a certain level of self-esteem in order to create and present an idea to the world, even to family and friends. As Branden points out, "Persons of low self-esteem tend to discount the productions of their mind. It is not that they never get worthwhile ideas. But they do not value them, do not treat them as potentially important, and often do not even remember them very long — *they rarely follow through with them*." Children need parents to value their inner signals and to model the behavior to them so they can learn to value their own work. This encourages kids to bring their own creative visions to fruition.

Value Independence

Researchers have found that you can promote your child's creativity by valuing his nonconformity and independence. When I was a child, a very creative friend of mine decided that he wanted to carry a purse to his first day of kindergarten. His parents, who were wildly creative and eccentric, took him to the store to find the prettiest purse a boy could carry. Even as an adult, this friend is one of the most creative people I know. As a teenager I used to go over to his house and make home movies in which we performed skits and had long, engaging dialogues until the early hours of the morning. It was not uncommon to come up with a wild idea at two in the morning and to see it through right then and there. While other kids were getting into trouble, we were making movies and being inventive at all hours of the day and night. Everyone wanted to hang out at his house; the creativity was contagious, and his parents kept a home that inspired it.

Encourage Independent Thought

Encourage your children to focus on themselves. Parents who are not focused on what other people think tend to produce creative kids. If you are too busy keeping up with the Joneses, your thinking may have become too conventional. You won't let your child carry a purse to school or wear plaids with stripes because you worry about what other parents and children will think. Choose your battles. Allow your child to do things that won't compromise his safety but may be a little bit off the beaten track. Along those lines, creative children tend to have parents who are not stuck in rigid gender stereotypes. Research has shown that creative kids, regardless of their genders, identify with adults of both sexes and view both men and women as role models.

Encourage Expression

Give your child enough freedom to find his own way; this breeds creativity. Parents who allow their children freedom and free expression tend to be authoritative. Perhaps that sounds strange to you, but authoritative parents don't try to control their children; rather, they tend to be more open to discussing and explaining things to their kids. Children need to learn how to find their own way naturally. If they are given the freedom to approach creating from new and different angles instead of just doing what they are told, children tend to discover their own creative passions and inspirations.

Encourage your child to make mistakes. Young children naturally have the curiosity and confidence to try new things until they become self-conscious and afraid to make mistakes. Parents can help their children avoid this fear by valuing the entire creative process and viewing "mistakes" as part of that process.

There is a lot that you as a parent can do to help your child's budding creativity. It is believed that of all our different personality characteristics, creativity is most influenced by the child's environment. A study of identical twins discovered that they scored very similarly on intelligence tests but were no more alike on measures of creativity than fraternal twins. In other words, creativity is not genetic. It is up to parents to create a family environment that encourages it.

Dealing with Sibling Rivalry

By a twist of fate, a child is born into a particular position in the family, and from this place, she will attempt to share her parents' love and attention and get her basic needs met. This setup naturally causes jealousies and resentment among siblings.

— Meri Wallace, *Birth Order Blues*

Sibling rivalry has existed for as long as there have been families. It is normal for children to feel anger, jealousy, and competition toward their siblings, regardless of how much they may love each other. Even when kids have a sense of abundance on a very primitive level, they still compete for food, goods, and, of course, their parents' love. It is totally normal to desire the exclusive love of one's parents.

Psychologists have found that the smaller the age gap between kids, the more competitive children tend to be. It is believed that this rivalry is a result of two (or more) children having similar needs and therefore vying for the same kind of attention.

How Parents Feel

Most parents feel pulled in many directions trying to meet the needs of more than one child. Erik Erikson, a psychoanalyst most known for his theories on psychosocial development, once said in reference to a mother who had multiple children, "When one child needs her, she feels she is ignoring the other. Then, when both need her, she feels she hasn't been able to satisfy either of them." This is the classic dilemma of parents with sibling children.

In addition, many parents of more than one child feel closer to one child than they do to the others. One 1950s study found that only one-third of the five- and six-year-olds in the study felt that they and their siblings received equitable treatment, and two-thirds felt that their mother preferred one sibling over another. Often, if you ask siblings who is the favorite, all of them will point to the same person. It is not uncommon for one child to be more like a certain parent, which can make it easier for that parent to relate to that child. Most parents feel ashamed of this very normal dynamic. You need to recognize these feelings so that you will be better able to give all your children the attention, love, and respect they need to grow. If you try to deny those feelings, you are more likely to act them out without realizing it.

How Kids Feel

In their book *Siblings without Rivalry*, authors Adele Faber and Elaine Mazlish provide parents with a great exercise to help them to have empathy for a child who is adjusting to a new sibling. They ask readers to imagine that a husband comes home and tells his wife that he loves her so much that he has decided to take another wife as well. When the new wife arrives, everyone makes a big deal about how cute she is. When she needs new clothing, the husband goes to the first wife's closet and takes some of her things, telling her that since she has grown out of them, the new wife will be wearing her old clothes. The new wife wants to use the first wife's stuff as well, and when the first wife tells the second that she can't, she gets into trouble. Faber and Mazlish then reverse the roles. This simple exercise can give you an idea of the normal feelings that come up for children around their siblings.

The Benefits of Siblings

All this is not to say that there are no benefits to having siblings. When researchers conducting a UNICEF study in Beijing compared four- and five-year-old only children to children of the same age from two-child households, they found that those with siblings scored higher in their willingness to share toys, in their ability to think of others first, and in how well other children responded to them and in less self-centered play. Another study of kindergartners conducted by researchers at Ohio State University found that children with siblings also negotiate peer relationships better than their only-children peers.

Sibling relationships are quite significant and typically outlast all other relationships. When they are good they can provide comfort and friendship to those involved. Even when their relationships are not so good, siblings still share a significant bond throughout their lives.

Raise the Odds

Most parents are willing to do anything they can to help their children get along and to have close relationships, but often they don't know what to do to increase the chance of positive interactions among their children. They can start by ensuring that the home is calm and peaceful, which naturally breeds peaceful sibling relationships. Children growing up in chaotic homes are more likely to fight with everyone, not just with their siblings. Anything you can do to make your relationship with your spouse calm and loving will increase your chances of having children who treat each other well. Researchers have found that sibling harmony has more to do with the example set by parents than with the children's personalities and temperaments. You need to be a good role model. If you treat your children and spouse with respect, empathy, and compassion, you are more likely to have children who treat each other that way too.

Siblings don't have to be alike to get along, but they must understand each other's feelings. Siblings who get along tend to be able to express empathy, respect, and compassion. It is up to a parent to impart these important values, which is best done through a combination of teaching and modeling behavior.

In addition to creating the proper mind-set for their children, there are many other things parents can do to prevent future sibling problems and to help to resolve ones that have already begun.

Set House Rules

Be clear about the consequences of undesirable behavior. Children should know what the consequences of their actions will be even before they act. Kids need to know that the punishments will be predictable and that they will be enforced. With older children who can read, it can help to post a written set of the rules someplace where they can refer to it when necessary.

When setting rules, you and your spouse should present a united front. Since children often try to divide and conquer their parents, both of you should be on the same page, regardless of whether you disagree in private. If you find that you are not getting the same response when disciplining your kids as your spouse does, this often means that your spouse needs to show the children that the two of you are in agreement. In other words, they need to learn that disobeying Mom will have the same consequences as disobeying Dad.

Birth Order Personalities

Individual personalities are very much a mixture of "nature and nurture." But experts argue that who we become is greatly influenced by where we fall in the birth order. None of the traits listed in the chart below, based on theory of birth order, are absolutes, but birth-order position does make certain traits more likely.

Birth Position	Strengths	Challenges
Firstborn	Is a natural leader; tends to be highly successful, focused, and detail oriented; works hard to please authority; is punctual and organized	Can be bossy and perfectionistic, tends to put enormous pressure on him- or herself to succeed, is picky and precise, can be moody, intimidating, bossy
Second born	Recovers from setbacks well; is creative, innovative, and playful; tries to be different; is more competent and independent	May feel inadequate next to older siblings, has a tendency to show off, can be very competitive
Middle child	Is able to nurture and lead, relates well, is able to share, is a good listener, gets along well with others, is rational and amiable, is a good mediator and negotiator	Often struggles for identity in the family, can become anxious or insecure, is a people pleaser, is uncomfortable with confrontation, can be codependent
Youngest	Is creative, fun-loving, affectionate, and outgoing; tends to be a cheerleader; has strong people skills; loves to entertain and talk to people; makes friends easily; is a risk taker	Is used to less responsibility, may have difficulty respecting authority, can be too dependent on others, gets onboard quickly, has a fear of rejection and a short attention span
Only child	Is a high achiever; is very motivated; matures faster; is well organized, dependable, and conscientious, comfortable with responsibility; enjoys facts and details	Can be self-centered; has a difficult time when he or she doesn't get his or her way; is demanding, unforgiving, and sensitive; doesn't take criticism well
Twins	Are natural team players; tend to be very emphathetic; are good at sharing	Can have intense personalities due to the need to differentiate; can find it more difficult to create an individual identity

Don't Allow Hitting

Hitting is never acceptable. By allowing children to hit each other, you teach them that violence is an acceptable form of communication among people they love. This rule is not gender specific. Boys should not be allowed to hit girls, and girls should not be allowed to hit boys. This goes for parents hitting children as well. When you spank Evan for hitting Lillie, you are still sending him the message that things get resolved by hitting. You are better off using your words, which will actually teach him how to use his.

Use Time-outs

Time-outs are a very useful technique for helping children deescalate a situation before it gets out of control. Time-outs give children the opportunity to learn how to calm themselves down and can help them to develop impulse control. To get maximum benefits, make sure that you put your child someplace without stimulation during a time-out. One parent I work with would send her daughter to her room. She couldn't understand why it had no effect until she walked into the bedroom during one of those time-outs and found her daughter quietly watching TV.

Remember that adults need time-outs, too! Sometimes it can be really helpful to call in a friend or relative to give you a few hours away from screaming kids so that you will be able to come back and think with a clear head. Doing this also allows you to demonstrate to your children how effective a time-out can be.

Honor Differences

Parents need to appreciate each child's strengths, which also means not putting your child down for his weaknesses. This helps enhance his self-esteem and identity. One of the most difficult aspects of this approach is avoiding comparison between children. Even favorable comparisons can be harmful.

Leah always told her oldest son, James, how impressed she was with his athletic ability and how much better his coordination was than that of his brother. As a result, James felt sorry for his brother and felt uncomfortable playing baseball in the backyard with him. Since he didn't play with his brother, his brother didn't improve his abilities, which only compounded the problem. James also felt a little guilty for being so much better than his brother, which made sports a little less enjoyable for him. If Leah had just told James how impressed she was with his athletic prowess, without comparing him to his brother, he would have felt good about himself, and his brother would not have been as affected by James's talents.

Avoid Labeling

It is all too easy to label Emma the "artistic one" and Madison the "mathematical one," but by doing that you place value judgments on each child, which will be very difficult for them to break out of. You also run the risk of giving one child the opportunity to develop talents that you may not give to the other one just because you have a preconceived notion that one has more skill than the other.

Shelby was a forty-year-old attorney who came to see me for psychotherapy. She was an identical twin and was very close to her sister, Shauna, who was an artist. As part of our work in stress reduction I starting talking to Shelby about relaxing activities that she could incorporate into her daily repertoire. When I asked her about painting she immediately responded by saying, "My sister is the artist, not me. I can't paint." On further questioning Shelby revealed that she found painting to be really relaxing but never did it because she considered it her sister's domain. Apparently, when they were young Shauna had shown artistic talent, and their parents gave her lessons but never offered them to Shelby. I asked Shelby to paint something for me as an experiment. When she brought in her work, I couldn't believe my eyes. She was incredibly talented. Once Shelby started painting she found that it came naturally and made her very happy. One interesting note is that Shelby has never told Shauna that she has started painting because she doesn't want to upset her.

Spend One-on-one Time

Children need to feel special. One of the best ways to help them feel important is to spend some devoted time alone with each child. Children who know they will have one-on-one time with each parent are less likely to fight for their parents' attention. Also, this special time gives you the chance to speak with your children in a safe, quiet place where they do not have to compete for your attention. If you do this consistently, you are likely to get to know your children on a whole new level.

Remain Neutral

Avoid taking sides as much as possible. It can be very difficult not to, especially when one child does something that is blatantly wrong. But when you avoid taking sides, you foster strong relationships among siblings, because you are preventing one child from becoming a parent's ally against another child. Sound impossible? Try giving attention to the child who has been wronged instead of focusing on the child who acted out. John and his brother Deryck were fighting when John, who is two years older and considerably larger and stronger, pushed Deryck. Instead of screaming at John, which he really wanted to do, the dad told John that it is never acceptable to push his brother and then focused on Deryck, taking him into his arms and kissing his shoulder where he had been pushed.

Differentiate between Feelings and Behavior

It is normal for children to feel anger and even hate toward one another. But while it is okay to feel that way toward a sibling, it is never okay to behave in an aggressive or hostile way. If your daughter tells you she hates her sister, you don't want to shame her by saying, "That's a terrible thing to say. You love your sister." Denying her feelings won't make them go away. Instead try saying, "It sounds like you are really angry at your sister. Did something happen that upset you?" This opens a dialogue, which helps you become closer to your daughter and lets her vent her emotions.

Help your children find the words to express themselves. Kids often have a difficult time comprehending their emotions and putting them into words. Often the emotions that come up are confusing or perceived as shameful, so children are reluctant to share them with their parents. It is the parent's job to normalize feelings of jealousy, anger, and rivalry and to help children express these feelings in productive ways. In other words, children should be taught that it is okay to have painful feelings but that it is not okay to physically hurt one another.

Don't Permit Name-calling

Name-calling and teasing should not be allowed. This rule applies to parents too. If your husband drops the bowl of popcorn on his way into the living room, and you call him a "klutz," you can expect your children to do the same with one another. Besides the fact that calling someone a name can make him or her feel bad, these names also tend to become self-fulfilling prophecies.

Whenever Danny got nervous he stammered, and his brother, David, called him "jabber jaw." The problem was that not only did this nickname make Danny feel bad, but he also started to think of himself as someone who wasn't articulate. When David teased him, he became nervous and would stammer more, which only seemed to confirm his brother's perspective. Once their parents stepped in and told David that it was unacceptable to call his brother names and made clear what his punishment would be if he disobeyed the rule, the teasing slowed down and eventually stopped. They also told Danny that they really believed that he was a very bright and articulate boy who just got nervous when he was teased. The change wasn't immediate but, over time, Danny became a very competent public speaker and many years later even tried out for the debate team.

Give Assignments

Hand out clear-cut assignments. If children know whose turn it is to feed the dog, clear the table, take out the trash, and so on, you will cut down on fights significantly. I always recommend rotating these assignments regularly, so that children don't feel like they get stuck with the "bad chores." Also, when we rotate tasks, children become well-rounded, since they are learning how to do a variety of household tasks.

Allow Kids to Have Their Own Belongings

Allow children to have their own possessions. Many parents are so worried their children will not learn to share that they forget that they are individuals who need to learn how to take care of their possessions and to make boundaries with others. Ownership helps create identity. Allow your children to have toys that they don't have to share unless they want to. Five-year-old Gary loved his drum set and took really good care of it. He identified as a drummer, and his drums were very important to him. When his sister expressed interest in playing with them, her parents made it clear that she would have to ask Gary. These parents demonstrated respect toward their son and his possessions by not automatically assuming that Gary should share them with his sister.

Prevent Escalation

When fights between siblings escalate, break things up. Many parents want their children to learn to work though conflict. While this is an admirable goal, your three-year-old cannot defend herself against your six-year-old. The age difference makes it impossible for the younger child to be effective. Children need help mediating their conflicts in a constructive way. This often means helping a child understand how it feels to be treated the same way he treats his siblings as well as encouraging him to use his words.

The good news is that most siblings develop healthy and fulfilling relationships with each other. As a parent you have the opportunity to help your children develop strong and loving relationships with each other by providing them with a loving, respectful foundation to build on.

 IS FOR TELETUBBIES

Understanding the Effects of TV on Your Child

The numbers on children and media consumption are downright shocking:

5: The average number of violent acts per hour during prime-time viewing

7.6: The average number of hours a day that a television is on with children watching

20: The average number of violent acts an hour during "children's television" programming

38: The number of hours the average child watches television per week

98: The percentage of families that own at least one television

8,000: The number of murders the average child has witnesses on television by the time she finishes elementary school

14,000: The average number of sexual references that a young viewer hears a year

33,500: The number of hours of television most children have watched by the time they graduate from high school (an amount equal to nearly four years)

100,000: The number of violent acts a child has viewed in the media before finishing elementary school

Who Holds the Remote Control?

With literally hundreds of broadcast, cable, and satellite stations to choose from, and what appear to be minimal standards of decency, the chances that your child will be exposed to information he or she is not ready for are high. Ever since Janet Jackson's now infamous "wardrobe malfunction" during the 2004 Super Bowl, we have an increased awareness that television viewing is not always safe for children. Children continue to need guidance in choosing shows to watch, and they need help in making emotional sense out of the images and situations they are exposed to. Even though the modern child is very savvy about the amount of information he possesses, developmentally he does not have the skills to integrate many of the messages he receives.

Often we give our children the latitude to make television viewing choices for themselves, but unfortunately, when we do, our kids are more likely to be exposed to programming that we wouldn't want them to see. Surprisingly, 65 percent of children who are eight or older and 33 percent of children between the ages of two and seven have television sets in their rooms. Even though 85 percent of parents say they always or often pay attention to what their kids are watching, 61 percent of kids say they watch what they want without any adult supervision. Children today are spending more time with various forms of media than they are with their parents. In fact, experts believe that most children spend seventeen hours each week with their parents but more than forty hours each week watching TV, playing games on a computer, or listening to radio, CDs, or an MP3 Player.

Clearly, whether or not parents know it, there is considerable competition for influence on their children's beliefs, values, and minds. In a study done by the Kaiser Foundation, nearly one-quarter of teens reported that they learned "a lot" about pregnancy and birth control from TV. In the book *The Other Parent: The Inside Story of the Media's Effect on Our Children*, James Steyer challenges parents to question their children's choices. He asks, If you discovered that another adult was spending five to six hours a day with your child exposing him to sex, drugs, violence, and commercial values, wouldn't you forbid that person from having contact with your kid?

Despite the fact that most parents would answer a resounding yes, most are not even taking advantage of some of the simplest ways of monitoring their children's viewing habits. In 1996 Congress asked the broadcasting industry to establish a voluntary ratings system for TV programs. As a result, the National Association of Broadcasters, the National Cable Television Association, and the Motion Picture Association of America created the ratings system known as "TV Parental Guidelines," which alert parents about the appropriateness, or lack thereof, of the material in each show. This information is shown for fifteen seconds before each program. In addition, as of January 1, 2000, the Federal Communications Commission (FCC) required all new television sets that are thirteen inches or larger to contain V-Chip technology. This chip gives parents the option of blocking out programming that they do not want their children to view. Studies show, however, that the number of parents who actually understand TV ratings has dropped from 70 percent in 1997 to 50 percent in 2000. Currently, nine out of ten parents asked don't even know the ratings for any of their children's favorite television shows.

Sticks and Stones

Many studies indicate a strong correlation between TV viewing and aggressive behavior in both young kids and teens. These studies have found that children who watch a lot of TV are becoming

- desensitized to the pain and suffering of others.
- more fearful of the world around them.
- more likely to behave aggressively toward others.

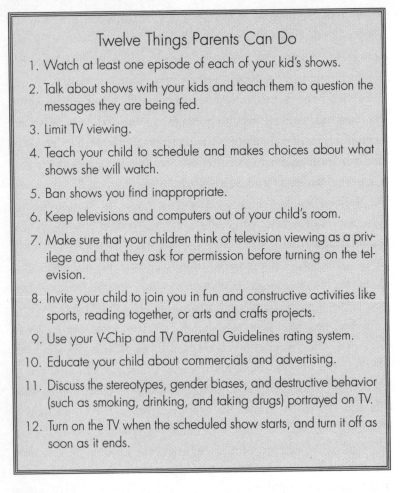

Twelve Things Parents Can Do

1. Watch at least one episode of each of your kid's shows.

2. Talk about shows with your kids and teach them to question the messages they are being fed.

3. Limit TV viewing.

4. Teach your child to schedule and makes choices about what shows she will watch.

5. Ban shows you find inappropriate.

6. Keep televisions and computers out of your child's room.

7. Make sure that your children think of television viewing as a privilege and that they ask for permission before turning on the television.

8. Invite your child to join you in fun and constructive activities like sports, reading together, or arts and crafts projects.

9. Use your V-Chip and TV Parental Guidelines rating system.

10. Educate your child about commercials and advertising.

11. Discuss the stereotypes, gender biases, and destructive behavior (such as smoking, drinking, and taking drugs) portrayed on TV.

12. Turn on the TV when the scheduled show starts, and turn it off as soon as it ends.

What these experts have found is that children who are frequently exposed to inappropriate images and messages are eleven times more likely to be disruptive, to fight with family members, to hit other kids, and to destroy property. To make that statistic stand out even more, those same researchers claim that children who watched a lot of TV when they were eight are more likely to be arrested and prosecuted for criminal acts as adults than their peers who did not watch as much TV.

One proof of the media's effect on children's behavior was found in a remote area in western Canada that did not receive broadcast television signals until relatively recently. Sociologists found a 160 percent increase in physical and violent acts, such as hitting and shoving, after television was introduced to the area. Other areas as well, both inside and outside the United States, have shown similar and significant behavior changes in children after exposure to television. However, just because your child is currently exposed to a lot of television does not mean that it is too late to effect change. In a recent Stanford University study of children whose TV time was reduced, it was found that these kids were, on average, 50 percent less likely to be physically aggressive with one another. Still need another reason to turn off the tube?

Monsters in My Closet and on My TV

Joanne Cantor, an internationally recognized expert on children and television, refers to television as "the number-one preventable cause of nightmares and anxieties in children." In fact, most children have been frightened by something they have seen on TV, sometimes very seriously. A random sampling of Madison, Wisconsin, parents with children who are in kindergarten through the sixth grade found that 43 percent of those parents reported that their children had been frightened by something on television and that the fear had outlasted the program. These fears can raise a child's level of anxiety and increase nightmares.

Nicolas was brought to my office after seeing a scripted television program in which a young boy was seen drowning. Nicolas, who had always been an enthusiastic swimmer, began to refuse to go into the water. He was haunted by visions of a boy, like himself, drowning and was having nightmares. He was really traumatized. Unfortunately, this is neither surprising nor unusual. Researchers examining the lasting effects of fear induced by media exposure asked three groups of children to watch a specific video, after which they gauged the impact of what the kids had seen. The first group watched a five-minute scene from *Little House on the Prairie* in which a school burns down and several people who are trapped inside die. The second group watched a scene from a movie in which people were enjoying cooking dinner over a campfire. The third group watched film clips of different benign activities with no specific connection to fire. Through having the kids fill out questionnaires, the researchers found that the children exposed to the *Little House* video were most worried about fires and being harmed by them and were not at all interested in participating in any positive fire-related activities such as building a fire in a fireplace or sitting around a campfire.

Sometimes it is difficult to know what will frighten a child, especially a younger one. In deciding whether something is appropriate for your child, it is always best to err on the side of caution. One thing to be aware of when making that determination is that preschool age children tend to be more influenced by the way things look than they are by whether the things are actually dangerous. For example, a young child is likely to be frightened by a movie about a person with deformities, even if the deformed character is kind and gentle, while older children are more likely to respond to situations that are actually dangerous. When trying to figure out if a specific television show or movie will be scary for your child who is six years old or younger, always preview the material yourself with an eye on the visual images.

Imagine All the People

Believe it or not, television can actually prevent children from developing their imaginations. Studies show that children who are heavy TV viewers, defined as those who watch at least three hours of television a day, are less imaginative than viewers who watch only one hour or less a day. Researchers also noticed that children who are less imaginative tend to watch more action and adventure programs, which commonly revolve primarily around rapid activity and violence. More imaginative children tend to watch television programs with greater educational benefits and have parents who value imagination. Studies also show that product-based programs, which derive their characters and storylines from toys, video games, or characters that are available in stores, tend to hinder creativity the most. This is most likely due to the fact that children are visually cued by the familiar characters; are given a script that tells them the toy's name, personality, and life story; and are not required to think or to imagine anything about the characters themselves.

All the News That's Not Fit to Print

Chelsea's parents had been sitting in bed been watching the eleven o'clock news for a good ten minutes before they realized that Chelsea had entered the room. The anchorwoman had just finished her summation of the kidnapping of seven-year-old Danielle Van Dam, who was taken from her bedroom while she slept and then murdered.

"Why did the bad man take that little girl out of her room, Mommy?" she asked, making her parents aware of her presence. That was the first of many nightmare-filled nights the parents faced before Chelsea was able to work through her anxiety and sleep through the night again.

News programs are always in the list of the top-ten shows that frighten children most. In fact, a 1994 study of parents with children in kindergarten through sixth grade found that 37 percent of parents reported that their children had been frightened by a news story that year. As children grow older they tend to become more affected by real-life reports of violence and crime. They are able to use more complex cognitive skills and are better able to distinguish between fantasy and reality, skills that tend to develop around the age of seven or eight. That same 1994 study noted that, of the children who were frightened by the news,

- one-third were frightened by stories portraying criminal violence.

- almost one-third were frightened by stories about war and famine.

- one-fourth were scared by stories about natural disasters.

- all the children were especially responsive to stories in which children were victimized.

Shortly after September 11, 2001, I was at a radio station answering questions from listeners about the emotional impact of trauma and terrorism. One caller, Mary, was clearly shaken. "My husband is a pilot," she told me, "and my son, Jake, has been having nightmares about my husband doing his job. He saw the planes crash into the buildings on the news, and now he is having nightmares about planes crashing into mountains and he is worried about his daddy. I don't know what to do."

During crises, people tend to watch a lot of news, which is often unedited and inappropriate for children to witness. On 9/11 many parents, engrossed in the unfolding events on television, were caught off guard by the devastation of the terrorist acts and were not as available to their children. As a result, many children who were watching with them became extremely confused by the footage, repeated over and over again, of the planes flying into the towers. Because young kids don't have a sense of time and don't really understand how television works, many children thought that multiple planes flew

into many buildings that day, which only added to their fear and anxiety. As a parent, it is crucial that you filter the information your kids
see and that you make certain that they view only appropriate shows.
You cannot count on television producers to do that for you.

TV Parental Guidelines Ratings System

According to the Federal Communications Commission, the TV
Parental Guidelines ratings system appears in the corner of your television screen during the first fifteen seconds of each television program and is included in the television listings of many newspapers.
Ratings is given to all television programming except news, sports,
and unedited movies on premium cable channels. A program can
receive six possible ratings:

- *TV-Y* (all children). Found only in children's shows, this rating means
  that the show is appropriate for all children.

- *TV-7* (directed to older children). Found only in children's shows,
  this rating means that the show is most appropriate for children
  ages seven and up.

- *TV-G* (general audience). This rating means that the show is suitable for all ages but is not necessarily a children's show.

- *TV-PG* (parental guidance suggested). This rating means that
  parental guidance is suggested and that the show may be unsuitable for younger children. (This rating may also include a *V* for
  violence, *S* for sexual situations, *L* for language, or *D* for sugges-
  tive dialogue.)

- *TV-14* (parents strongly cautioned). This rating means that the show
  may be unsuitable for children under fourteen. (A *V, S, L,* or *D* may
  accompany a rating of *TV-14*).

- *TV-MA* (mature audience only). This rating means that the show is
  for mature audiences only and may be unsuitable for children under
  seventeen. (A *V, S, L,* or *D* may accompany a rating of *TV-MA*.)

I Want One!

Children influence their parents to spend approximately $50 billion a year. These numbers are not lost on advertisers, who are determined to seduce young viewers into buying their products. It is to these companies' benefit to make children feel bad if they don't have the clothes, toys, or products that they are selling. But children don't understand the concept of the sales pitch and don't grasp that many of the commercials they see are meant to make them feel deprived. To complicate matters, young children aren't able to differentiate between television shows and commercials, and they believe what they see. Therefore, it is crucial that you educate your children when they are young and that you help them understand how commercials work.

Analyze commercials with your child. Advertisers are counting on children's underdeveloped analytical skills. If you can help your children question those messages, you will also be helping them to develop their analytical minds.

Fat Chance of Having a Healthy Kid!

Research shows that television viewing is detrimental to your child's long-term physical health. According to the Dunedin Multidisciplinary Health and Development Research Unit in New Zealand, children who watch more than two hours of television a night are at a higher risk of becoming smokers and of turning out to be overweight, physically unfit, and suffering from high cholesterol as adults — which leads to being at an increased risk for heart disease, diabetes, and other diseases. As few as one or two hours of television viewing a night for five- to fifteen-year-olds was associated with higher BMIs, lower cardiorespiratory fitness, increased cigarette smoking, and elevated cholesterol later in life.

It is not just the fact that children are sedentary while they watch

TV that makes them more likely to become overweight. As mentioned earlier, television viewing actually slows down metabolic rates. Studies show that normal-weight children experience a 12 percent decline in metabolic rates, while obese children experience a 16 percent decline. The fact that 95 percent of television food ads are for low-nutrient foods doesn't help children make healthy choices either.

Television is not all bad. There are many great educational shows out there for kids to watch. But parents need to monitor their children's viewing in order to guard their children's well-being.

Parenting Your Only Child

Single-child families are the fastest-growing type of family in the United States. The percentage of women who give birth to only one child has more than doubled in the past twenty years, up from 10 percent to over 23 percent. It is now estimated that there are over 20 million single-child households in the United States.

There are many reasons for this shift in family size. Some are situational, while others are due to choice: Parents are waiting longer to have children and are running out of childbearing years; more women are working outside the home in careers they hope to continue; it is becoming more socially acceptable to have a smaller family; many couples are marrying later in life; many couples are now divorcing before they have time to have a second child; and the cost of raising a child is higher than ever.

Only You: Parenting an Only

Many parents of only children appreciate the advantages of having one child. For them, parenting an only child allows them the time to focus their parenting skills on one person, while maintaining a marriage and a career. As a friend of mine, a mother of one child, says, "I'd rather parent one and do it well."

Many women are concerned about the effects that motherhood will have on their careers. Julie went to therapy to seek help with deciding whether she wanted children at all. She was a partner at a law firm and had worked very hard to get there. Julie didn't feel an urgent need to have a baby, but turning thirty-six, along with being pushed by her gynecologist, made her realize that time was not on her side and that she needed to make some decisions. Julie ultimately chose to have just one child so she could still "have it all."

Many parents worry that having an only child will leave their child lonely, selfish, or unsocialized. But that is certainly not the norm for children in single-child households.

Smarty-pants

Many studies have shown only children to have better cognitive abilities, verbal skills, and even higher IQ scores. According to a study conducted by the American Institutes for Research, only children from two-parent homes exhibited higher intelligence than their peers with one sibling. Another study that measured the cognitive abilities in the areas of math, reading, abstract reasoning, creativity, and reasoning found that children with no siblings did significantly better than children with one sibling in twenty-five out of thirty-two areas. In follow-up studies done eleven years later, the only children scored higher in forty-eight out of fifty-six topics.

There are a number of explanations for these findings. One obvious reason is that parents have a finite amount of resources — financial, emotional, intellectual — and energy to devote to their child. Since only children are the recipients of 100 percent of those resources, they do have an advantage over children who have to share their parents' resources. Only children are also exposed to adult language more frequently than their peers. As a result of this discrepancy, these children learn language from adults instead of siblings, so they have a more accurate and sophisticated model of language to learn from. In addition, the intellectual environment in a one-child home tends to be more mature and adult oriented than that of homes with more children, a circumstance that has been proven to expedite the learning of language skills.

A Wealth of Experience

Only children who were measured for what researchers call "richness of experience" also scored higher than children with siblings who were tested. Tenth-grade boys in the Youth in Transition program were asked to check off from a list of forty-six activities those they had engaged in at least once, such as making a long-distance phone call, taking a taxi, buying a book, visiting a zoo, attending summer camp, traveling to Europe, playing ping-pong, going to a museum, or writing a letter to someone. The sample collected indicated a clear advantage for the average only child, who had more varied experiences than the other children in the study. Why are these experiences so valuable for your child? The ultimate benefit of these types of life experiences is that it leaves children more confident and prepared for the world, a goal shared by all parents.

The Sky's the Limit

While no studies have confirmed this, many people believe that only children are more ambitious than other kids. These children have the sole attention of their parents, allowing them to develop a strong sense of self within the confines of a safe and contained relationship. They also have more resources with which to explore their hobbies and interests than would have been available to them in a larger family. As a result, many only children are able to focus on themselves and to discover their passions earlier in life. Because they are often "adultified," that is, exposed to adult conversation and treated like adults prematurely, they tend to take themselves seriously and start thinking about life goals and their futures earlier than other children.

On the negative side, however, because only children are the sole receptacles of their parents' hopes and dreams, a great deal of pressure can also be put on them to succeed. As a result, many only children never discover their passion in life because they desperately want their parents' approval, and they follow paths they believe will please their parents instead of finding and pursuing what pleases them. Mason, an adult only child, came to see me in therapy because he hated his job as an investment banker. He was making a lot of

Famous Only Children

Kareem Abdul-Jabbar	Lillian Hellman
Ansel Adams	John Lennon
Hans Christian Anderson	Joe Montana
Lauren Bacall	Cole Porter
Candice Bergen	Natalie Portman
Ada Byron	Elvis Presley
Truman Capote	Franklin D. Roosevelt
Leonardo da Vinci	Brooke Shields
Albert Einstein	Frank Sinatra
Rudy Giuliani	John Updike
Tipper Gore	Robin Williams
Cary Grant	Tiger Woods

money but dreaded going to work each day. Both his parents had pushed him into this line of work because of their own unfulfilled dreams. He felt trapped and depressed and, even at the age of twenty-eight, he stayed in a job he hated because he was still trying to please his parents. Mason was afraid that if he left his job and tried to become a writer, as he had always wanted to do, his parents would be crushed. It wasn't until he became willing to disappoint his folks and become his own person that he was able to follow his dream, which ultimately resulted in a successful career writing for television.

Going Solo

Heather's daughter, Justine, preferred finger painting by herself to playing in the sandbox with her kindergarten peers. This panicked Heather, who worried that her daughter would never make friends. Many parents of only children fear that their children are so accustomed to being alone that they will not develop social skills or close relationships with other kids. While only children tend to enjoy their own company, according to a study done by the National Center for Health Statistics, children without siblings and children from small families tend to be more popular than kids from large families. Only children, when asked to rate themselves, tend to consider themselves less sociable than their peers, which experts attribute to an apparently diminished need to connect with others.

This conclusion might lead you to believe that these children lead solitary lives. But further studies show that most only children are not lonely. They do, however, tend to enjoy solitary activities more than other children. This enjoyment continues later in life as well. In a study of 1,800 college students, those who identified themselves as only children reported that they do not feel especially lonely.

Parenting Your Singular Sensation

The stereotypical problems associated with being an only child are more a result of poor parenting than of a child not having siblings. In a *Los Angeles Times* article aptly titled "The One and Only: Children without Siblings Are Not Destined to Be Selfish, Spoiled, or Lonely," Susan Newman, psychologist and author of *Parenting an Only Child*, was quoted as saying, "The presence or absence of siblings has much less influence on the outcome of the child than the way that parents parent."

Parents of only children are more vulnerable to making mistakes, owing to the intense relationship they have with their child. In addition, when parents do make mistakes, these errors tend to be magnified because there are fewer familial relationships to dilute the interactions. Parents of only children tend to make some common mistakes. In her book *The Seven Common Sins of Parenting an Only Child*, Carolyn White says the seven biggest mistakes parents make are overindulgence, overprotection, failure to discipline, overcompensation, seeking perfection, treating your child like an adult, and overpraising. These parenting snafus can harm your child's development and give having an only child a bad name.

Avoiding the Little Emperor: Tips for Parents

While all parents can benefit from the following tips, they are especially useful for parents of only children.

Set Boundaries

Set clear and consistent boundaries with your child. She needs to know that when you say no, you really mean it. Children who can talk their parents out of keeping their word and manipulate their parents into giving them whatever they want do not feel satisfaction or happiness — quite the contrary. When parents give in repeatedly and do not maintain appropriate boundaries, their children, especially only children, feel unsafe and tend to act out. This dynamic can also lead to the development of an inflated sense of power that is inappropriate, and uncomfortable, for a child.

Let Kids Be Kids

Your child is not a little adult. While I do believe that children's thoughts and ideas should be heard and appreciated, I do not believe that children should be in control. I once worked with a couple whose only son held the remote control hostage. When I asked them why they didn't take away the remote and watch what they wanted, they told me, "Sam is an equal in our house." While children deserve to have their opinions taken into account, parents must always have the final say.

Maintain Grown-up Time

Parents need to have time alone. Not only is adult time good for parents, it is also good for a child who is used to being the focus of the triad to be reminded of the distinction between grown-ups and kids. Children need to learn to entertain themselves, and adults need time together. Finding that balance on a regular basis makes families healthier.

Provide One-on-one Time

Spend alone time with your child. It is important for him to develop a relationship with his father and a relationship with his mother. These relationships develop best when the child is given specific one-on-one time together with each parent. Children need that focused time with an individual parent to feel important and to develop self-esteem.

Don't Overpathologize

Don't assume that your child's bad behavior is a result of being an only child. Sometimes children get cranky or need a "time-out" simply because they are kids who don't yet know how to regulate their emotions or calm themselves down, not because of some imaginary only-child pathology.

Let Your Kids Chart Their Own Course

Help your child discover herself. Encourage her to pursue her own interests, even if you don't find those pursuits interesting. This helps a child's emerging identity form. It also helps her feel in control of her life. Children who are encouraged to follow their passions tend to be more confident.

Don't Push Too Hard

Because your child is your only chance to fulfill your fantasy of having a kid who is an Academy Award–winning actor, successful lawyer, or famous plastic surgeon, you are more vulnerable to pushing too hard. Since the parent of an only child has essentially put all her eggs in one basket, she is more likely to try to control the outcome, which is detrimental to her child's well-being. Fulfilling a parent's dreams is too heavy a burden for any child. Allow your child to fulfill his or her own fantasies, not yours.

Letting Your Child Have Downtime

Lola loves to perform and aspires to have a career on Broadway. On Mondays and Wednesdays she has dance class, on Tuesdays and Thursdays she has acting lessons, on Friday she has piano lessons, on Saturday she has singing class, and on Sunday she goes to church with her family. Lola also manages one hour each week of homework and one hour each month of volunteer work, as required by her school. Her brother, Max, is the family athlete. He plays soccer every Monday, Wednesday, and Friday and basketball every Tuesday and Thursday; he has a conditioning and calisthenics class every Saturday; and he goes to church with his family on Sunday. He does an hour of homework each night and is also responsible for doing one hour of volunteer work each month. Have I mentioned that Lola is six years old and Max is ten?

Kids today are under tremendous pressure to accomplish more and at higher levels than ever before. This pressure comes from their parents, coaches, educators, and peers. Children are encouraged to "get ahead" by learning to read and write before their peers and to start preparing for college while still in grade school. It is increasingly common to see very young children taking multiple extracurricular classes after preschool.

How Bad Is It?

A study performed at the University of Michigan's Institute for Social Research followed the lives of over 3,500 children in 1997 to examine how they spent their free time. The study found a 16 percent decrease in unstructured activities when compared to data from 1981. Unstructured activities are considered anything left over after sleeping, eating, and grooming and going to school, daycare, and after-school classes. The study found that in 1997, involvement in sports and other structured activities rose by 50 percent and that even children as young as six years old were spending eight more hours in school each week as well as more time on homework. It has been estimated that, as of 1997, children only had an average of three hours left a week of unstructured time — and that time may continue to shrink. According to a poll of almost nine hundred children ages nine to thirteen conducted by KidsHealth, more than four out of ten kids feel stressed "most of the time" or "always" and cited having "too much to do" as the primary reason for their stress. More than three-quarters of those polled said they longed for more free time.

The frantic scramble to accomplish and perform has left little time for family life. In fact, a study conducted by the University of Minnesota found that family time is disappearing at an alarming rate. Since the 1970s, family vacations, a prime source of family bonding and communal memories, have declined by 28 percent and family dinners, vital to family communication and unity, have decreased by more than 30 percent. Additionally, a national poll of teens reported the surprising result that the number-one concern among teens (tied with school worries) was "not having enough time with their parents."

Ten Signs That Your Child Is Getting Enough Downtime

1. He sleeps in one morning a week.

2. She tells you about her solo playtime.

3. He comes up with creative projects to do on his own.

4. She seems relaxed.

5. His calendar is not full.

6. She daydreams.

7. He asks for books, materials for projects, or art supplies.

8. She spends time outdoors.

9. He can entertain himself.

10. She builds things.

All Work and No Play Makes Jack a Dull Boy

"Downtime," or time when children are able to freely choose their own activities (or "inactivities"), is important for your children's overall mental health and development. Here are some specific reasons why children need this unstructured time:

1. Children need free time to "recharge their batteries."

2. Children who can spend their free time doing what they want will gravitate toward activities they enjoy, which helps them discover their passions.

3. Free time helps kids learn to regulate themselves. They will naturally be drawn to physical activities when they need to let off steam, to creative activities when they need to explore their imaginations, and to reading or scientific experimentation when they have a need to explore the more cerebral side of themselves.

4. Children who have freedom to choose their own activities are more likely to get in tune with themselves and their bodies, which will help them take better care of themselves as adults.

5. Unstructured time allows children quiet time, which increases their ability to focus and concentrate.

6. Free time allows children to become creative.

7. Children (and adults) tend to get to know themselves best when they spend time alone.

8. Daydreaming helps children to create a sense of future and helps them to set goals.

Running on Empty

Cathy brought her six-year-old daughter, Grace, to me after her pediatrician had ruled out all possible physical causes of her frequent stomachaches. Cathy suspected that something emotional might be going on but couldn't figure out what exactly. When I met with Grace she told me all about her friends at school, her homework, and her favorite topic, gymnastics. Grace loved gymnastics and had begged her mom to let her take classes. One class had turned into two, and before they knew it, Grace was training twenty hours a week. While Grace loved training, she missed the free time she used to have and didn't get any joy out of competing. She wasn't developmentally ready for the stress of competition and didn't know how to tell her mother, who had become quite invested in her career.

What many adults don't realize is how much children want their approval and what a strong need kids have to please them. Too often, parents get caught up in the excitement of their children's success, whether it is academic or athletic, and lose their objectivity about how their kids are handling the pressure. Understandably, Cathy was confused when she realized that Grace's stress was related to gymnastics, since Grace had begged to participate in it more and more frequently. Only when Cathy pulled back on her own involvement in Grace's gymnastics and limited Grace's training did her daughter's stomachaches miraculously disappear.

More and more, I see children in my practice who are overtraining, overstudying, and generally taking on too much. Some kids are able to tell their parents how they feel, but sadly, many are not. Among those who don't tell their parents are kids who are too young even to understand themselves why they feel so terrible. Many children who aren't able to tell their parents that they need to cut back on an activity or sport experience stress symptoms, such as headaches, bed wetting, stomachaches, sleep problems, anxiety, nightmares, clinginess, or agitation. If you see these symptoms in your child, it may be time to reassess your child's schedule and allow for some unstructured time.

Peer Pressure

Everyone knows that kids are notorious for falling prey to peer pressure, but it isn't just kids who experience it. Parents put pressure on each other regarding the accomplishments and talents of their children, and this dynamic tends to start very early. It is hard to keep up with the Joneses not only financially but, often, in the opportunities we give our children. In *Perfect Madness*, Judith Warner captures this anxiety well: "Parents know all too well that if they don't groom their children to be winners they will end up, de facto, as losers."

We all want what is best for our children, but at some point we need to look in the mirror and determine what we are doing for our children and what we are doing for ourselves. Pushing too hard doesn't usually create geniuses, but it does tend to create anxious children.

We need to pay attention to our children's natural talents and passions, understand where they are in their development and, most of all, pay attention to their cues. When children are overwhelmed and stressed they always let us know, sometimes by telling us and other times by showing us.

When It's Time to Change, You've Got to Rearrange

To give their children the downtime they need and to avoid overscheduling, most parents have to reexamine the choices they have made so far. This often means making changes. These changes are usually both logistic and emotional. Here are some suggestions to get you started:

- Take your cues from you child's behavior.
- Give your child the opportunity to develop skills in areas that interest her the most without imposing your own judgments.
- Give your child technology-free time in which she can do anything she wants (not including television, video games, the Internet, the radio, and so on).
- Create unstructured family time to give playing games, being creative, and talking to one another a valued place in the family repertoire.
- Limit extracurricular activities to no more than two at any given time.
- Give your child a daily dose of free time.
- Make sure your child's activities are age appropriate.
- Don't get pressured into signing your child up for activities by teachers, coaches, or other parents.

- Be a good role model, and show your child that you know how to have unstructured time yourself.

- Talk to your child about the benefits of downtime.

- Spend unstructured time with your child in which you do whatever activities she wants; this will allow you to get to know her even better.

The world we live in is very high pressured, and it can be difficult to go against the norms. The trick is finding the perfect balance for *your* child.

Keeping Your Marriage Strong

Your relationship with your spouse or partner is the emotional foundation of your family. Your children are counting on you not only to demonstrate what a healthy relationship looks like but also to provide them with the safety and security they need to create their own healthy attachments as they get older.

Four No-no's

Dr. John Gottman, founder of the Gottman Institute and a therapist who studies couples over the long term in his "love lab," found that the most important predictor of the success or failure of a marriage was not whether a couple fights, but the ratio of positive interactions to negative interactions. According to Gottman, for a marriage to work there must be five positive interactions for every negative one.

Gottman also identified four common predictors of divorce in married couples: criticism, contempt, defensiveness, and stonewalling.

He explains that couples who discuss their grievances are able to work through conflict, while those that criticize or attack each other's characters do not. According to his research, showing contempt for your partner can cause tremendous damage to a relationship. As Gottman defines it, contempt is an interaction that contains sarcasm, cynicism, name-calling, eye rolling, sneering, mockery, or hostile humor. In one study, in fact, Gottman found that wives who make sour facial expressions during conversations, which he views as an example of contempt, are likely to be separated from their husbands within four years. When a relationship has devolved to the point where a couple is regularly demonstrating their contempt for each other, they are no longer trying to get along; they are simply communicating their disgust toward one another.

Gottman identifies defensiveness as a predictor of divorce because it quickly and quietly erodes a marriage. When partners are defensive, they are blaming each other without taking responsibility for their own actions. This stalemate makes it impossible to work through conflicts. Stonewalling (ignoring your partner and refusing to be responsible), similar to defensiveness, is equally damaging, although it can take more time for the full effects to become apparent. When even one member of a couple is guilty of stonewalling, it makes any sort of dialogue impossible, resulting in an inability to communicate and work through problems.

All's Fair in Love and War?

You can do many things to improve your relationship. While few couples avoid fighting completely, all can learn to fight fairly. Communicating well and fighting fairly are crucial to a healthy marriage.

1. *Use "I" statements.* Instead of blaming your partner, use what therapists call "I" statements. They look like this: "When you

_____ [fill in the blank with a behavior], I feel _____ (fill in the blank with a feeling or two). For example "When you raise your voice to me, I feel scared and hurt."

2. *Try reflective listening.* Reflective listening means repeating back to your partner what he or she just said using your own words. For example, "Let me see if I understand you correctly. When I yell at you, you find it threatening and it makes you feel hurt and scared?" Often when couples fight they are so busy constructing their next argument while their partner is talking that they don't really listen to what the other person is saying. Feeling heard in a relationship is vital to good communication.

3. *Change the way you begin a discussion.* Gottman found that 96 percent of the time the way a discussion begins will predict the way it will end. If you can start from a loving place rather than an accusatory or attacking one, the odds are better that you will resolve the conflict in a positive way.

4. *Take a time-out.* Time-outs are not just for kids. Sometimes adults can benefit from a cool-down period during an argument as well. You need to establish that you are doing this before taking the break, so your partner doesn't think you are simply walking away. It is helpful to say something like, "I think I need a time-out right now. I am too upset to think straight and need some time to calm down. Let's check back with each other in an hour." Learning to take a loving time-out is a valuable skill.

5. *Do a daily check-in.* Take some time during your day to check in and see how you are both doing. Try to touch base about your thoughts and feelings as well as about how your partner's day is going. Make sure you ask if it is a good time if you are calling.

6. *Put the romance back into the relationship.* Sharing specific information about what pleases you and agreeing to do things to please each other regularly is a very good idea. If you are not sure what your partner would like, ask him or her to complete the following sentences: "I feel loved and cared about when you _____," "I used to feel loved and cared about when you _____," and "I would love it if you would _____."

7. *Let your partner influence you.* Let your partner influence your decisions. Gottman found that, even in the first few months of marriage, men who allow their wives to influence them have happier marriages and are less likely to want a divorce than men who resist their wives. Statistically speaking, when a man is not willing to share power with his partner, there is an 81 percent chance that his marriage will self-destruct.

8. *Make a date night.* Go out on regular dates, even if that means hiring a babysitter. Make sure to pick something you both enjoy. Keep the pressure low, but make sure it is adults only.

Make Time for Each Other

Date night has gotten a bad rap. Most couples think it has to be an elaborate, expensive evening in order to be successful. But that assumption misses the true intention of the event. Date night is meant to be about reconnecting and just being together, not trying to impress your spouse. It is for sharing and being intimate with each other and staying connected.

Most couples start out with good intentions when it comes to setting up a date night, but then the realities of careers, money, and childcare often get in the way. Sometimes it is the fantasy of what date night is "supposed" to be about that gets in the way. The fantasy of the candlelit dinner and romantic glances pales in comparison to your dress that becomes food splattered when you feed the kids before leaving and the sitter who arrives so late that you lose your dinner reservations.

Susan and Dave both work full-time jobs, have been married for ten years, and have three children. They started to go out on regular dates as a way to stay connected, but they are starting to wonder if they are on the right track. "I love the *idea* of date night. On Fridays, it starts out really well. He'll call me and say, 'Let's do something special.' I'm really into it. Then we get home, get comfortable, and we just don't feel like going out," laments Susan.

Brad and Nicole, considered the most romantic couple among their group of friends, vowed to keep the romance alive in their relationship. "Saturday is our date night," says Nicole. "Brad works all week long, so we don't get to see each other as much as I would like, and I really look forward to that time together. But whenever we start getting ready to go out, Mason, our four-year-old, starts crying. Before I know it, he is sobbing. I calm him down, but it's really hard to feel sexy when you have a hysterical toddler tugging on your dress." Basically, Nicole struggles to make the transition from mommy to wife when she and Brad go out on dates.

Sean and Delana keep vowing to make a date night happen. "The last time we went out, the babysitter cost us fifty dollars, dinner was forty-five dollars, and parking was five dollars. That's a hundred bucks! We can't afford to have a weekly date night. If we do, we'll never put Emma through college! Not to mention, have you ever tried to get reliable babysitters on a weekend? It's impossible!"

So what is a couple to do? Here are some suggestions.

Make It a Priority

Make going out on dates a priority. The parental relationship is the foundation of the healthy family and needs to be at the top of the list.

If the two of you are not feeling connected and close, your family will not be close either. You must demonstrate to your children that your relationship is a priority. One way to accomplish this is to have date night on the same day and at the same time every week. Put it on your calendar in ink, and let your children know that it is happening. If once a week is not feasible, try for once every other week or even once a month. It is better to do it less often but consistently than it is to go out more often at unpredictable times.

Make the Connection

Focus on connecting, not on wining and dining. Change the name! Instead of date night, call it *couple's night*, which has less of a connotation of getting "dressed up" and leaving the house. You still want to arrange childcare, but your evening doesn't have to be very formal. Sometimes just cuddling together at home in front of a movie that doesn't involve any talking animals is just what the two of you need to feel close.

Plan

Plan childcare in advance, and have backups. Getting reliable childcare can be more difficult than getting the newest PlayStation during the holiday season. To make couple's night work, you need help. One way to reduce resistance from your children is to get babysitters with whom they are comfortable. Try out different people while you are at home, and observe how well the children relate to them. Nicole discovered that Mason didn't get as upset once she started having Grandma come over to take care of him. If reliable family or babysitters aren't available, plan alternate nights out with another couple. This takes the pressure off of finding childcare and reduces the financial pressure on both couples.

Ten Things You Can Do to Strengthen Your Relationship

1. *Be appreciative* of the good things your partner does to please you, support you, or make your life a little easier. Reinforce the behaviors you like.

2. *Tolerate differences* in parenting styles, but do your best to find common ground.

3. Find time every day to *check in* with each other so you can stay connected.

4. *Do something nice for no reason.* Send him flowers at the office or give her a foot rub just because you care.

5. *Be direct about what you need from one another.* Mind reading should not be a prerequisite for being a couple. Tell your partner exactly what you want in specific terms so that he or she stands a chance of meeting your expectations.

6. *Make time for intimacy.* Spontaneity can be hard to come by, especially when at any minute someone could walk in on you and ask for a glass of water. Schedule adult time together.

7. *Take good care of yourself.* Your marriage doesn't stand a chance if you regularly don't get enough sleep, eat foods that fuel you, or find a few minutes to yourself on a regular basis.

8. *Give your partner a compliment.* Don't hold back from telling him or her the qualities you enjoy in your relationship.

9. *Make boundaries.* Say no to activities you don't absolutely need to do or care a lot about. Each time you say no, you are making time for your partner, yourself, or your kids.

10. *Address communication problems before they snowball.* If you find that you and your partner are repeatedly having the same fights, take a communication class for couples, make an appointment with a therapist, or sit down with a clergy member who is skilled at counseling.

Look Good to Feel Good

Get dressed for a grown-up night out. You don't have to put on a ball gown or a tux. Even putting on a nice clean pair of jeans and some lipstick, or your pressed khakis and some aftershave can make a big difference in your mind-set. Some parents find that tending to themselves and their personal appearance gets them in the mood for a grown-up evening. A lace Wonderbra can lift more than your breasts; it can also lift your spirits! "I spend all day in sweats schlepping my daughter from class to class. I never put on makeup anymore," says Lori. "I found that on date night with my husband, the one thing I do differently that makes me feel romantic is lingerie!"

Don't Overreach Financially

Make your date night financially feasible. It doesn't have to be expensive. You can picnic in the backyard, see a movie, or just go out for a cup of coffee, as long as it is adults only and you can talk and connect with each other. If money is an issue, send your kids to a grandparent's house or take turns babysitting with a friend who has kids too. Start a date night piggy bank into which you and your spouse throw loose change that you will use for a night out.

It doesn't matter how you do it, but you need to do whatever it takes to make sure your relationship is a priority. Communication and connection are essential for a healthy relationship between parents, but they both take effort. The time and energy you put into your relationship is well worth it, and you will reap its rewards both immediately and for years to come. After all, it is an investment in your relationship and your family's future.

IS FOR X CHROMOSOME

Raising a Girl

These days it seems like it is difficult to turn on a television or pick up a newspaper without reading a story about girls with poor self-esteem. These self-esteem problems often manifest as eating disorders, drug problems, drinking, social problems, and premature sexual experiences. Many parents feel helpless to change the course of their daughters' futures, thinking that these issues are inevitable. While sometimes being a parent to a daughter can seem like being on a runaway train and at other times like a psychological minefield, there is a lot you can do, especially in early childhood, to pave the way for your daughter to become a healthy, happy, young woman.

Girl Power: Self-esteem

Despite the fact that women today are more powerful and successful and have more rights than ever before, adolescent girls seem to be suffering more than ever. Compared to boys, girls grow up less confident and more insecure. In *Reviving Ophelia*, author and psychotherapist

Mary Pipher states that in their early adolescence, girls' IQ scores drop, their math and science scores plummet, they lose resiliency and curiosity, and they become less inclined to take risks. But do not panic: there are steps you can take to help prevent these things from happening to your daughter.

To begin with, parents must appreciate their daughters and teach them to appreciate themselves. Girls also need to be taught to be themselves, to listen to their instincts, and to find their passions in life. Patricia Freedman said it best in her online article "A Girl's Place Is in the Universe," printed in *EQ Today*, when she said, "Girls should be immunized with empowerment. By finding their own voices, girls identify their talents and capabilities. This provides a direction and a shelter to revisit when faced with the pervasive negative messages they may encounter in adolescence." These messages must start early. Early childhood is when people start to build a sense of self. Young girls are constantly looking to their parents to be positive mirrors reflecting back who they are and what their strengths are.

Parents need to have a "the sky is the limit" attitude about their daughters, and they must be aware of their own gender stereotypes. Recently a close friend of mine took her six-year-old daughter out of gymnastics classes. "I watched her doing handstands and thought to myself that if her arms get tired she could fall on her head and break her neck." For some reason she did not express the same concern about her four-year-old son taking classes at the same school. Most young girls need to be encouraged to take risks; they need to be given the room to fall down once in a while.

Falling and failing are important steps to learning any new behavior. When your child was first learning to walk, she fell down a lot, but you encouraged her to get up again and keep walking. Life is no different. Falling down is all part of the learning curve, and girls must be taught to understand that it is part of the process of achieving success. In 1982 nearly all the girls on my rhythmic gymnastics team made the United States Rhythmic Gymnastics team that year except me. This difficult experience taught me about hard work, discipline, and sportsmanship, skills that have served me well ever since. If I had not had that experience I would not have accomplished as much as I did in that sport years later.

Teaching a daughter about her own competence is crucial to the growth of her independence and sense of self-efficacy. If girls are taught to evaluate risks appropriately, they won't let fear prevent them from being all they can be. But if they are taught only to see danger, they will never grow. In other words, you must teach your daughter to swim, not to fear drowning.

Whatever You Say: People Pleasing

Legendary psychologist Carol Gilligan was the first to talk about what she called the "tyranny of niceness," that is, the way American culture encourages girls to be people pleasers at their own expense. This cultural pressure to put others' needs first, to ignore one's own gut feelings, and to avoid asking for what one wants because it might make other people uncomfortable has traditionally harmed girls. Girls tend to be raised to be relationship oriented, and because they receive praise for pleasing other people instead of themselves, they subvert their own desires and are less likely to pursue their own dreams. This is because, despite the fact that they enjoy the positive attention and accolades they receive, the more a girl pushes her own needs and desires underground to please others, the more likely her self-esteem will suffer. Each time a girl denies her own needs to make someone else happy, she sends a subtle message to her own unconscious that she is not important enough and worthy of caring for.

It is crucial that we teach our girls to say no in order to raise strong women who know how to take care of themselves and who

Raising Strong Girls

- *Encourage your daughter to say no.* Respect your daughter's boundaries, and encourage her to express her feelings. Encourage your daughter to speak her mind, regardless of her position and/or the circumstance.

- *Give her permission to make mistakes.* Girls need encouragement to take risks and to understand that mistakes are an important part of the learning curve.

- *Teach her to self-sooth.* Girls who never learn to calm themselves are more likely to turn to drugs or alcohol when they are older. Teach your daughter how to relax and calm herself down when she is upset.

- *Teach her to take care of herself.* Girls who know how to take care of themselves, which includes everything from recognizing her hunger pangs to knowing how to pack her own lunch to calming herself down, tend to feel a greater sense of confidence and self-efficacy.

- *Teach her to love her body.* Trust your daughter to listen to her body's signals, and help her appreciate the strength, flexibility, and endurance her body has to offer. Teach her to accept what she considers her imperfections too.

- *Encourage your daughter to negotiate.* Don't see her attempts at negotiation as insubordination; rather, view them as early attempts to learn an important skill. Participate in negotiations with your daughter about issues that have some wiggle room.

- *Help her find role models.* Read and talk about women in history so your daughter has an awareness of women's accomplishments. Point to the role models all around you.

- *Monitor her media exposure.* Studies show a direct correlation between how much media exposure a woman is subject to and the frequency of eating disorder symptoms she experiences.

- *Get her involved in sports.* High school girls who participate in sports are 40 percent less likely to drop out of high school and 33 percent less likely to become teen mothers. They are also less likely to smoke cigarettes.

- *Monitor your comments about yourself.* Mothers must staunch their own self-criticism in order to help their daughters develop a healthy self-image.

- *Get dads involved.* Girls with active dads are more likely to attend college, more ambitious, more successful in school, more likely to attain careers of their own, less dependent on others, more self protective, and less likely to date abusive men.

- *Watch your stereotypes.* Encourage girls, as well as boys, to question stereotypes. Have dinner table discussions about gender stereotypes.

- *Suggest activities and experiences for girls that may be traditionally reserved for boys.* Girls may not ask for the chance to change a tire, fix a leaky pipe, or explore the cause of an electrical short. But when they are given the opportunity, they are often enthusiastic participants. Encourage girls to explore nontraditional areas of interest.

- *Recognize your daughter for her mind, ideas, skills, and creativity instead of for her looks.* Reinforce her strengths outside of the superficial.

are capable of keeping themselves safe. While having a compliant and obedient child can make the job of a parent immeasurably easier, keep in mind that from the point of view of a child molester, this is very convenient behavior to find in a new victim. Stephanie and Mike brought their five-year-old daughter, Sara, across the country for a family vacation with Stephanie's brother and his children. Sara had only met these relatives a few times when she was much younger. At the end of the family weekend, when Stephanie told Sara to kiss her Uncle Burt good-bye, Sara said no. Stephanie, a people pleaser, was mortified. Sara said that she wasn't "comfortable" kissing Uncle Burt and reached out to shake his hand instead. The truth is that Sara was listening to her instincts, which is one of the healthiest things a young girl can do. Sara was very polite about it. If Sara is taught to continue to listen to her inner voice, she is likely to grow up with good self-esteem and is more likely to stay out of harm's way.

Rachel was a seventeen-year-old girl who came to my office after being in a terrible car crash with her boyfriend and two other friends. The four of them had plans that Saturday night. When Rachel's boyfriend, Steve, arrived at the house to pick her up he was clearly intoxicated. Before Rachel got into the car she asked if he had been drinking, and he replied, "Not anymore. Come on. Get in." When Rachel hesitated, the two other teens in the car made fun of her and told her she was "chicken" and a "big baby." Rachel didn't want to upset her cute new boyfriend or be thought of as "uncool" by the rest of the kids, so she got into the car, even though her gut told her not to. Fortunately Rachel did put on her seat belt, which is ultimately what saved her life. It took a long time for Rachel to forgive herself for not listening to her instincts.

My Body, Myself: Body Image and Eating Disorders

Girls are hungry for role models. Since the first woman any girl attempts to emulate is her mother, one of the greatest gifts a woman can give her daughter is the gift of positive self-image and body acceptance. A parent who loves her own body and appreciates her daughter's body is teaching her an important lesson. The ability to embrace imperfections and curves is an important part of self-esteem for girls.

During the normal adolescent growth spurt, a girl's body fat increases by 125 percent, compared to her lean body mass, which only increases by 42 percent. This normal, healthy growth can be shocking and scary for adolescent girls, especially when they are not prepared for this change. It can be even scarier for moms who haven't worked through their own body-image issues. I recommend celebrating developmental changes and preparing young girls for the positive changes that their bodies will go through as far in advance as possible.

In a world in which girls are constantly told they are not thin enough or perfect enough, in which the five-billion-dollar-a-year diet industry lies in wait to seduce your daughter, a parent must learn very quickly to identify the signs of eating problems. "My daughter is so young, I don't need to start thinking about that stuff now," you may think to yourself. You are wrong. Studies show that 50 percent of eight-year-old girls and 80 percent of ten-year-old girls report having already been on a diet. There is a lot you can do to help your daughter learn healthy behaviors. You may not realize, for instance, that the risk of developing an eating disorder is eight times higher in dieting fifteen-year-old girls than it is among nondieting fifteen-year-old girls. Since girls usually learn to diet from their mothers, it is important to be a good role model.

Teaching your daughter to listen to her body's signals of hunger and satiety empowers her. It is a metaphor for listening to her gut. Girls who listen to their bodies tend to listen to their instincts. They trust themselves on every level, which allows them to make good decisions in other areas of their lives and to feel good about those decisions.

Ask and You Shall Receive: Getting What She Wants

A study of students graduating from Carnegie Mellon University with a master's degree in a business-related field found that the starting salaries of men were, on average, 8 percent, or about $4,000, more than those of women. On closer examination researchers found out that only 7 percent of the women had asked for more money during the job interview, compared with 57 percent of the men. Students who actually asked for more money received on average $4,053 more than those who did not. Over time the gap between those who asked for more money and those who didn't only became bigger. In the book *Women Don't Ask* Linda Babcock and Sara Laschever report that men ask for what they want twice as often as women, and they initiate negotiations four times as often. Girls must be taught to take risks, to recognize challenges, and to negotiate. It is the only way to close the gender gap in income. Until that changes, women will still be earning seventy-six-and-half cents to the dollar.

Girls tend to silence themselves to avoid conflict. Encourage your daughter to speak up and ask for what is fair. Give her the room to negotiate her allowance or her bedtime. Encourage her to strengthen those negotiating muscles early on so she will be prepared to duke it out when she enters the workforce.

Madam President?: Career

Tracey had planned to take a few years off from her career as a television producer when her daughter, Katherine, was born. One day, while she was playing make-believe with Katherine, Tracey said that her character, a mother of two, was going to go to "the office." Katherine turned to her mother and said, "She can't go to the office. Mommies go to the gym, and daddies go to the office." Tracey almost fell over. She hadn't considered the impact her daily choices could have on her daughter.

Girls must not only be told that they can be anything they want to be; they must also be shown by example. This is not to say that every mother needs to work, but every mother does need to introduce career role models into her daughter's life if she wants her daughter to aspire to have a career outside the home. There are all sorts of positive role models: models of strength, courage, honor, and risk taking. Female role models help girls to identify their own strengths and potential and offer them motivation to be their best.

Be aware of the messages that your daughter is receiving from the Internet, music, books, movies, and television, and be open to discussing those messages openly. In *Growing a Girl*, author and mother Barbara Mackoff tells the story of how she handled her daughter's request for the book *Sleeping Beauty*. Despite her reservations about the sexist message that sleeping beauty needed a prince to rescue her, she allowed her daughter to get the book but used it as an opportunity to talk about how Sleeping Beauty could have helped herself. Children are greatly influenced by the messages they receive. A study of three- to seven-year-old children found that brief presentations of picture books with egalitarian gender role models actually reduced stereotypical thinking.

Girls who grow up feeling that they make a difference in the world and have the power to create change tend to feel good about themselves. Throw in connected relationships with parents and friends, and you have the ingredients for a daughter with healthy self-esteem. Girls thrive when they feel good about themselves and when they have room to explore and make mistakes without criticism.

IS FOR Y CHROMOSOME

Raising a Boy

Because boys and girls are treated as equals (in many ways), people assume that we raise them the same way. But science and psychology have shown us that boys and girls are actually different and as a result have different triggers and vulnerabilities that parents need to be aware of. Insightful parents must be conscious of cultural biases in order to avoid buying into harmful ideas of masculinity and femininity.

Dirty Harry and Superman

Somehow masculinity has become equated with destruction, fighting, and toughness. Boys are taught to "be tough," to avoid emotions, and never to cry. They are given responsibility prematurely, hugged less frequently, and encouraged to fight more often. In essence, they are taught to resemble the tough, stoic male stereotypes visible in television and the movies.

Kim and her husband, Bob, came to see me because their five-year-old son, Brody, was having nightmares. Bob was a pilot and

231

traveled frequently for work. Recently he had begun doing more international travel, which kept him away from home for longer periods than had been the case in previous years. When I asked them how they prepared Brody for those periods when his father was not around, Bob said they didn't do anything special. He would just say "good-bye" and tell Brody when he would be home. "And you always tell him to take good care of his mother while you are gone," added Kim.

I asked Bob why he would ask a five-year-old to take care of a grown woman. "Well," he answered, "I wanted him to feel like the man of the house while I was gone. I wanted him to feel strong and powerful, even though I expected him to do whatever his mother told him to do." But Brody was a boy, not a man. He was already experiencing a separation from his father that made him anxious, and on top of that he was being asked to take on a responsibility that he was totally unprepared for and that was not appropriate for a boy of his age. In addition, Bob's flip comment left Brody feeling like his mother wasn't capable of taking care of him, which only served to raise his anxiety. Strangely enough, Bob and most men like him would never have made that same comment to a daughter.

After a few sessions together, Bob and Kim prepared to make changes in their approach to Bob's future absences. They decided that the next time Bob was about to leave, he would give Brody a big hug, say good-bye, and tell him that his mother would take good care of him, reminding him that his daddy was only a phone call away. In addition, each time he would go away, he would mark the trip on a calendar so that Brody would understand when his dad would be back. I also had Bob record himself reading some of Brody's favorite bedtime stories so that Brody could hear his dad's voice every night before going to sleep. In addition, Bob and Kim decided to arrange a nightly bedtime call whenever possible and to let Brody know when to expect that call. After his parents had instituted these steps during

Bob's next trip, Brody felt very taken care of by his mother and connected to his father even though he was far away. He no longer had
nightmares, and his separation anxiety decreased. This change in
Brody brought about by his parents' actions demonstrates the deep
impact the often subtle messages that boys receive from their parents,
peers, and society have on boys and on their budding sense of self.

From Boys to Men

Boys and girls start out with primary attachments to their principle
caregivers who, even in modern times, still tend mostly to be their
mothers. This makes the process of separation and individuation,
which is already problematic for all children, particularly complicated
for boys. Freud believed that a boy must reject his mother in order to
identify with his father and become a man. While there does come a
time in every boy's life when he shifts his central attachment from
his mother to his father in order to identify with a male role model,
there is no age at which a boy must "give up" his mother. A healthy
mother-son relationship allows that son to leave his mother without
ever losing her completely, allowing him to return to her as needed.
This process can take place at any point from early childhood through
adulthood and can be difficult for mothers to experience, in part because many moms mistake individuation for rejection. It can be particularly painful because it can manifest itself quite suddenly, catching
the unsuspecting mother off guard.

   Gavin and Deena had been married for fifteen years when they
decided to call it quits. Their divorce was a surprisingly cordial division of the assets. They even decided to let each of their thirteen-
year-old twin sons decide which parent he would like to live with. As
is often the case with adolescent boys, they both opted to live with
their dad. Even though their mother would still have them at her

house three days a week, she was devastated. She felt completely rejected. Deena's feelings are understandable. What mother wouldn't feel that way? But what mothers need to understand is that it is normal developmental behavior for a boy to pick his father over his mother, because most adolescent boys are hungry to connect with their same-sex parent and desperately need that role model.

This is not to say that boys don't need their mothers. On the contrary, boys who are cut off from their moms tend to have more difficulties later in life. No matter how old a boy is, he always needs his mother's love and acceptance, which are vital to a boy's self-esteem and his sense of security. In order to grow, boys need to be both dependent and independent, which can be very confusing to a mother.

In *Raising Boys*, Steve Biddulph looks at male development in three stages. The first is from birth to age six, when a boy's primary attachment is to his mother. According to Biddulph, boys at this stage need a lot of affection so they can learn how to love. The second stage is from age six to fourteen, when a boy starts to increasingly look to his father to help discover new interests and activities. The third stage is from age fourteen to adulthood, when boys make the transition to becoming men. This is a time when they need to learn new skills, responsibility, and self-respect by joining with the adult community more and more. Male mentors are particularly important at this stage.

Chalkboards and #2 Pencils

A client of mine once described her son's first day of preschool to me. The wise teacher told all the parents to stick around in case their children needed them. Within hours all the boys were crying at their mothers' sides, while the girls sat and played. This experience is not unusual. Studies show that boys are more prone to feel separation anxiety than girls. Fortunately this teacher knew enough to encourage the parents to remain in the building to help their young children cope with the difficult task of separation. Many teachers are not that wise and actually force the parents to leave. This can be extremely traumatic for a child who is not ready to make this kind of separation. I always encourage parents of children going to school for the first time to stay nearby so their kids can come to them as needed. Children separate at their own paces, and boys should never be pushed to do it more quickly than they are ready.

The early academic world is often a bit more difficult for boys than girls. To begin with, from kindergarten through third grade, the teachers are predominantly female. While women are more than capable of teaching boys, they often teach the way they themselves would like to be taught, which may not always work for boys. In the book *Raising Cain*, authors Dan Kindlon and Michael Thompson take this a step further: "Grade school is a largely feminine environment, populated predominantly by women teachers and authority figures, that seems rigged against boys, against the higher activity level and lower level of impulse control that is normal for boys."

The things that are valued by schools — sitting still, reading, and concentrating — are difficult for most young boys. In addition, the early school curriculum now focuses on reading and writing, which isn't always developmentally appropriate for boys. A Virginia Tech study of brain development in boys and girls found that the areas of the brain involved in language and fine motor skills mature approximately six years later in boys than they do in girls. In other words, boys may have a more difficult time performing tasks such as writing the alphabet. A Louisiana State University study of infants' hearing found that boys' hearing is also not as sensitive as that of girls of the same age. This is especially apparent in the 1,000–4,000 Hz range, which is the range at which speech discrimination occurs. Follow-up studies show that girls of all ages tend to have finer hearing

What You Can Do for Your Son

- *Don't be too quick to pathologize your son.* Many parents are quick to diagnose their boys with ADD or other psychological disorders when they exhibit typical high-energy behavior or when they struggle in school.

- *Encourage the expression of feelings.* Teaching boys how to identify and express their feelings earlier in life puts them at an advantage. Boys who internalize their stress and pain tend to have more physical and emotional problems later on.

- *Give him run-around time.* Make sure to give boys time to burn off energy, especially if you know they will be in situations where they have to sit still for a long period of time (car trips, religious services, and so on).

- *Reduce risk.* When your son is learning a new sport or activity, like snowboarding, Sax recommends that you do three things: (1) Insist that your son receive lessons, (2) Don't allow your son to participate without supervision, (3) Assert your authority. When it comes to potentially risky behavior, tell your son the way it is going to be without leaving him any room for negotiation.

- *Encourage your son to sit where he can hear his teacher.* It is probably best for your son to sit in the front of the classroom. Since we know that boys tend not to pick up on sounds in the 1,000–4,000 Hz range, it is especially important that they sit where they can hear the teacher.

- *Make discipline fair and age appropriate.* Since parents have a tendency to be tougher on boys than on girls, make sure you treat your son with the same fairness with which you would treat a daughter.

- *Provide your son with father-son time alone.* Boys need both their mothers and their fathers, but too often they don't get to spend quality time with their fathers, owing to divorce, work, or unavailability. No matter how young or old a boy is, he needs his father's attention.

> • *Avoid gender bias.* Expose your son to the same sports, arts, and activities that you would a daughter. Allow him to do what he enjoys, even if goes against your ideas of what is traditionally male. When you let your son participate in household chores, you are helping to create a well-developed man. In their book *Raising a Son*, Don and Jeanne Elium recommend that parents teach their sons how to cook. They pick that skill because cooking encourages boys to cooperate, be sensitive to the needs of others, use forethought, pay attention to detail, and be creative. Teaching boys to cook also challenges sexist notions that cooking is for girls.

abilities. So what does this have to do with boys in school? Often boys are accused of not paying attention or, even worse, they are diagnosed with Attention Deficit Disorder (ADD), when in fact they are simply not sitting close enough to the teacher to make out the words that are being spoken.

If You're Happy and You Know It, Clap Your Hands

Researchers believe that most boys come into the world more sensitive than girls. In fact, studies have shown that male babies are more emotionally reactive than female babies and even tend to cry more frequently. However, somewhere along the line boys are discouraged from exhibiting this sensitivity and are encouraged to dissociate from their emotions. In a study in which both boys and girls listened to the sound of a crying baby over a loudspeaker while their physiological responses were monitored, the boys were found to be most upset by the crying baby and most likely to act aggressively toward the baby or to turn down the volume. The researchers concluded that boys are more likely to have trouble managing their own feelings and therefore are more likely to tune out other people's emotional distress.

In my psychotherapy practice I use a set of magnets, each of which has a face expressing a different emotion; each magnet is labeled with its corresponding emotion. Clients can place an additional magnet that reads "Today I feel" on top of the first magnet. This tool helps the users to identify their emotions. I noticed that many of my (mostly female) clients with eating disorders had a very difficult time identifying their emotions. After years of disconnecting from unpleasant emotions and using food to cover them up, many of these women found the magnet to be a simple way to check in with themselves and to identify their feelings.

One day, a teenage male athlete who was seeing me for sports psychology (the use of cognitive behavioral interventions to improve performance) started to realize that a lot of the feelings he was holding inside were affecting his baseball game. This smart young guy realized that his inability to identify and express his feelings was harming him. Once he started to use his new skills (and his magnet!) he was better able to talk through issues that were bothering him and to perform better as an athlete.

Kindlon and Thompson posit that to avoid "emotional illiteracy," boys must learn how to do the following three things:

1. Identify and name emotions

2. Recognize the emotional content of voice, facial expressions, and body language

3. Understand the situations and reactions that produce emotional states

Studies show that older boys have a more difficult time identifying and expressing emotions. To make matters more difficult for men, the part of the brain where emotions originate is not well connected to the part of the brain where verbal processing takes place. This, on top of societal pressure on boys not to express their feelings, makes it even more difficult for most boys and men to express themselves.

Soldiers, Guns, and Spitballs

Boys are notorious risk takers and tend to be naturally more aggressive than most girls. There are many reasons for this, the most common being that boys are more likely to overestimate their abilities. In a University of Missouri study of gender differences and children's responses to risk, researchers asked subjects to sit on a stationary bike in front of a very realistic interactive video screen. As subjects rode their bicycles, hazards were suddenly thrown in their way, while researchers measured how quickly these children stepped on their brake pedals. The boys consistently were slower to brake than the girls and, if the situation had been real, many of the boys would have been killed. When interviewed the boys were more likely to report feeling exhilarated, whereas the girls were more likely to report feeling fearful. It appears that boys are actually wired to enjoy risk.

Another reason is that boys who partake in risky behavior improve their social status with their peers. A boy who climbs onto the highest limb of a tree is considered cool by his friends. A girl in the same situation does not generally gain any social status. Boys are also more likely to do something dangerous when they are in a group, as opposed to girls, who are more likely to be more responsible in a group setting. In his book *Why Gender Matters*, Leonard Sax proposes two other reasons based on observations of monkeys: that aggressive play serves a primal imperative originating from the need to chase and hunt and that it is necessary to blow off steam. Sax goes so far as to hypothesize that boys who are not given the opportunity to be appropriately aggressive are more likely to experience violent outbursts.

Crime and Punishment

One Saturday afternoon Lynn caught her five-year-old twins drawing on the living room wall with crayons. She punished them, sending both her son, Landon, and her daughter, Regan, to their separate rooms. She told them they would have to stay there until dinnertime. An hour later she let Regan come out of her room and go play because she was worried that her "sensitive" daughter would get too distraught if she was punished for so long. Landon was not invited out of his room until supper. Many parents give their sons harder punishments or use a more severe disciplinary style than they do with their daughters. But boys should be given equal punishments for equal crimes. Some parents assume that their sons are tougher and can handle more punishment or need tougher discipline in order to learn, but that is just not the case. In fact, the opposite has been found to be true; boys who are punished unfairly are not likely to learn from their punishments.

On the flip side parents often underestimate the importance of love, nurturing, and affection for boys. Some parents worry that if they are too loving with their sons, they will create "sissies" or "weak" boys but, again, the reverse is true. Sons who grow up feeling loved and cared for by their parents and who are permitted to share the full range of their emotions grow up to be stronger and more confident men.

 IS FOR GETTING ZZZS

Helping Your Child Get a Good Night's Sleep

The first question most new parents are asked, immediately after "Is it a boy or a girl?" is, "Are you getting any sleep?" This, as we all know, is because babies feed at short intervals, need their diapers changed regularly, and cry when they are not comfortable, keeping their parents up all night. But just because your child is no longer an infant or even a toddler does not mean that sleep will come easily to him or her.

In fact, sleep problems among young children are extremely common. According to a 2004 sleep poll performed by the National Sleep Foundation, most children get less sleep during a twenty-four-hour period than recommended by sleep experts. In addition, 69 percent of parents with a child under the age of ten reported that their child had at least one sleep problem.

The Importance of Those ZZZs

While parents may be tempted to think that their child's loss of an hour or two of sleep isn't a big deal, the studies show that it is actually quite problematic. According to Jill Spivack and Jennifer Waldburger, renowned pediatric sleep specialists and authors of *The Sleepeasy Solution*, a child who isn't sleeping isn't developing well physically, cognitively, and emotionally. Once children start getting the right amount of sleep they start to thrive and can stay on an even keel throughout the day.

One study of middle-school-age children who were limited to six and a half hours of sleep a night found that these children had learning problems, poor attention spans, difficulty solving problems, and a decrease in both the speed and efficiency of completing tasks. A Harvard Medical School study found that sleep allows people to process, consolidate, and retain new memories and skills. The study investigated the effects on learning of reduced sleep by teaching students complex finger-tapping tasks after depriving them of one night's sleep. The researchers found that this one lost night of sleep significantly limited how well the subjects remembered new skills for as many as *three days*.

Most parents tend to underestimate the amount of sleep their children need and to overestimate how much sleep their children are actually getting. How do you know if your child isn't getting enough sleep? Here is a list of signs to look for. Some of them might surprise you:

- hyperactivity
- irritability
- depression
- clinginess
- tendency to be easily distracted
- forgetfulness
- excessive talking

- fidgeting

- aggressive behavior

- decreased motor skills

- trouble recovering from illness

- poor hand-eye coordination

- problems with memory

- poor impulse control

- inability to fall asleep

- nightmares or sleepwalking

- falling asleep during the day

- regressive behavior like thumb sucking

- tantrums

- difficulty waking

- inability to regulate actions, responses, and emotions

- resisting bed time or nap time

- repeated injuries

- seeking stimulation to stay alert

What You Can Do to Help Them Sleep

Sleep problems start early and, if not resolved, can last throughout adulthood. Children who are sleep trained, or in the words of Spivack and Waldburger, who "are taught the skill of self-soothing in order to learn how to fall asleep or fall back to sleep" are at an advantage over those who are not. In a study of three-year-olds receiving treatment for sleep problems, the American Academy of Pediatrics found that

84 percent have struggled with their problem since infancy, and college students who complain of sleep problems stated that they have experienced similar difficulties since childhood. Even if you did not teach your child good sleep habits when he was an infant, it is never too late to start him on a good sleep program. Here are some specific actions you can take.

Set a Sleep Schedule

Set a consistent sleep schedule and bedtime routine. Your child needs to have regular sleeping and waking times seven days a week so that he can regulate his internal clock. Children need that kind of consistency to get adequate rest. Further, a set schedule helps them to prepare their bodies and minds to go to sleep at the proper time each night, which in turn ensures that they get enough rest.

Children need transition time from energetic activities so that they can wind down. They are not capable of going from wrestling on the floor with a sibling to jumping into bed and going to sleep. They need time to calm down and prepare for sleep, both physically and mentally. The best way to make sure this happens is to create a series of consistent bedtime rituals. In addition to preparing your child for sleep, these rituals create a sense of security and predictability for him. These activities need to be relaxing and enjoyable and to be the same every night. Experts recommend three or four activities such as a bathing, putting on pajamas, washing up, and being read to. All the activities should take place in your child's bedroom or bathroom, and your child should not be allowed to wander around in between activities. In other words, little Jimmy shouldn't run downstairs to say goodnight to Mom after Dad has helped him wash up and get into his pajamas and is about to read him a bedtime story. Jimmy needs to say his goodnights before the evening ritual begins.

Address Anxieties

Give your child a chance to talk through his anxieties. Bedtime is a good time to connect with your child and to learn about what is going on in his life. According to Jodi Mindell, sleep specialist and co-author of *Take Charge of Your Child's Sleep*, "five- to eight-year-olds worry a lot. Setting aside time each day to talk about what worries them can help prevent sleep disturbances." This also gives you the opportunity to help your child work through his angst. Rosie's seven-year-old son, Teddy, started talking to his mom about his fear of earthquakes one night before bed. He had learned about them in school and was worried about what would happen to him and his family if one struck at home. Rosie was able to show him how the furniture was bolted to the wall and that the family had an earthquake preparedness kit and to talk to him about a family disaster plan. This quelled his anxiety enough for him to fall asleep.

Provide Kid Comforts

Give your child a transitional love object, something that comforts her in your absence. Many children have a teddy bear, blanket, special pillow, or other toy that helps sooth them to sleep after they go to bed. This added security can help a child go to sleep and can even help her self-sooth if she awakens in the middle of the night.

Regulate Darkness and Light

Set up your child's room so that he can have light in the morning and darkness at night. This way he will be more able to regulate his sleep. The easiest and most effective way to do this is by installing black-out blinds or drapes. The reason this step is so important is that bright light triggers the release of hormones that help create a wakeful state, and darkness triggers the release of other hormones that help aid sleep. Having your child spend time in the sunlight during the day, especially in the early morning, can help regulate his internal clock and make it easier for him to sleep at night. If you think of the lighting in your child's room on a 1-to-10 scale, with 10 being completely dark, then, according to Spivack and Waldberger, your child's room should be an 8 or a 9 during daytime or nighttime sleep. Remember to take into account that small sources of light such as a digital clock or the light from under a door bring light into the room. The darker the room is during daytime or nighttime sleep, the better.

Spivack and Waldberger point out that light reminds children that exciting activities are taking place outside their rooms and can make it harder for them to fall asleep. It is also believed that the additional light can cause physical problems. When researchers in the Department of Ophthalmology at the University of Pennsylvania tested the vision of 479 children between the ages of two and sixteen, they found that 34 percent of the children who slept with a night-light and 55 percent of the children who slept with the lights on became nearsighted. In contrast, only 10 percent of the children who slept in darkness were found to be nearsighted.

Regulate Bedroom Temperature

Keep the bedroom cool. While experts disagree on the ideal temperature for sleep, most recommend a cool room that is somewhere between 60 and 70 degrees Fahrenheit. Many children benefit from using an air purifier, humidifier, or dehumidifier. In addition, children often respond well to the sounds created by white-noise machines.

Keep Your Child Active

Children who are healthy, fit, and active also tend to sleep better than those who are not. Active children sleep well not only because they have tired themselves out but also because the physical activity increases the amount of time they spend in stage-3 and stage-4 sleep, the deepest and most restful sleep stage, when the body and brain are most able to rejuvenate.

Blockades to the Sandman

Sometimes it may seem like you are doing everything right, and your child still won't go to sleep. Here are a few more issues to take into account.

The Cortisol Connection

Spivack and Waldberger stress the importance of getting your child to bed before you miss her natural sleep window, which is when she is tired but not overtired. They point out that when that window has shut, your child produces a stress hormone called cortisol, a stimulant similar to adrenaline that can produce hyperactive behavior. Elevated levels of cortisol have three primary effects on kids: (1) It makes it difficult for them to settle down and go to sleep, (2) It makes their sleep more fragmented, and (3) It makes them wake up earlier.

Testing, One, Two, Three

Slightly older children who have developed cognitive skills and have an awareness of the rules are likely to test their limits. This is a normal part of child development but can be tough on parents. Often this dynamic is played out at bedtime, with children refusing to get into bed, repeating requests for water, getting out of bed throughout the night, and so forth.

Night Owls and Early Birds

Most children (and adults) have distinct sleep personalities. In other words, most people have a tendency toward being a "morning person" or a "night person." If left to our own devices we tend to naturally follow those patterns. It can be especially difficult for a night-owl child to go to sleep earlier than he is ready. This does not mean that he should stay up till all hours of the night. It just means that it may take him a little longer to adjust to a regular appropriate bedtime.

Sleep Thieves

Parents today need to be aware of a few other sneaky factors so they can help their children sleep well.

The Overscheduled Child

Kids today are involved in so many exciting activities at such an early age, and the list just seems to get longer. In addition, schools are now giving more and more homework, starting in the earlier grades. All this activity and overscheduling can prevent a child from getting a good night's rest. The simple mathematics are that there are only twenty-four hours in a day, and each activity eats away at time left for sleeping. Additionally, parents now work later hours and spend more time commuting from work but still want to spend time with their children when they get home, which often results in their keeping their kids up too late.

Too Much TV Time

Television viewing eats away at time that could be spent sleeping or engaging in relaxing activities. Children who watch a lot of television are more likely to have sleep problems. There are many reasons for this. Television is a stimulating activity that is not conducive to sleep. Kids who become used to falling asleep with the television on become dependent on it to fall back to sleep if they wake up in the middle of the night. The light from the television can prevent the body from producing melatonin, a hormone that helps regulate sleep cycles. Children who watch a lot of TV are more likely to be overweight, and overweight children are more likely to have difficulty sleeping.

Chubby Children

Overweight children are at a higher risk for snoring and sleep apnea, which can be dangerous. Sleep apnea in obese children has been associated with insulin resistance, increased risk of heart disease, high triglyceride levels, and diabetes. In addition, studies have shown a link between obesity and later bedtimes and fewer hours of sleep.

It is difficult to know which comes first when it comes to childhood sleep problems and obesity. One Japanese study of six- and seven-year-olds who got less than eight hours of sleep a night found they ran a nearly three times greater risk of being obese compared to children who got ten or more hours of sleep. Another study found that the risk of being obese decreased with each additional hour of sleep a child gets.

Caffeine Consumption

Many parents forbid their children to drink coffee but don't realize that caffeine is also present in many sodas, teas, chocolate desserts, and even some medications. In addition to keeping your children wired, caffeine is a diuretic, which means that your child may have to get up multiple times throughout the night to go to the bathroom. Do not give your kids a big mug of hot chocolate right before bedtime!

Food before Bed

Do not give your child a really large snack right before bedtime. It is difficult for children to sleep on a full stomach, especially when they have eaten foods high in protein or fat. In addition, children cannot

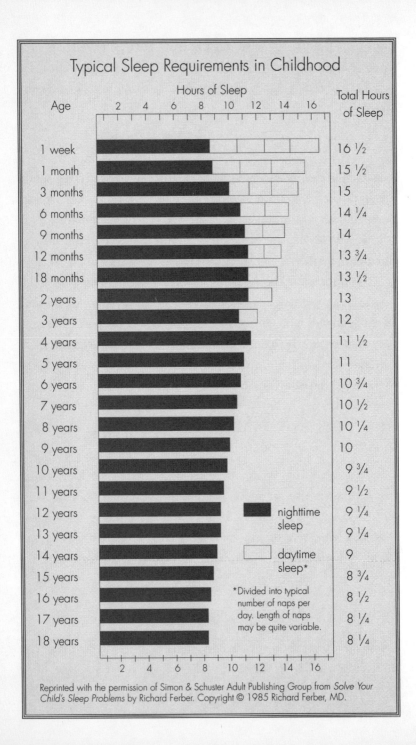

Typical Sleep Requirements in Childhood

Age	Total Hours of Sleep
1 week	16 ½
1 month	15 ½
3 months	15
6 months	14 ¼
9 months	14
12 months	13 ¾
18 months	13 ½
2 years	13
3 years	12
4 years	11 ½
5 years	11
6 years	10 ¾
7 years	10 ½
8 years	10 ¼
9 years	10
10 years	9 ¾
11 years	9 ½
12 years	9 ¼
13 years	9 ¼
14 years	9
15 years	8 ¾
16 years	8 ½
17 years	8 ¼
18 years	8 ¼

nighttime sleep

daytime sleep*

*Divided into typical number of naps per day. Length of naps may be quite variable.

Reprinted with the permission of Simon & Schuster Adult Publishing Group from *Solve Your Child's Sleep Problems* by Richard Ferber. Copyright © 1985 Richard Ferber, MD.

sleep if they are too hungry. Check in with your child before bedtime
to make sure that he is satisfied but not too full.

Nighty-night

Studies show that an early bedtime is ideal for children and promotes
healthy blood pressure, heart rate, and cortisol regulation. Spivack
and Waldberger indicate that most children successfully fall asleep
between 7:00 and 8:00 p.m., and they caution parents to not allow
their children younger than seven to have a bedtime past 8:30.

Most children stop napping between the ages of three and five.
According to statistics in Judy Owens and Jodi Mindell's book *Take
Charge of Your Child's Sleep*, only 27 percent of five-year-olds still
nap. It is important to be flexible and to pay attention to your child's
cues so that you can figure out what your child needs. Some children
cut out their naps at an earlier age, and some can at a later age. Either
way, the most important thing is to be in sync with your child's sleep
needs and to be flexible enough to meet them.

ACKNOWLEDGMENTS

I would like to thank Leif Reinstein for being the greatest attorney I could ever ask for. Thank you for always supporting my dreams. Your attention to detail and your willingness to fight for my projects always amazes me. Thank you for always having my back.

Also a special thanks to Georgia Hughes for believing in this book from the start. Your vision and inspiration took my work to the next level. Thank you for giving me enough autonomy to write from the heart but enough guidance to create a book I am truly proud to have written.

To my talented editing team, thank you for your great suggestions and terrific editing. Alexander Slagg, your kind words and encouragement made the whole editing process painless. Mimi Kusch, I am grateful for your eye to detail and amazing memory. It constantly amazed me how you noticed the smallest details and made my writing so much better. Thank you for all your hard work on this project.

I want to thank Joshua for being the most supportive husband I could ever ask for. Thank you for waking up at three thirty in the morning for months to do my hair for the morning news. Thank you for proofreading and formatting my five-hundred-page doctoral dissertation. Thank you for looking over all my contracts. Thank you for editing all my work before I turn it in so no one knows quite how bad my spelling really is. But most of all, thank you for loving me the way you do.

I would like to thank the crew at *Los Angeles Family* magazine for giving me a meaningful platform for my "Dr. Jenn" column. Thank you for your support over the past five years. I especially want to thank Andy Wexler, Merry Potter, and Mac Duffy.

Thank you, Donna Corwin, for encouraging me to write about parenting issues, and for your friendship and advice. You inspire me as a writer, a woman, and a parent.

Thank you, Toni Mendez, for being my role model and my inspiration. I know how proud you would be of this book.

I thank my daughters Quincy and Mendez for their warm hearts and generous smiles that inspire me to walk the walk. I love you both more than I ever could have imagined.

BIBLIOGRAPHY
AND RECOMMENDED BOOKS

A Is for Apple: Helping Your Children Form
a Healthy Relationship with Food

Becker, Anne. *Body, Self, and Society: The View from Fiji*. Philadelphia: University of Pennsylvania Press, 1995.

Fomon, Samuel. *Nutrition of Normal Infants*. St. Louis: Mosby, 1993.

Mellin, L. M., C. E. Irwin, and S. Scully. "Prevalence of Disordered Eating in Girls: A Survey of Middle-Class Children." *Journal of the American Dietetic Association* 92 (1986): 851–53.

Roth, Geneen. *Breaking Free from Emotional Eating*. New York: Plume, 2003.

Satter, Ellyn. *Child of Mine: Feeding with Love and Good Sense*. Boulder, CO: Bull Publishing, 2000.

———. *How to Get Your Kids to Eat . . . But Not Too Much*. Boulder, CO: Bull Publishing Company, 2000.

———. *Your Child's Weight: Helping without Harming*. Madison: Kelcy Press, 2005.

Tribole, Evelyn, and Elyse Resch. *Intuitive Eating: A Revolutionary Program That Works*. New York: St. Martin's Griffin, 2003.

Utter, Jennifer, et al. "Reading Magazine Articles about Dieting and Associated Weight Control Behaviors among Adolescents." *Journal of Adolescent Health* 32, no. 1 (2003): 78–82.

Vandereycken, Walter, and Roth van Deth. *From Fasting Saints to Anorexic Girls: The History of Self-Starvation*. New York: New York University Press, 1994.

Waterhouse, Debora. *Like Mother, Like Daughter: How Women Are Influenced by*

Their Mother's Relationship with Food—And How to Break the Pattern. New
York: Hyperion Books, 1997.

B Is for Bogeyman: Understanding and Addressing Childhood Fears

Brazelton, Berry T. *Touchpoints Three to Six: Your Child's Emotional and
Behavioral Development.* Cambridge, MA: Perseus, 2001.

Brown, Jeffrey, and Julie Davis. *No More Monsters in the Closet: Teaching Your
Children to Overcome Everyday Fears and Phobias.* New York: Prince
Paperbacks, 1995.

Crist, James. *What to Do When You're Scared and Worried: A Guide for Kids.*
Minneapolis: Free Spirit Publishing, 2004.

Feiner, Joel, and Graham Yost. *Taming Monsters, Slaying Dragons: The
Revolutionary Family Approach to Overcoming Childhood Fears and Anxieties.*
New York: Arbor House, 1988.

Garber, Stephen, Marianne Daniels Garber, and Robyn Freedman Spizman.
*Monsters under the Bed and Other Childhood Fears: Helping Your Child to
Overcome Anxieties, Fears, and Phobias.* New York: Villard, 1993.

Huebner, Dawn. *What to Do When You Worry Too Much: A Kid's Guide to
Overcoming Anxiety.* Washington, DC: Magination Press, 2006.

Lite, Lori. *The Goodnight Caterpillar: The Ultimate Bedtime Story.* Atlanta: Books
of Lite Publishing, 2001.

Lobby, Ted. *Jessica and the Wolf: A Story for Children Who Have Bad Dreams.*
Washington, DC: Magination Press, 1990.

Manathasis, Katharina. *Keys to Parenting Your Anxious Child.* Hauppauge, NY:
Barron's Educational Series, 1996.

Marans, Steven. *Listening to Fear: Helping Kids to Cope, from Nightmares to the
Nightly News.* New York: Owl Books, 2005.

Marcus, Irene Wineman, Paul Marcus, and Susan Jeschke. *Scary Night Visitors: A
Story for Children with Bedtime Fears.* Washington, DC: Magination Press, 1991.

Mayer, Mercer. *There's a Nightmare in My Closet.* New York: Puffin (Penguin),
1992.

Rapee, Ronald, et al. *Helping Your Anxious Child: A Step-By-Step Guide for
Parents.* Oakland: New Harbinger, 2000.

C Is for Cheering: Being a Great Sports Parent

Burnett, Darrell J. *It's Just a Game: Youth, Sports & Self Esteem — A Guide for
Parents.* Lincoln, NE: Authors Choice Press, 2001.

Cohn, Patrick. "An Exploratory Study on Sources of Stress and Athlete Burnout
in Youth Golf." *Sport Psychologist* 4 (June 1990): 95–106.

Corwin, Donna. *Pushed to the Edge: How to Stop the Child Competition Race So Everyone Wins.* New York: Berkley Books, 2003.

Fish, Joel, with Susan Magee. *101 Ways to Be a Terrific Sports Parent.* New York: Fireside, 2003.

Murphy, Shane. *The Cheers and the Tears: A Healthy Alternative to the Dark Side of Youth Sports Today.* San Francisco: Jossey-Bass, 1999.

Wolff, Rick. *The Sports Parenting Edge.* Philadelphia: Running Press, 2003.

D Is for Double Trouble: Raising Twins

Ainslie, Ricardo. *The Psychology of Twinship.* Lanham, MD: Rowman & Littlefield, 2005.

Bowman, Katrina, and Louise Ryan. *Twins: A Practical Guide to Parenting Multiples from Conception to Preschool.* Australia: Allen & Unwin, 2005.

Gromada, Karen, and Mary Hurlburt. *Keys to Parenting Multiples.* Hauppauge, NY: Barron's, 2001.

Lage, Cheryl. *Twinspiration: Real Life Advice from Pregnancy Through the First Year.* Lanham, MD: Taylor Trade, 2006.

Laut, Willaim, and Sheila Laut. *Raising Multiple Birth Children: A Parent's Survival Guide: Surviving the First Three Years of Twins and Supertwins.* Worcester, MA: Chandler House, 1999.

Lyons, Elizabeth. *Ready or Not . . . Here We Come: The Real Experts' Cannot-Live-Without Guide to the First Year with Twins.* Finn-Phyllis Press, 2003.

Malmstrom, Patricia, and Janet Poland. *The Art of Parenting Twins: The Unique Joys and Challenges of Raising Twins and Other Multiples.* New York: Ballantine, 1999.

Moskwinski, Rebecca. *Twins to Quints: The Complete Manual for Parents of Multiple Birth Children.* Nashville, TN: Harpeth House, 2002.

National Center for Health Statistics. "National Vital Statistics Reports" 50, no. 5 (2002): 18–19.

Pearlman, Eileen, and Jill Ganon. *Raising Twins from Birth Through Adolescence: What Parents Want to Know (and What Twins Want to Tell Them).* New York: HarperResource, 2000.

Sandbank, Audrey. *Twin and Triplet Psychology: A Professional Guide to Working with Multiples.* New York: Routledge, 1999.

Segal, Nancy. *Entwined Lives: Twins and What They Tell Us about Human Behavior.* New York: Plume, 2000.

Tinglof, Christina. *Double Duty: The Parent's Guide to Raising Twins from Pregnancy Through the School Years.* Chicago: Contemporary Books, 1998.

Wright, Lawrence. *Twins and What They Tell Us about Who We Are.* New York: Wiley, 1997.

E Is for Eenie Meanie: Helping Children Become Good Decision Makers

Cline, Foster, and Jim Fay. *Parenting with Love and Logic: Teaching Children Responsibility.* Colorado Springs, CO: Piñon Press, 2006.

De Becker, Gavin. *The Gift of Fear: Survival Signs That Protect Us from Violence.* New York: Little, Brown and Company, 1997.

Fay, Jim. *Tickets to Success: Techniques to Lead Children to Responsible Decision-Making.* Golden, CO: Love & Logic Press, 1995.

Gladwell, Malcolm. *Blink: The Power of Thinking without Thinking.* New York: Little, Brown and Company, 2005.

Green, Joey. *The Road to Success Is Paved with Failure: How Hundreds of Famous People Triumphed Over Inauspicious Beginnings, Crushing Rejection, Humiliating Defeats, and Other Speed Bumps along Life's Highway.* New York: Little, Brown and Company, 2001.

Hammond, John, Ralph Keeney, and Howard Raiffa. *Smart Choices: A Practical Guide to Making Better Decisions.* New York: Broadway Books, 2002.

Jacobs, Janis, and Paul Klaczynski. *The Development of Judgment and Decision Making in Children and Adolescents.* Mahwah, NJ: Lawrence Erlbaum Associates, 2005.

Schwartz, Barry. *The Paradox of Choice: Why More Is Less.* New York: Ecco, 2004.

F Is for Free to Be Me!: Raising Kids with Great Self-esteem

Branden, Nathaniel. *The Six Pillars of Self-esteem.* New York: Bantam, 1994.

Briggs, Dorothy Corkille. *Your Child's Self-esteem: Step-by-Step Guidelines for Raising Responsible, Productive, Happy Children.* New York: Little Brown and Company, 1988.

Brooks, Robert, and Sam Goldstein. *Raising Resilient Children: Fostering Strength, Hope, and Optimism in Your Child.* New York: McGraw-Hill, 2002.

Coopersmith, Stanley. *The Antecedents of Self-Esteem.* San Francisco: Freeman, 1967.

Farber, Adele, and Elaine Mazlish. *Liberated Parents, Liberated Children: Your Guide to a Happier Family.* New York: Collins, 1990.

Ginott, Haim. *Between Parent and Child.* London: Macmillan, 1966.

Gordon, Thomas. *Parent Effectiveness Training: The Proven Program for Raising Responsible Children.* New York: Three Rivers Press, 2000.

Hartley-Brewer, Elizabeth. *Raising Happy Kids: Over 100 Tips for Parents and Teachers.* Cambridge, MA: Da Capo Press, 2003.

Heinlein, Robert. *Stranger in a Strange Land.* New York: Ace, 1987.

Kaufman, Gershen, Lev Raphael, and Pamela Espeland. *Stick Up for Yourself: Every Kid's Guide to Personal Power and Positive Self-Esteem.* Minneapolis: Free Spirit Publishing, 1999.

Loomans, Diane, and Julia Loomans. *100 Ways to Build Self-Esteem and Teach Values.* Novato, CA: H J Kramer, 2003.

Ramsey, Robert. *501 Ways to Boost Your Child's Self-Esteem.* New York: McGraw-Hill, 2002.

Rosemond, John. *John Rosemond's Six-Point Plan for Raising Happy, Healthy Children.* Riverside, NJ: Andrews McMeel, 1989.

Sears, William, Martha Sears, and Elizabeth Pantley. *The Successful Child: What Parents Can Do to Help Kids Turn Out Well,* 1st ed. New York: Little, Brown and Company, 2002.

Seligman, Martin. *The Optimistic Child: Proven Program to Safeguard Children from Depression & Build Lifelong Resilience.* New York: HarperPerennial, 1996.

G Is for Gimme, Gimme: Raising Down-to-earth Children

Buffone, Gary W. *Choking on the Silver Spoon: Keeping Your Kids Healthy, Wealthy, and Wise in a Land of Plenty.* Jacksonville, FL: Simplon Press, 2003.

Clarke, Jean Illsey, Connie Dawson, and David Bredehoft. *How Much Is Enough: Everything You Need to Know to Steer Clear of Overindulgence and Raise Likable, Responsible and Respectful Children: From Toddlers to Teens.* New York: Marlowe & Company, 2004.

Gallo, Eileen, and Jon Gallo. *Silver Spoon Kids: How Successful Parents Raise Responsible Children.* New York: Contemporary Books, 2002.

Guthrie, Elizabeth, and Kathy Matthews. *The Trouble with Perfect: How Parents Can Avoid the Overachievement Trap and Still Raise Successful Children.* New York: Broadway Books, 2002.

Hausner, Lee. *Children of Paradise: Successful Parenting for Prosperous Families.* New York: Tarcher, 1990.

Kindlon, Dan. *Too Much of a Good Thing: Raising Children of Character in an Indulgent Age.* New York: Talk Miramax Books, 2001.

Samalin, Nancy, with Catherine Whitney. *Loving without Spoiling: And 100 Other Timeless Tips for Raising Terrific Kids.* New York: Contemporary Books, 2003.

Willis, Thayer Cheatham. *Navigating the Dark Side of Wealth: A Life Guide for Inheritors.* Zanesville, OH: New Concord Press, 2005.

H Is for Hero: Being a Great Dad

Brott, Armin. *The New Father: A Dad's Guide to the First Year.* New York: Abbeville Press, 2004.

Lamb, Michael. *The Role of the Father in Child Development.* Hoboken, NJ: Wiley, 2004.

Leman, Kevin. *What a Difference a Daddy Makes: The Lasting Imprint a Dad Leaves on His Daughter's Life.* Nashville, TN: Thomas Nelson Publishers, 2000.

Parke, Ross, and Armin Brott. *Throwaway Dads: The Myths and Barriers That Keep Men from Being the Fathers They Want to Be.* Boston: Houghton Mifflin, 1999.

Poulter, Stephan. *The Father Factor: How Your Father's Legacy Impacts Your Career.* Amherst, NY: Prometheus Books, 2006.

Pruett, Kyle. *Fatherneed: Why Father Care Is as Essential as Mother Care for Your Child.* New York: Broadway Books, 2001.

I Is for "I Don't Wanna Go": Helping the Child Who Doesn't Want to Go to School

Balaban, Nancy. *Everyday Goodbyes: Starting School and Early Care: A Guide to the Separation Process.* New York: Teacher College Press, 2006.

Brown, Jeffrey. *No More Monsters in the Closet: Teaching Your Children to Overcome Everyday Fears and Phobias.* New York: Three Rivers Press, 1995.

Eisen, Andrew, and Charles Schaefer. *Separation Anxiety in Children and Adolescents: An Individualized Approach to Assessment and Treatment.* New York: Guilford Press, 2007.

Eisen, Andrew, Linda Engler, and Joshua Sparrow. *Helping Your Child Overcome Separation Anxiety or School Refusal: A Step-by-Step Guide for Parents.* Oakland: New Harbinger, 2006.

Feiner, Joel, and Graham Yost. *Taming Monsters, Slaying Dragons: The Revolutionary Family Approach to Overcoming Childhood Fears and Anxiety.* New York: Arbor House, 1988.

Goldstein, Sam, Kristy Hagar, and Robert Brooks. *Seven Steps to Help Your Child Worry Less: A Family Guide.* Plantation, FL: Specialty Press, 2002.

Heyne, David, and Stephanie Rollings. *School Refusal: Parent, Adolescent and Child Training Skills* 2. Oxford, Eng.: BPS Blackwell, 2002.

Jervis, Kathe. *Separation: Strategies for Helping Two to Four Year Olds.* Washington, DC: National Association for the Education of Young Children, 1989.

Manassis, Katherina. *Keys to Parenting Your Anxious Child.* Hauppauge, NY: Barron's Educational Series, 1996.

McEwan, Elaine. *When Kids Say No to School.* Colorado Springs, CO: Shaw, 2000.

J Is for Jumping Jacks: Helping Your Children Love Exercise

Cederquist, Caroline J., MD. *Helping Your Overweight Child: A Family Guide.* Naples, FL: Advance Medical Press, 2002.

Gavin, Mary L., MD; Steven A. Dowshen, MD; and Neil Izenberg, MD. *Fit

Kids: A Practical Guide to Raising Healthy and Active Children — From Birth to Teens. New York: DK Publishing, 2004.

Pica, Rae. *Your Active Child: How to Boost Physical, Emotional, and Cognitive Development through Age-Appropriate Activity*. New York: Contemporary Books, 2003.

Satter, Ellyn. *Your Child's Weight: Helping without Harming*. Madison, WI: Kelcy Press, 2005.

Tribole, Evelyn, and Elyse Resch. *Intuitive Eating: A Revolutionary Program That Works*. New York: St. Martin's Griffin, 2003.

K Is for Kitty Cat: Keeping Pets in the Home

Arambasic, L., and G. Kerestes. "The Role of Pet Ownership as a Possible Buffer Variable in Traumatic Experience." Paper presented at the Eighth International Conference on Human-Animal Interactions, "The Changing Roles of Animals in Society," Prague, September 10–12, 1998.

Becker, Marty. *The Healing Power of Pets: Harnessing the Ability of Pets to Make and Keep People Happy and Healthy*. New York: Hyperion, 2002.

Bierer, Robert. "The Relationship between Pet Bonding, Self-Esteem, and Empathy in Preadolescents." Pub# 9993506, Arizona State University, 2000.

Endenburg, Nienke, and Ben Baarda. "The Role of Pets in Enhancing Human Well-being: Effects on Child Development." In *The Waltham Book of Human-Animal Interactions: Benefits and Responsibilities*, ed. I. Robinson. Oxford, Eng: Pergamon Press, 1995.

Guttman, Predovic, and M. Zemanek. "The Influence of Pet Ownership in Non-Verbal Communication and Social Competence in Children." *IEMT Proceedings of the International Symposium on the Human-Pet Relationship* (1985): 58–63.

Kilcommons, Brian, and Sarah Wilson. *Childproofing Your Dog: A Complete Guide to Preparing Your Dog for the Children in Your Life*. New York: Warner Books, 1994.

McDaniel, Colleen, and Jack McDaniel. *Pooches & Small Fry: Parenting in the 90s*. Wilsonville, OR: Doral Publishing, 1995.

Melson, G. F. "The Role of Companion Animals in Human Development." Paper presented at the Seventh International Conference on Human-Animal Interactions, *Animals, Health and Quality of Life*, Geneva, September 6–9, 1995.

Melson, Gail. *Why the Wild Things Are: Animals in the Lives of Children*, rev. ed. Cambridge, MA: Harvard University Press, 2005.

Poresky, Robert H. "Companion Animals and Other Factors Affecting Young Children's Development." *Anthrozoos* 9, no. 4 (2002): 159–68.

Salomon, A. "Animals as Means of Emotional Support and Companionship for Children Aged 9 to 13 Years Old." Paper presented at the Seventh International

Conference on Human-Animal Interactions, *Animals, Health and Quality of Life*, Geneva, September 6–9, 1995.

Silvani, Pia, and Lynn Eckhardt. *Raising Puppies & Kids Together: A Guide for Parents*. Neptune City, NJ: TFH Publications, 2005.

Swint, Sean. "Owning a Cat in Childhood May Lower Adult Allergies." Available at www.webmd.com/content/article/20/1728_53222.

Teacher Support Network. "New Research Says Pet-Owning Children Spend Significantly More Time at School." Available at www.teachersupport .org.uk/index.cfm?p=1563.

Toeplitz, Zuzanna, et al. "Impact of Keeping Pets at Home upon the Social Development of Children." Paper presented at the Seventh International Conference on Human-Animal Interactions, *Animals, Health and Quality of Life*, Geneva, September 6–9, 1995.

Triebenbacher Sandra. "Pets as Transitional Objects: Their Role in Children's Emotional Development." Department of Child Development and Family Relations, School of Human Environmental Sciences. Greenville, NC: East Carolina University, 1994.

————. "The Relationship between Attachment to Companion Animals and Self-Concept: A Developmental Perspective." Paper presented at the Seventh International Conference on Human-Animal Interactions, *Animals, Health and Quality of Life*, Geneva, September 6–9, 1995.

L Is for Lovebug: Teaching Your Child about Love

Chapman, Gary, and Ross Campbell. *The Five Love Languages of Children*. Chicago: Moody Press, 1997.

Gottman, John. *Why Marriages Succeed or Fail: And How You Can Make Yours Last*. New York: Simon & Schuster, 1995.

Gottman, John, and Nan Silver. *The Seven Principles for Making Marriage Work: A Practical Guide from the Country's Foremost Relationship Expert*. New York: Three Rivers Press, 2000.

Siegel, Judith. *What Children Learn from Their Parents' Marriage: It May Be Your Marriage, but It's Your Child's Blueprint for Intimacy*. New York: HarperPerennial, 2001.

M Is for Mary Poppins: Finding Good Childcare

Carlton, Susan, and Coco Myers. *The Nanny Book: The Smart Parent's Guide to Hiring, Firing, and Every Sticky Situation in Between*. New York: St. Martin's Griffin, 1999.

Carroll, Deborah, and Stella Reid, with Karen Moline. *Nanny 911: Expert Advice for All Your Parenting Emergencies*. New York: Regan Books, 2005.

De Becker, Gavin. *Protecting the Gift: Keeping Children and Teenagers Safe (and Parents Sane)*. New York: Dell, 1999.

Douglas, Ann. *Choosing Childcare for Dummies*. Hoboken, NJ: Wiley, 2004.

Ehrich, Michelle. *The Anxious Parents' Guide to Quality Childcare*. New York: Perigee, 1999.

Hernan, Frances Anne. *The ABC's of Hiring a Nanny: How to Find a Nanny without Losing Your Mind*, exp. ed. Olathe, KS: McGavick Field Publishing, 2003.

Raffin, P. Michele. *The Good Nanny Book: How to Find, Hire and Keep the Perfect Nanny for Your Child*. New York: Berkley Books, 1996.

N Is for Noodles and Nuggets: Eating Meals Together

Bennett, Steve, and Ruth Bennett. *Table Talk!: 365 Ways to Reclaim the Family Dinner Hour*. Holbrook, MA: Bob Adams, 1994.

Duke, M. P., et al. "Of Ketchup and Kin: Dinnertime Conversations as a Major Source of Family Knowledge, Family Adjustment and Family Resilience." Working paper # 26. Emory Center for Myth and Ritual in American Life, 2003.

Eisenberg, M. E., et al. "Correlations between Family Meals and Psychosocial Well-being among Adolescents." *Archives of Pediatrics and Adolescent* 158 (2004): 792–96.

Neumark-Sztainer, Dianne, et al. "Are Family Meal Patterns Associated with Disordered Eating Behaviors among Adolescents?" *Journal of Adolescent Health* 35 (2004): 350–59.

———. "The 'Family Meal': Views of Adolescents." *Journal of Nutrition Education*. 32 (2000): 329–34.

———. "Family Meal Patterns: Associations with Sociodemographic Characteristics and Improved Dietary Intake among Adolescents." *Journal of the American Dietetic Association* 103, no. 3 (2003): 317–22.

———. "Family Meals among Adolescents: Findings from a Pilot Study." *Journal of Nutrition Education* 32 (2000): 335–40.

Roth, Geneen. *Breaking Free from Emotional Eating*. New York: Plume, 2003.

Satter, Ellyn. *Your Child's Weight: Helping without Harming*. Madison, WI: Kelcy Press, 2005.

Squires, Sally. "It's Better Together." *Los Angeles Times*, March 7, 2005.

Tarkan, Laura. "Benefits of the Dinner Table Ritual." *New York Times*, May 7, 2005.

Weinstein, Miriam. *The Surprising Power of Family Meals: How Eating Together Makes Us Smarter, Stronger, Healthier, and Happier*. Hanover, NH: Steerforth Press, 2005.

O Is for Ouch: Making Visits to the Doctor Painless

Berenstain, Stan, and Jan Berenstain. *The Berenstain Bears Go to the Doctor.* New York: Random House Books for Young Readers, 1981.

Brazelton, T. Berry. *Doctor and Child.* New York: Delta Books, 1976.

Brazelton, T. Berry, Alfred Womack, and Sam Ogden. *Going to the Doctor.* Reading, MA: Addison-Wesley, 1996.

Chambliss, Maxie, and Kathryn Siegler. *I'm Going to the Doctor: A Pop-Up Book.* New York: HarperCollins, 2005.

Civardi, Anne. *Going to the Doctor* (Usborne First Experiences). Tulsa, OK: EDC Publishing, 1992.

Cole, Joanne, and Maxie Chambliss. *My Friend the Doctor.* New York: Harper-Collins, 2005.

Hayward, Linda. *Jobs People Do — A Day in a Life of a Doctor.* New York: DK Children, 2001.

Krauss, Ronnie. *Captain Kangaroo: Just Say "Ahhh!"* New York: HarperPerennial, 1998.

London, Jonathan. *Froggy Goes to the Doctor.* New York: Puffin (Penguin), 2004.

Moses, Amy. *Doctors Help People.* Plymouth, MN: Child's World, 1997.

Robbins, Beth. *It's OK: Tom and Ally Visit the Doctor!* New York: Dorling Kindersley, 2001.

Thorpe, Kiki, and Tom Brannon. *The Big Blue House Call (Bear in the Big Blue House).* New York: Simon Spotlight, 2000.

Zoehfeld, Kathleen, A. A. Milne, and Robbin Cuddy. *Pooh Plays Doctor.* New York: Disney Press, 1997.

P Is for Priorities: Spending Time with Loved Ones

Corwin, Donna. *Pushed to the Edge: How to Stop the Child Competition Race So Everyone Wins.* New York: Berkley Books, 2003.

Cox, Meg. *The Book of New Family Traditions: How to Create Great Rituals for Holidays and Every Day.* Philadelphia: Running Press, 2003.

Crain, William. *Reclaiming Childhood: Letting Children Be Children in Our Achievement-Oriented Society.* New York: Owl Books, 2004.

Doherty, William. *The Intentional Family: Simple Rituals to Strengthen Family Ties.* New York: Quill, 2002.

Doherty, William, and Barbara Carlson. *Putting Families First: Successful Strategies for Reclaiming Family Life in a Hurry-Up World.* New York: Owl Books, 2002.

Elkind, David. *The Hurried Child: Growing Up Too Fast Too Soon.* Cambridge, MA: Perseus, 2001.

Fiese, Barbara, et al. "A Review of 50 Years of Research on Naturally Occurring

Family Routines and Rituals: Cause for Celebration?" *Journal of Family Psychology* 16, no. 4 (2002): 381–90.

Friedman, Jenny. *The Busy Family's Guide to Volunteering: Do Good, Have Fun, Make a Difference as a Family.* Beltsville, MD: Robins Lane Press, 2003.

Hofferth, S. L. "How American Children Spend Their Time." *Journal of Marriage and the Family* 63 (2001): 295–308.

Imber-Black, Evan. *Rituals for Our Times: Celebrating, Healing, and Changing Our Lives and Our Relationships.* Lanham, MD: Rowman & Littlefield, 1998.

McGraw, Dr. Phil. *Family First: Your Step-by-Step Plan for Creating a Phenomenal Family.* New York: Free Press, 2004.

Niven, David. *The 100 Secrets of Happy Families: What Scientists Have Learned and How You Can Use It.* New York: HarperSanFrancisco, 2004.

Parents Magazine and Ann Pleshette Murphy. *It Worked for Me: From Thumb Sucking to Schoolyard Fights, Parents Reveal Their Secrets to Solving the Everyday Problems of Raising Kids.* New York: Golden Books, 1999.

Putnam, Robert. *Bowling Alone: The Collapse and Revival of American Community.* New York: Simon & Schuster, 2000.

Rosenfeld, Alvin, and Nicole Wise. *The Over-Scheduled Child: Avoiding the Hyper-Parenting Trap.* New York: St. Martin's Griffin, 2001.

Thompson, Michael, and Teresa Barker. *The Pressured Child: Helping Your Child Find Success in School and Life.* New York: Ballantine, 2004.

Warner, Judith. *Perfect Madness: Motherhood in the Age of Anxiety.* New York: Riverhead Books, 2005.

Q Is for Quarters: Teaching Your Kids about Money

Bodnar, Janet. *Raising Money Smart Kids: What They Need to Know about Money — and How to Tell Them.* Chicago: Dearborn Trade, 2005.

Gallo, Eileen, and Jon Gallo. *Silver Spoon Kids: How Successful Parents Raise Responsible Children.* Chicago: Contemporary Books, 2002.

Godfrey, Joline. *Raising Financially Fit Kids.* Berkeley: Ten Speed Press, 2003.

Godfrey, Neale, and Carolina Edwards. *Money Doesn't Grow on Trees: A Parent's Guide to Raising Financially Responsible Children.* New York: Fireside, 1994.

Mayr, Diane. *The Everything Kids' Money Book: From Saving to Spending to Investing — Learn All about Money!* Holbrook, MA: Adams Media, 2000.

McCurrach, David. *Allowance Magic: Turn Your Kids into Money Wizards.* Kids' Money Press, 2003.

Owen, David. *The First National Bank of Dad: The Best Way to Teach Kids about Money.* New York: Simon & Schuster, 2006.

Pearl, Jayne. *Kids and Money: Giving Them the Savvy to Succeed Financially.* New York: Bloomberg Press, 1999.

R Is for Riddles and Rainbows: Promoting Creativity in Your Child

Amabile, Teresa M. *Growing Up Creative: Nurturing a Lifetime of Creativity*. New York: Crown, 1989.

Branden, Nathaniel. *The Six Pillars of Self-esteem*. New York: Bantam, 1994.

Cassou, Michele. *Kids Play: Igniting Children's Creativity*. New York: Tarcher, 2004.

Csikszentmihalyi, Mihaly. *Creativity: Flow and the Psychology of Discovery and Invention*. New York: HarperPerennial, 1996.

Dacey, John S., and Kathleen H. Lennon. *Understanding Creativity: The Interplay of Biological, Psychological, and Social Factors*. San Francisco: Jossey-Bass, 1998.

Diamond, Marian, and Janet Hopson. *Magic Trees of the Mind: How to Nurture Your Child's Intelligence, Creativity, and Healthy Emotions from Birth Through Adolescence*. New York: Plume Books, 1999.

Einon, Dr. Dorothy. *Creative Child: Recognize and Stimulate Your Child's Natural Talent*. Hauppauge, NY: Barron's Educational Series, 2002.

Gardner, Howard. *Art, Mind & Brain: A Cognitive Approach to Creativity*. New York: Basic Books, 1982.

Root-Bernstein, Robert, and Michele Root-Bernstein. *Sparks of Genius: The 13 Thinking Tools of the World's Most Creative People*. New York: Mariner Books, 1999.

S Is for SOS (Save Our Siblings): Dealing with Sibling Rivalry

Borden, Marian. *The Baffled Parent's Guide to Sibling Rivalry*. New York: McGraw-Hill, 2003.

Brazelton, T. Berry, and Joshua Sparrow. *Understanding Sibling Rivalry: The Brazelton Way*. Cambridge, MA: Da Capo Press, 2005.

Downey, Douglas B., and Dennis J. Condron. "Playing Well with Others in Kindergarten: The Benefits of Siblings at Home." *Journal of Marriage and Family* 66 (2004): 333–50.

Faber, Adele, and Elaine Mazlish. *Siblings without Rivalry: How to Help Your Children Live Together So You Can Live Too*. New York: Collins, 2004.

Goldenthal, Peter. *Beyond Sibling Rivalry: How to Help Your Children Become Cooperative, Caring and Compassionate*. New York: Owl Books, 2000.

———. *Why Can't We Get Along?: Healing Adult Sibling Relationships*. Collingdale, PA: Diane Publishing Company, 2002.

Shulan Jiao, Guiping Ji, and Qicheng Jing (C. C. Ching). "Comparative Study of Behavioral Qualities of Only Children and Sibling Children." *Child Development* 57, no. 2 (April 1986): 357–61.

Sonna, Linda. *The Everything Parent's Guide to Raising Siblings: Eliminate Rivalry, Avoid Favoritism, and Keep the Peace*. Avon, MA: Adams Media, 2006.

Wallace, Meri. *Birth Order Blues: How Parents Can Help Their Children Meet the Challenges of Their Birth Order.* New York: Owl Books, 1999.

Wolf, Anthony. *"Mom, Jason's Breathing on Me!": The Solution to Sibling Bickering.* New York: Ballantine, 2003.

T Is for Teletubbies: Understanding the Effects of TV on Your Child

Cantor, Joanne. *"Mommy, I'm Scared": How TV and Movies Frighten Children and What We Can Do to Protect Them.* San Diego: Harcourt, 1998.

Manathasis, Katharina. *Keys to Parenting Your Anxious Child.* Hauppauge, NY: Barron's Educational Series, 1996.

Marans, Steve. *Listening to Fear: Helping Kids Cope, from Nightmares to the Nightly News.* New York: Owl Books, 2004.

Singer, Dorothy, and Jerome Singer. *Imagination and Play in the Electronic Age.* Cambridge, MA: Harvard University Press, 2005.

Steyer, James. *The Other Parent: The Inside Story of the Media's Effect on Our Children.* New York: Atria, 2002.

U Is for Uno: Parenting Your Only Child

Nachman, Patricia, with Andrea Thompson. *You and Your Only Child: The Joys, Myths, and Challenges of Raising an Only Child.* New York: Skylight Press, 1997.

Newman, Susan. *Parenting an Only Child: The Joys and Challenges of Raising Your One and Only.* New York: Broadway Books, 2001.

Pickhardt, Carl. *Keys to Parenting the Only Child.* Hauppauge, NY: Barron's Educational Series, 1997.

Szegedy-Maszak, Marianne. "The One and Only." *Los Angeles Times,* July 11, 2005.

White, Carolyn. *The Seven Common Sins of Parenting an Only Child: A Guide for Parents and Families.* San Francisco: Jossey-Bass, 2004.

V Is for Vegging Out: Letting Your Child Have Downtime

Corwin, Donna. *Pushed to the Edge: How to Stop the Child Competition Race So Everyone Wins.* New York: Berkley Books, 2003.

Crain, William. *Reclaiming Childhood: Letting Children Be Children in Our Achievement-Oriented Society.* New York: Owl Books, 2004.

Doherty, William, and Barbara Carlson. *Putting Families First: Successful Strategies for Reclaiming Family Life in a Hurry-Up World.* New York: Owl Books, 2002.

Elkind, David. *The Hurried Child: Growing Up Too Fast Too Soon.* Cambridge, MA: Perseus, 2001.

Rosenfeld, Alvin, and Nicole Wise. *The Over-Scheduled Child: Avoiding the Hyper-Parenting Trap*. New York: St. Martin's Griffin, 2001.

Thompson, Michael, and Teresa Barker. *The Pressured Child: Helping Your Child Find Success in School and Life*. New York: Ballantine, 2004.

Warner, Judith. *Perfect Madness: Motherhood in the Age of Anxiety*. New York: Riverhead Books, 2005.

W Is for Wedded Bliss: Keeping Your Marriage Strong

Craker, Lorilee. *We Should Do This More Often: A Parents' Guide to Romance, Passion, and Other Pre-Child Activities You Vaguely Recall*. Colorado Springs, CO: Waterbrook Press, 2005.

Fisher, Helen. *Anatomy of Love: A Natural History of Mating, Marriage, and Why We Stray*. New York: Ballantine, 1994.

———. *Why We Love: The Nature and Chemistry of Romantic Love*. New York: Henry Holt and Company, 2004.

Gottman, John. *Why Marriages Succeed or Fail: And How You Can Make Yours Last*. New York: Simon & Schuster, 1995.

Gottman, John, and Nan Silver. *The Seven Principles for Making Marriage Work: A Practical Guide from the Country's Foremost Relationship Expert*. New York: Three Rivers Press, 2000.

Hendrix, Harville. *Getting the Love You Want: A Guide for Couples*. New York: HarperPerennial, 1990.

Hendrix, Harville, and Helen Hunt. *Couples Companion: Meditations and Exercises for Getting the Love You Want*. New York: Atria, 1994.

Lindquist, Carol Ummel. *Happily Married with Kids: It's Not a Fairy Tale*. New York: Berkley Books, 2004.

Salazar, Linda. *Parents in Love: Reclaiming Intimacy after Your Child Is Born*. Rolling Hills Estates, CA: Kystar Publishing, 1998.

Siegel, Judith. *What Children Learn from Their Parents' Marriage: It May Be Your Marriage, but It's Your Child's Blueprint for Intimacy*. New York: HarperPerennial, 2001.

X Is for X Chromosome: Raising a Girl

Babcock, Linda, and Sara Laschever. *Women Don't Ask: Negotiation and the Gender Divide*. Princeton: Princeton University Press, 2003.

Beck, Carol. *Nourishing Your Daughter: Help Your Child Develop a Healthy Relationship with Food and Her Body*. New York: Perigee, 2001.

Deak, JoAnn, with Teresa Barker. *Girls Will Be Girls: Raising Confident and Courageous Daughters*. New York: Hyperion, 2002.

Elium, Jeanne, and Don Elium. *Raising a Daughter: Parents and the Awakening of a Healthy Woman*, 2d ed. Berkeley, CA: Celestial Arts, 2003.

Freedman, Patricia. "A Girls' Place Is in the Universe." *EQ Today*. Available at www.eqtoday.com/archive/jpcgirls1.html.

Gilligan, Carol. *In a Different Voice: Psychological Theory and Women's Development*. Cambridge, MA: Harvard University Press, 1993.

Hartley-Brewer, Elizabeth. *Raising Confident Girls: 100 Tips for Parents and Teachers*. Cambridge, MA: Da Capo Press, 2001.

Institute for Women's Policy Research. "The Gender Wage Ratio: Women's and Men's Earnings" (August 2005). Available at www.iwpr.org/pdf/C350.pdf.

Littman, Barbara. *Everyday Ways to Raise Smart, Strong, Confident Girls: Successful Teens Tell Us What Works*. New York: Thomas Dunne Books, 1999.

Mackoff, Dr. Barbara. *Growing a Girl: Seven Strategies for Raising a Strong, Spirited Daughter*. New York: Dell, 1996.

Pipher, Mary. *Reviving Ophelia: Saving the Selves of Adolescent Girls*. New York: Ballantine, 1994.

President's Council on Physical Fitness and Sports. "Physical Activity and Sport in the Lives of Girls." Minneapolis: University of Minnesota, Center for Research on Girls & Women in Sports, May 1997.

Richardson, Brenda Lane, and Elane Rehr. *101 Ways to Help Your Daughter Love Her Body*. New York: Quill, 2001.

Rimm, Dr. Sylvia. *See Jane Win for Girls: A Smart Girl's Guide to Success*. Minneapolis, MN: Free Spirit Press, 2003.

Rimm, Dr. Sylvia, with Sara Rimm-Kaufman, and Dr. Ilonna Rimm. *See Jane Win: The Rimm Report on How 1,000 Girls Became Successful Women*. Philadelphia: Running Press, 2001.

Sax, Leonard. *Why Gender Matters: What Parents and Teachers Need to Know About the Emerging Science of Sex Differences*. New York: Doubleday, 2005.

Simmons, Rachel. *Odd Girl Out: The Hidden Culture of Aggression in Girls*. New York: Harvest Books, 2002.

Warshaw, Robin. *I Never Called It Rape: The "Ms." Report on Recognizing, Fighting and Surviving Date and Acquaintance Rape*. New York: Harper & Row, 1988.

Wiseman, Rosalind. *Queen Bees and Wannabes: Helping Your Daughter Survive Cliques, Gossip, Boyfriends & Other Realities of Adolescence*. New York: Three Rivers Press, 2002.

Y Is for Y Chromosome: Raising a Boy

Biddulph, Steve. *Raising Boys: Why Boys Are Different — and How to Help Them Become Happy and Well-Balanced Men*. Berkeley, CA: Celestial Arts, 1997.

Buchanan, Andrea J., ed. *It's a Boy: Women Writers on Raising Sons.* Emeryville, CA: Seal Press, 2005.

Elium, Jeanne, and Don Elium. *Raising a Son,* 3d ed. Berkeley, CA: Celestial Arts, 2004.

Hartley-Brewer, Elizabeth. *Raising Confident Boys: 100 Tips for Parents and Teachers.* Cambridge, MA: Da Capo Press, 2001.

Kindlon, Dan, and Michael Thompson. *Raising Cain: Protecting the Emotional Life of Boys.* New York: Ballantine, 2000.

Macmillan, Dr. Bonnie. *Why Boys Are Different and How to Bring Out the Best in Them.* Hauppauge, NY: Barron's Educational Series, 2004.

Newberger, Eli H. *The Men They Will Become: The Nature and Nurture of Character.* Cambridge, MA: Da Capo Press, 1999.

Pollack, William. *Real Boys: Rescuing Our Sons from the Myths of Boyhood.* New York: Owl Books, 1998.

Sax, Leonard. *Why Gender Matters: What Parents and Teachers Need to Know About the Emerging Science of Sex Differences.* New York: Doubleday, 2005.

Silverstein, Olga, and Beth Rashbaum. *The Courage to Raise Good Men: You Don't Have to Sever the Bond with Your Son to Help Him Become a Man.* New York: Penguin Books, 1994.

Z Is for Getting ZZZs: Helping Your Child Get a Good Night's Sleep

American Academy of Pediatrics. *American Academy of Pediatrics Guide to Your Child's Sleep: Birth through Adolescence.* New York: Villard, 1999.

Ferber, Richard. *Solve Your Child's Sleep Problems.* New York: Fireside, 1986.

Kurcinka, Mary Sheedy. *Sleepless in America: Is Your Child Misbehaving or Missing Sleep?* New York: HarperCollins, 2006.

Lite, Lori. *The Goodnight Caterpillar: The Ultimate Bedtime Story.* Atlanta: Books of Lite Publishing, 2001.

Mindell, Jodi. *Sleeping through the Night, How Infants, Toddlers, and Their Parents Can Get a Good Night's Sleep,* rev. ed. New York: Collins, 2005.

Mindell, Jodi, and Judith Owens. *Take Charge of Your Child's Sleep: The All-in-One Resource for Solving Sleep Problems in Kids and Teens.* New York: Marlowe & Company, 2005.

Pantley, Elizabeth. The *No-Cry Sleep Solution: Toddler and Preschooler.* Columbus, OH: McGraw-Hill, 2005.

Spivack, Jill, and Jennifer Waldburger. *The Sleepeasy Solution: The Exhausted Parent's Guide to Getting Your Child to Sleep: From Birth to Age Five.* Deerfield Beach, FL: Health Communications, 2007.

Weissbluth, Marc. *Healthy Sleep Habits, Happy Child.* New York: Ballantine, 1999.

INDEX

A

alcohol and drug use
    family meals and reduced risk of, 128–29
    father's presence and reduced risk of, 72
    girls', reducing risk of, 224
    parental, 130
    spoiling/spoiled children and, 62
allergies, pets and, 105
allowance, 157–59, 161
Amabile, Teresa, 166
anxiety. *See* fears and anxieties
apologies
    love and, 113
    by parents, 54
attachments. *See* relationships

B

Babcock, Linda, 62–63
Becker, Marty, 99
bedtime. *See* sleep
behavioral problems
    boys', normal, 236
    in school, 65
    doctor visits and, 138–39
    family meals and reduced risk of, 135, 150
    father's presence and reduced risk of, 72
    house rules and, 176
    only children and, 204
    pets and reduction in, 102–3
    spoiling/spoiled children and, 62
    television viewing and, 187–89
Berenstain, Stan and Jan, 140
Berenstain Bears Go to the Doctor, The (Berenstain), 140
Biddulph, Steve, 234
Big Blue House Call, The (Thorpe and Brannon), 140
Birth Order Blues (Wallace), 173
birth order personalities, 177
body image, 1, 8–9, 10–11, 92
    girls, and eating disorders, 226–27
    media influence, 10–11
    parental role model and self-acceptance, 98
    parental role model and self-criticism, 98, 225
    sports and, 28
bonding
    father-child, 73, 78, 79
    mother-child, 73
    parental, 40
    siblings, 175
    ten overlooked opportunities for, 147
    twins, 39–40

boundaries
    and only children, 202–3
    setting clear, 63–64
boys, raising, 231–40
    behavioral problems, normal, 236
    cultural expectations, problems with,
        231–33
    discipline, 236, 239–40
    emotions, identifying and expressing, 236,
        237–38
    father-son relationship, 233–34, 236
    fears and anxieties, 232–33, 234–35, 237
    gender stereotyping and, 231–32, 237, 240
    hearing ability and, 235, 236
    mothers, separation, individuation and,
        233–34
    nurturing and, 240
    physical activities and, 236
    risky behavior and, 236, 239
    role models, 233–34
    tips for parents, 236–37
Branden, Nathaniel, 51, 169
Brannon, Tom, 140
Brazelton, T. Berry, 13–14, 140
Breaking Free of Emotional Eating (Roth), 129
Briggs, Dorothy Corkille, 56–57
Brown, Jason, 166, 167
Buffone, Gary, 66–67

C

Campbell, Ross, 110
Cantor, Joanne, 189
Captain Kangeroo: Just Say "Ahhh!" (Krauss),
    140
Chambliss, Maxie, 140
Chapman, Gary, 110
childcare, 117–26
    au pair services, 119, 126
    detailed job description for, 121–22
    fears about, 117–18
    helpful organizations, 126
    interviewing the caregiver, 122–25
    nanny contract, 125–26
    parenting philosophy and, 120–21
    references/background check, 118, 122
    sources for nannies, 118–20
Child's Nutrition Research Center (CNRC),
    129–30

Choking on the Silver Spoon (Buffone), 66–67
chores and tasks, 66–67, 182
    earning an allowance and, 157–59, 161
Civardi, Anne, 140
Cole, Joanne, 140
communication skills
    family meals and, 136
    helping your child speak up, 114–15
    listening and, 112–13
    one-on-one time and, 146
    pets and better skills, 104
    reflective listening, 215
    using "I" statements, 214–15
computer, limiting use of, 94, 95, 148
Connely, Sandy, 32
consequences
    behavioral problems and, 64–65
    cause and effect, teaching, 65–66
    decision making by children and, 45–47
    discipline and, 64
    for negative behavior, 69
    rescuing behavior by parent versus, 69
Coopersmith, Stanley, 53, 56
Couric, Katie, 48
Cox, Michael, 75
Crary, Elizabeth, 17
creativity, 165–71
    Akiane Kramarik, 165, 169
    believing in your child and, 166–67
    encouraging expression, 171
    encouraging independent thought, 170
    Jason Brown, 166, 167
    parental support for, 167, 169
    respecting the creative instinct, 169–70
    specific things parents can do to inspire at
        home, 168
    Stephanie Taylor, 165, 167
    television, negative effect of, 190–91
    valuing independence and, 170
    valuing process over results, 167
Cuddy, Robbin, 140

D

death and grieving, pet ownership and, 101–2
de Becker, Gavin, 49–50, 122
decision making by children, 43–50
    facing consequences and, 45–47
    five steps to help children solve problems, 50

five tips for parents for teaching about
    good and bad decision making, 48–49
  intuition and, 49–50
  making mistakes and, 47–48, 50
  offering clear options for, 43–45
  questions for parents to ask their child,
    46
delayed gratification, teaching, 63, 65, 68–69,
  162
  advertising awareness, 163
diets and dieting, 3–4, 9, 130
  girls, eating disorders and, 226
discipline
  allowing child to face consequences,
    45–47, 64–66, 69, 154–55
  boys, 239–40
  consistency and, 64
  father's presence and, 72
  house rules and, 176, 182
  time-outs, 178
divorce, boys and, 233–34
*DK Readers: Jobs People Do — A Day in a Life
  of a Doctor* (Hayward), 140
Doctors Help People (Moses), 140
doctor visits, 137–42
  anxiety, dealing with, 138–39
  books recommended, 140
  fears and, 141
  parental role model and, 138
  preparing for, playing doctor, 141
  preparing for, reading books, 142
  questions children can ask, 137–38
  telling the truth about, 139–40
  tips for, 142
downtime, 205–11
  signs your child is getting enough, 207
  suggestions to avoid overscheduling,
    210–11

E

Eating Disorder Awareness and Prevention
  (EDAP), 8
eating disorders (ED), 1, 4, 8–9, 10–11
  emotions, difficulty identifying, and, 238
  girls and, 226–27, 238
  media exposure and, 224
  preventing, 131–32
  sports and, 27

emotions
  family rituals and, 144–45
  identifying and expressing, 57, 87, 236,
    237–38
  self-esteem and, 57
  sharing feelings within the family, 112
  worst thing a parent can say and, 57
empathy, 65, 72
  pet ownership and, 104
  siblings and, 176
  twins and, 38
Erikson, Erik, 174
exercise, 91–98
  age appropriate, 92–93
  emphasizing fun, 92–93
  father's influence and, 98
  importance of play, 93–95
  intelligence and, 97
  limiting television viewing and, 94, 95–96
  motor skill development and, 96, 105
  parental activity and, 98
  peer acceptance and leadership, 97
  pets and increased activity, 105
  self-critical children and, 97–98
  tips to having an active family, 94
  weight regulation and, 9, 91, 97

F

Faber, Adele, 174–75
family life
  activity-friendly home, 94, 96
  chaotic setting and sibling rivalry, 175–76
  chores and tasks, 66–67, 157–59, 161, 182
  constructive disagreements, 79, 113
  family history lessons, 150
  family meals, 8, 127–36, 149–50
  home atmosphere, 54
  house rules and family laws, 63–64, 176,
    178, 181–82
  one-on-one time, 145–46
  parental modeling of loving relationships,
    79, 111, 213–20
  parental presence and, 63, 134–35
  pet-friendly home, 107–8
  physical activities and closeness, 98
  priorities, 143–51
  rituals, 144–45, 149, 244
  routines, importance of, 135

family life (*continued*)
single child households, 197–204
specific things parents can do to inspire
creativity at home, 168
television viewing and, 186–95
turning off technology, 148, 210
vacations, 150–51
volunteer work and, 151
See also love; sleep
family meals, 8, 11, 127–36
academic success and, 132
communication skills and, 136
don'ts, 130
do's, 133
fathering and, 71–79
improved nutrition and, 135
manners and, 136
nurturing and, 127–28
parental presence and, 134–35
preventing eating disorders, 131–32
prioritizing, 149–50
reduced risk of destructive behaviors and,
128–29
reduced risk of medical problems and, 135
weight problems and, 129–31
family rituals, 144–45
bedtime, 149, 244
fathering, 71–79
bonding with child, 73, 78, 79
boys, 233–34, 236
family rituals and, 145
father as primary caregiver, 71
getting involved in a child's life, 78
girls, 225
impediments to involvement by fathers,
73–75, 77
influence in child's life, 72, 78
influence on child's future intimate relationships, 73, 78–79
job demands and, 77
lack of role models for, 75
listening to a child, 79
media depiction of, 75
misconceptions about, 74–75
mothers as impediments to, 73–74
physically active children and, 98
websites for dads, 76–77
Fay, Jim, 50
fears and anxieties, 13–23
acknowledging the child's, and respond-
ing, 14–15

"behavioral inhibition" and, 23
boys and, 232–33, 234–35, 237
common childhood fears, by age, 20–22
of the dark, 13, 19, 20, 21
deep breathing techniques for, 18
of doctor visits, 138–39, 141
of dogs, 16, 21
eight steps to overcome, 14–15
family history and, 23
of first day of school, 19
guided imagery, 18–19
inborn temperament and, 22–23
peer and parental pressure and, 209–10
preparation for new experiences, 16–17
prevention of, 15–19
providing information about the feared
object or event, 16
recommended books, 17
relaxation exercises for, 18
school-related, 87
separation anxiety, 20, 72, 81, 86, 232–33,
234–35
serious, trauma and, 19
of sleepovers, 17
sleep problems and, 245
stranger anxiety, 20
television and, 189–90, 191–93
Fienberg, Dan, 155–56, 157–58, 163
financial education, 67–68, 153–63
and advertising awareness, 163, 194
basic lessons of, 156–57
and charitable contributions, 162, 165
earning an allowance, 157–59, 161
explaining and allowing child's participation in money matters, 155–56
games about money, 160
Internet sites, 160
savings, 161–62
"three little piggy banks" approach,
161–62
Fit Kids (Gavin et al), 93
Five Love Languages of Children, The (Chapman
and Campbell), 110
food and nutrition, 1–12
binge eating, 4
body image and, 1, 8–9, 10–11
child's choice of foods, 133
deprivation mentality, 2, 7
diets and dieting, 3–4, 9

education about, 135
exercise and, 97
family meals, 8, 11, 127–36
food before bedtime, 249, 251
girls and, 226
hunger scale, 5
intuitive eaters, 3, 6, 97
letting go of parental control, 6–8
media and, 10–11
metabolic changes and, 4
normal eating, 4–6
parental model and, 12
restricted eating, 2–4
television viewing and, 9, 95, 129, 194–95, 249
tips for the whole family, 11
varied and healthy diet, 3
weight problems, 1–2, 3–4, 9
Freedman, Patricia, 222
Froggy Goes to the Doctor (London and Remkiewicz), 140
frustration
ability to tolerate, 65
decision making by children and developing a tolerance for, 45

G

Gallo, Eileen, 154
Garber, Stephen W., 19
Gavin, Mary, 93
Gift of Fear, The (de Becker), 49–50
Gilligan, Carol, 223
"Girl's Place in the Universe, A" (Freedman), 222
girls, raising, 221–29
assertiveness, need for, 227–28
career choices and, 228–29
and eating disorders, 224, 238
father-daughter relationship, 225
gender stereotyping and, 222, 225
independence, encouraging, 224
media exposure, monitoring, 224
negotiating skills and, 224, 228
reinforcing strengths over appearance, 225
role models, 224, 226, 227, 228–29
self-esteem, 221–23
sports participation, 225
tips for parents, 224–25
"tyranny of niceness," 223, 225–26

Gleicher, Jamie, 61
Going to the Doctor (Brazelton, Womack, and Ogden), 140
Going to the Doctor (Civardi), 140
Goldberg, Alan, 30
Goodnight Caterpillar, The: The Ultimate Bedtime Story (Lite), 17, 18
Gottman, John, 213–14
Grant, Ulysses S., 48
Growing a Girl (Mackoff), 229
Growing Up Creative (Amabile), 166
guided imagery, 18–19

H

Hayward, Linda, 140
Healing Power of Pets, The (Becker), 99
Heinlein, Robert, 53
Hilfiger, Ally, 61
Hilton, Paris, 61
Hudson, Rock, 48

I

identity development, 27
in boys, 233–34
decision making by children and, 43–45
father's presence and reduced gender-role stereotyping, 72
in girls, 221–26
individuation, 45, 233–34
self-definition, 45
twins and, 36–37
I'm Going to the Doctor: A Pop-Up Book (Chambliss and Siegler), 140
I'm Scared: Dealing with Feelings (Crary), 17
Internet sites
banks and piggy banks, 161
educational games, 160
nanny specific sites, 119, 126
websites for dads, 76–77
intuition
decision making by children and, 49–50
intuitive eaters, 3, 6
parental, interviewing a caregiver and, 122–23
thirteen signs of, 49–50
trusting instincts, 114, 222
Intuitive Eating (Resch and Tribole), 3, 6, 97

It's OK: Tom and Ally Visit the Doctor (Robbins and Stuart), 140

J

Jessica and the Wolf: A Story for Children Who Have Bad Dreams (Lobby), 17
Jordan, Michael, 33, 48

K

Kindlon, Dan, 235, 238
Kramarik, Akiane, 165, 169
Krauss, Ronnie, 140

L

language development, 41
  secret twin language, or idioglosia, 41
Laschever, Sara, 228
Licata, Lisa, 26
Lite, Lori, 17, 18
Lobby, Ted, 17
London, Jonathan, 140
love, 109–16
  five conveyors of, 110
  helping your child speak up, 114–15
  listening and, 112–13
  "love bank," 110–11
  love notes, leaving for child, 54
  mirroring a healthy relationship, 111
  modeling conflict resolution, 111
  myths and realities, 113
  parent availability and, 115
  self-esteem and, 109–10
  sharing feelings within the family, 112
  teaching kids to expect respect, 115–16
  telling the truth, 114
  trusting instincts, 114
  unconditional parental, 109–11

M

Mackoff, Barbara, 229
manners, 136
Marcus, Irene Wineman and Paul, 17
marital stability
  changing approach to discussions, 215
  daily check-in, 215
  as emotional foundation for your child, 213
  four predictors of divorce, 213–14
  letting your partner influence you, 216
  making a date night, 216–18, 220
  putting romance back in, 216
  reflective listening, 215
  ten things to strengthen your relationship, 219
  time-outs, 215
  using "I" statements, 214–15
Mayer, Mercer, 17
Mazlish, Elaine, 174–75
Mead, Margaret, 74–75
Michoacán State Institute for Youth Sports, 32
Milne, A. A., 140
Mindell, Jodi, 245, 251
mistakes
  encouraging expression and making, 171
  financial, 162
  girls, permission to make, 224
  importance of failure and frustration, 68–69
  learning process and, 47–48, 50, 65
  taking responsibility for, 65
  teaching child successful failure, 55–56
Monsters under the Bed and Other Childhood Fears (Garber et al), 19
Moses, Amy, 140
My Friend the Doctor (Cole and Chambliss), 140

N

name-calling, 52–53, 181–82
National Alliance for Youth Sports (NAYS), 26
National Center on Addiction and Substance Abuse (CASA), 128–29
negative feedback, 65
Newman, Susan, 202

O

obesity and weight problems, 1–4
  acceptance and encouragement of over-weight children, 92
  contributing factors, 9
  exercise and, 91, 97
  family meals and healthy eating, 129–31
  television viewing and, 9, 95, 129, 194–95, 249

Ogden, Sam, 140
"One and Only, The: Children without Siblings
    Are Not Destined to Be Selfish, Spoiled, or
    Lonely" (Newman), 202
only children (single child households),
    197–204
    bad behavior as normal, 204
    benefits, 197–201
    famous only children, 200
    letting them discover themselves, 204
    maintaining grown-up time, 203
    mistake of treating as an adult, 203
    not pushing too hard, 204
    providing one-on-one time, 203
    setting clear boundaries, 202–3
    social skills, 201
Other Parent, The: The Inside Story of the
    Media's Effect on Our Children (Steyer),
    186–87
overscheduling of children, 146–47, 205–11
    sleep problems and, 248
Owens, Judy, 245, 251

P

Paradox of Choice, The (Schwartz), 45
parenting philosophy, 120–21
Parenting with Love and Logic (Fay), 50
Parke, Ross, 75
Perfect Madness (Warner), 209
pets, 99–108
    age-appropriate responsibilities, 103
    allergies and, 105
    benefits, psychological and emotional, for
        a child, 99–100, 102–5, 105
    benefits for adults, 107
    better grades and school attendance,
        104–5
    motor skill development and, 105
    pet-friendly home, steps to make, 107–8
    physical activities and, 105
    preparing for a new baby and, 106
Pica, Rae, 92
Pipher, Mary, 221–22
play, 93–95, 207–8.
    See also downtime; exercise
Pooh Plays Doctor (Zoehfeld, Milne, and
    Cuddy), 140
Poresky, Robert, 104–5
Protecting the Gift (de Becker), 122

R

Raising Boys (Biddulph), 234
Raising Cain (Kindlon and Thompson), 235, 238
relationships
    attachments, forming healthy, 62–63
    boys, parental attachments and self-
        esteem, 234
    family rituals and, 144–45
    father-child and future attachments, 73,
        78–79
    fathering, 71–79
    keeping your marriage strong, 213–20
    mirroring a healthy relationship, 111
    modeling conflict resolution, 111
    sibling, 173–83
    teaching kids to expect respect, 115–16
    ten things to strengthen your marital rela-
        tionship, 219
relaxation exercises, 18
    deep breathing techniques, 18
    guided relaxation, 88–89
    rhythmic breathing, 88
    for school anxieties, 87, 88–89
Remkiewicz, Frank, 140
Resch, Elyse, 3, 6, 97
responsibility
    chores and tasks, 66–67, 157–59, 161, 182
    decision making by children and, 45–47
    earning an allowance, 157–58, 161
    meal preparation, 133
    money and, 154–55
    pet ownership, 100–101, 103
    rescuing behavior by parent versus, 69
Reviving Ophelia (Pipher), 221–22
Rich Girls, 61
Richie, Nicole, 61
Robbins, Beth, 140
role models
    for boys, 233–34
    caregiver and, 121–22
    for girls, 224, 226, 227, 228–29
    lack of, for fathering, 75
    media, "spoiled princess," 61
    media, thin image, 10–11
    parental, and alcohol use, 130
    parental, of conflict resolution, 111
    parental, and doctor visits, 138
    parental, of healthy eating, 12

role model (*continued*)
    parental, of loving relationships, 79
    parental, of money management, 155–56
    parental, of respect for creativity, 169–70
    parental, of self-acceptance, 98
    parental, and self-criticism, 98, 225
    parental, of self-esteem, 52, 58–59
    parental, and sports, 28, 33–34
    parental, and television viewing, 98
    parental, and values, 63
Roth, Geneen, 129
rules
    bedtime and testing of, 247
    consistent, 54
    family laws, 63–64
    house, 176, 182

S

Satter, Ellyn, 91, 92, 128, 131
Sax, Leonard, 239
Scary Night Visitors: A Story for Children with Bedtime Fears (Marcus and Marcus), 17
school
    activity limit recommendation, 147
    boys and, 234–35, 237
    disruptive behavior, 65
    family meals and academic success, 132
    first day of kindergarten, 19, 81
    girls and early adolescence, 222
    only children and academic success, 198–99
    overscheduling of children and, 205–6
    parental presence, first day, 234–35
    personality traits and vulnerability to school refusal, 84
    pet ownership and better grades/attendance, 104–5
    professional help and, 90
    refusal to attend, 81–90
    refusal to attend, techniques to resolve, 86–87, 89–90
    relaxation exercises, 88–89
    school anxiety scale, 83
    separation anxiety, 81, 86, 234–35
    signs and symptoms of school-attendance problems, 82–83
    sleep and academic performance, 242
Schwartz, Barry, 45

Sears, William, 52
self-critical children, 97–98
self-esteem, 51–59
    boys, parental attachments and, 234
    creativity and, 169
    family meals and, 135, 150
    in girls, raising, 221–23
    goal-setting by child and, 67–68
    high parental standards and, 56–57
    identifying and expressing feelings and, 57
    love and, 109–10
    name-calling and, 52–53, 181–82
    parental acceptance and, 53
    parental love and, 63
    parental presence and, 63, 115
    parental role model of, 52, 58–59
    paying attention to, 55
    respect for child's thoughts and feelings, 55
    sports and, 27–28
    teaching kids to fail, 55–56
    teaching kids to expect respect, 115–16
    ten tips for parents, 54
    twins and, 38
    volunteer work and, 67, 151
    worst thing a parent can say and, 57
self-regulation, 62–63
Seven Common Sins of Parenting an Only Child, The (White), 202
sexuality
    reduced risk of destructive behaviors and family meals, 128–29
    sex education, pet ownership and, 101
sibling rivalry, 173–83
    allowing kids to have their own belongings, 182–83
    assigning household tasks, 182
    avoiding labeling, 38, 179–80
    benefits of siblings, 175
    birth order personalities, 177
    causes of, 173
    children's feelings and, 174–75
    competition between twins, 37–39
    forbidding hitting, 178
    forbidding name-calling, 181–82
    honoring differences, 178–79
    house rules and, 176
    parental neutrality and, 180

parents' feelings and, 174
preventing escalation, 183
time-outs, 178
Siblings Without Rivalry (Faber and Mazlish),
    174–75
Siegler, Kathryn, 140
Silver Spoon Kids (Gallo), 154
Simple Life, The, 61
Six Pillars of Self-Esteem, The (Branden), 51, 169
sleep, 241–51
    academic success and, 242
    activities and soundness of, 246–47
    bedroom temperature, 246
    bedtime, ideal, 251
    bedtime routine/ritual, 149, 244
    caffeine consumption and, 249
    child's sleep personality and, 247–48
    cortisol and stress, problem of, 247
    enforcing bedtime, 148–49, 244
    and fears and anxieties, 245
    food before bedtime, 249, 251
    importance of, for emotional, cognitive,
        and physical development, 242
    issues preventing, 247–49, 251
    light, regulation of, 245–46
    naps, 251
    overscheduling of children and, 248
    problems, frequency of, 241, 243–44
    rule-testing and, 247
    signs of sleep deprivation in children,
        242–43
    sleep requirements chart, 250
    "sleep-training," 243–47
    television and sleep problems, 248–49
    transitional object for, 245
Sleepeasy Solution, The (Spivack and Wald-
    burger), 242, 246, 247, 251
smoking, 128–29
Snow, Catherine, 132
social skills
    exercise, peer acceptance, and leadership,
        97
    family rituals and, 144–45
    only children, 201
    twins and, 38
Spike TV, 71
Spivack, Jill, 242, 243, 246, 247, 251
spoiling/spoiled children, 61–70
    cause and effect, teaching, 65–66

curbing through work and chores, 66–67
delayed gratification, teaching, 63
and discipline, 64–65
goal-setting by child and, 67–68
importance of failure and frustration,
    68–69
"little emperor syndrome," 64, 202–4
parental presence vs. presents, 62–63
parental role model and, 63
rescuing behavior by parent, 69
risks to child of, 62
setting clear boundaries, 63–65
tips for parents, 202–4
sports, 25–34
    age-appropriate activities, 29–30, 93
    age to begin, 26–27
    avoiding overscheduling, 146–47, 210
    boys and risky behavior, 236
    burnout and stress, 32
    coach, monitoring, 33
    exposing to different activities, 26–27,
        93–95
    focusing on process not outcome, 30
    girls participating in, 225
    goal-setting by child and, 30–31
    identity development and, 27
    "in utero classroom," 26
    parental role model, 28, 33–34
    pushing child into parental choice, 58, 92
    questions for parents, 31
    self-esteem and, 27–28, 58
    sixteen do's and don'ts for parents, 28
    unconditional parental support, 32
    winning or losing gracefully, 33–34
Stranger in a Strange Land (Heinlein), 53
stress
    cortisol and sleep problems, 247
    overscheduling of children and, 208–9
    sports burnout and, 32
Stuart, Jon, 140
Successful Child, The (Sears), 52
Surprising Power of Family Meals, The (Snow et
    al), 132

T

Take Charge of Your Child's Sleep (Owens and
    Mindell), 245, 251
Taylor, Stephanie, 165, 167

television, 185–95
    advertising, effect of, 194
    aggressive behavior and, 187–89
    bedroom, removing from, 94
    body image and, 10–11
    children making viewing choices, 186
    limiting viewing, 94, 95–96, 148
    negative effect on creativity, 190–91
    news broadcasts, effect of, 191–93
    nightmares and anxieties and, 189–90,
        191–93
    parental viewing, 98
    sleep problems and, 248
    time spent watching vs. time with parents,
        186
    tips for reducing viewing time, 96
    TV Parental Guidelines, 187, 188, 193
        (ratings chart)
    twelve things a parent can do, 188
    V-Chip technology, 187, 188
    weight problems and, 9, 95, 129, 194–95,
        249
There's a Nightmare in My Closet (Mayer), 17
Thompson, Michael, 235, 238
Thorpe, Kiki, 140
time-outs, 178
    for parents, 215
toilet training,
    twins and, 38
transitional object(s), 87, 142, 245
trauma
    fears and anxieties following, 19
    pets and help dealing with, 103
    television viewing and, 189–90
Tribole, Evelyn, 3, 6, 97
twins, 35–42
    advantages for, 38
    avoiding labeling, 38, 179–80
    birth order personalities for, 177
    bonding between, 39–40
    competition between, 37–38

    creating individuals, 36–37
    increasing number of, 35
    language development, 41
    parental bonding with, 40
    secret twin language, or idioglosia, 41
    self-esteem, 38
    ten tips for parents, 42

V

vacations, 150–51
values, teaching, 61–70
    down-to-earth child, 62–70
    financial education, 155–56, 162
    parental role model, 62–63
video games, limiting use of, 94, 95
volunteer work, 67, 151

W

Waldburger, Jennifer, 242, 243, 246, 247, 251
Wallace, Meri, 173
Warner, Judith, 209
White, Carolyn, 202
Why Gender Matters (Sax), 239
Womack, Alfred, 140
Women Don't Ask (Babcock and Laschever), 228
work ethic, 65
    chores and tasks, 66–67, 182
    earning an allowance, 157–59, 161
    goal-setting by child and, 67–68

Y

Your Active Child (Pica), 92
Your Child's Self-Esteem (Briggs), 56–57
Your Child's Weight (Satter), 91, 92, 131

Z

Zoehfeld, Kathleen, 140

ABOUT THE AUTHOR

D r. Jenn Berman is a licensed marriage, child, and family therapist in private practice in Beverly Hills, California. She has appeared as a psychological expert on hundreds of television shows,
including *Oprah*, *The Today Show*, *Intervention*, *48 Hours*, and *The
Tyra Banks Show*. Dr. Jenn has spoken on various radio programs
and spent one year cohosting *On the Couch*, a call-in advice show on
Clear Channel's Star 98.7 in Los Angeles. Her popular "Dr. Jenn"
column, which is published in *Los Angeles Family* magazine and
reprinted in five other magazines, has been running for five years
and won the 2005 Parenting Publications of America Silver Medal in
the area of Child Development and Parenting. Dr. Jenn lives in Los
Angeles, California, with her husband and two children. For more
information about Dr. Jenn, visit www.DoctorJenn.com.